The Complete

LEGAL GUIDE

GUIDE

to SENIOR

CARE

Second Edition

The Complete

LEGAL GUIDE

to SENIOR

CARE

Second Edition

BRETTE McWHORTER SEMBER
Attorney at Law

SPHINX® PUBLISHING
AN IMPRINT OF SOURCEBOOKS, INC.®
NAPERVILLE, ILLINOIS
www.SphinxLegal.com

Second Edition: 2008

Published by: **Sphinx® Publishing, An Imprint of Sourcebooks, Inc.®**
Naperville Office
P.O. Box 4410
Naperville, Illinois 60567-4410
(630) 961-3900
Fax: 630-961-2168
www.sourcebooks.com
www.SphinxLegal.com

This publication is designed to provide accurate and authoritative information in regard to the subject matter covered. It is sold with the understanding that the publisher is not engaged in rendering legal, accounting, or other professional service. If legal advice or other expert assistance is required, the services of a competent professional person should be sought.

*From a Declaration of Principles Jointly Adopted by a Committee of the
American Bar Association and a Committee of Publishers and Associations*

This product is not a substitute for legal advice.

Disclaimer required by Texas statutes.

Library of Congress Cataloging-in-Publication Data

Sember, Brette McWhorter
  The complete legal guide to senior care / by Brette McWhorter Sember. -- 2nd ed.
    p. cm.
  Includes index.
  ISBN 978-1-57248-659-1 (pbk. : alk. paper) 1. Older people--Legal status, laws, etc.--United States. 2. Older people--Long-term care--Law and legislation--United States. 3. Old age assistance--Law and legislation--United States. I. Title.
  KF390.A4S446 2008
  344.7303'26--dc22
                                        2008020342

Printed and bound in the United State of America.
SB — 10 9 8 7 6 5 4 3 2 1

Contents

Handling Finances from a Distance
Staying in Touch
When to Visit

INTRODUCTION

Caring for and assisting an aging parent as he or she faces important decisions is difficult. Suddenly your whole world has shifted and instead of the senior being someone you view as older and wiser, you are in the position of having to help him or her make long-term decisions, assist with his or her daily care, and plan for eventualities you would probably rather not think about.

This book often refers to "your parent," since many seniors are cared for by their children. However, this book is for *anyone* who is involved in caring for, assisting, or helping a senior, whether it is a spouse, an aunt or uncle, a parent, a neighbor, or another close friend or relative. It can be a huge change to take on a caretaking role in your relationship with your parent. Spouses often also find themselves taking on this kind of role with their husband or wife. It is also not uncommon for adult grandchildren, nieces or nephews, brothers or sisters, and even close neighbors or friends to step into the role of caring for an elderly person and helping him or her plan for the future. Again, this book will be able to assist anyone who finds him- or herself in any of these roles.

You may also start to realize that you need to begin planning now so that your own elderly years can be comfortable and as well-prepared for as possible. While you may have some years before these decisions become imminent for you, the farther ahead you can begin planning, the more prepared you will be.

When you become a primary caregiver or decision maker for an elderly person you love or care about, or when you begin to consider the choices that lie ahead for you, you first have to get your bearings in this new world. This book will help you understand the programs, regulations, living options, and health care terms you need to understand both to help your elderly parent *and* to make plans for your *own* future.

This book contains many tips within the chapters to help you get organized and cope. There are also a lot of worksheets at the end of the chapters. These worksheets are designed so that you may photocopy and use them. Take them along with you as you meet with doctors, visit facilities, and talk to other professionals.

The worksheets will help you ask the right questions and give you a place to write all your information down. This book is designed to be easy to understand and is divided into chapters so you can easily find what you need to know. The book also contains a glossary so you can look up words and terms that you may not understand.

An important portion of this book is the appendixes. They are filled with the names, addresses, phone numbers, and websites of organizations that can help you get more information, find people or agencies who can assist you, obtain publications, and offer you support both in your role as a caretaker and in your own life. Appendix A provides state-specific resources, such as agencies for aging, long-term care ombudsmen, and home and hospice care organizations. Appendix B provides general resources, including organizations, websites, and magazines. Appendix C lists books to consult for more information. Appendix D provides the Nursing Home Resident's Bill of Rights. Appendix E contains a Nursing Home Checklist. Finally, Appendix F contains sample forms that may prove helpful.

There's certainly nothing easy or unemotional about the situation you are thinking about and facing. It is hard to watch someone you love age and change. It is even harder to be in the position of having to help that person face difficult decisions and be the person who carries the burden of caretaking on your own shoulders. It is difficult to imagine yourself as someday needing assistance with daily life. As with all things, if you approach the situation armed with knowledge and coping skills, everything is easier.

Coming to grips with your parents' aging is something you may never really be able to do, but you can find ways to help him or her, help yourself through it, and gather the information you need to make rational and informed decisions. Facing the fact that you, too, will age is an uneasy feeling and one that is difficult to absorb. However, you will find that, as you have been throughout your life, you will be able to cope with the gradual changes and demands that age makes upon you.

The information in this book is as up-to-date as possible, but laws and regulations are always changing, as is contact information for agencies and organizations. Always do your own research to get current information. Because this book is not a substitute for legal advice, consult with an attorney to get up-to-date information about laws in your own state.

Understanding and Facing the Situation

Understanding Aging

As you age, you will notice changes in every aspect of your life. If you are caring for your parent, you will have noticed changes in his or her lifestyle as well as his or her abilities. You may also have noticed some change in his or her mental and emotional outlook. Aging is a comprehensive process, one that involves the entire person, and one that affects every aspect of a person's life. We all logically understand that there is no way to prevent or reverse aging, yet we all still hope to find ways to do so for our loved ones and for ourselves. It is important to remember that aging is natural. Aging does not have to mean the end. People live longer lives now than ever before, which is why it is even more important to understand how you can help make those elderly years comfortable and happy.

When people become elderly, they undergo gradual physical changes and often experience some changes to their personalities or mental abilities. However, it is important to remember that your parent is an adult with needs, thoughts, opinions, and desires, and is not a baby or child who only needs physical care. The simple fact of aging does not take away a person's right to be as independent as possible and the right to self-determination. Your aging parent may feel at times as if he or she is losing these rights or having them taken away by you or by other caregivers. It is a fine line between offering care and taking away decision-making power.

Dealing with these conflicts is one of the most difficult parts of caring for an elderly parent. In thinking about your own future, you probably feel horrified at the thought of someone interfering in your life or making decisions for you that you disagree with. Keeping your feelings in mind will help you understand the feelings your parent is going through as you help him or her face some of the choices discussed in this book.

Assessing

One of the reasons you bought this book is that you need information about how to cope with the changes in your parent's life and because you need to understand the choices and options you both have. Before you can begin to make any real decisions, you need to first determine the stage your parent is in and what kind of assistance he or she needs. This can be done through an *assessment*—either an informal one that you do or a professional one. When an elderly person's abilities and needs are assessed, they are broken down into two categories:

    1. Activities of Daily Living (ADLs); and,

    2. Instrumental Activities of Daily Living (IADLs).

ADLs are the basics of life and include:

- personal hygiene and bathing;

- eating;

- using the bathroom;

- dressing;

- basic speech;

- breathing; and,

- walking.

IADLs are activities that are, in essence, the next level of physical and mental abilities and include:

- handling money;

- cooking and food preparation;

- reading;

- using the phone;

- shopping;

- taking medications;

- cleaning and housekeeping;

- driving or using transportation; and,

- complex communication.

When Help Is Needed

If your parent is having difficulty with an ADL, it has probably become obvious to you. You have likely noticed if your parent has trouble walking, cannot bathe, or has difficulty chewing. Difficulties with IADLs may be more difficult to spot. Sometimes it is easy to miss this, particularly if your parent is married. Often elderly spouses can compensate for each other, in essence covering up these difficulties. Other times, elderly people purposefully cover up changes in their abilities out of fear of losing their independence. Some of the warning signs of difficulty with IADLs can include:

- medication mistakes;

- late payment of bills or misplacing paperwork;

- gradual decline in home cleanliness;

- lack of appropriate food in the home;

- communication mix-ups; and,

- trouble driving.

If you notice difficulties with ADLs, you need to get some professional assistance (explained later in this chapter). If you notice difficulties with some IADLs, you shouldn't immediately jump to conclusions. There can be many causes for IADL problems and many of them can be solved. A problem with an IADL does not always mean a person cannot live independently. For example, your parent may be unable to push a heavy grocery cart and thus does not purchase a lot of food at one time, explaining why there never seems to be enough food in the house. Or he or she may need to get new glasses or hearing aids so that communication, reading, or bill paying can be handled more effectively.

Look at the situation yourself and think about what you are seeing and the possible reasons for it. Sometimes an elderly person is reluctant to admit that he or she is having difficulty with an IADL, or the difficulty has evolved so gradually that he or she has not truly noticed. If you see it happening, you need to think about what is causing it and what the possible simple solutions are. If your parent is experiencing difficulty with many IADLs, it is a good idea to get a *professional assessment*. (See the following section.) It is difficult to know when you need to become involved in helping your parent manage things and make decisions about future care. Unless there is an immediate urgent need to make changes, it is often best to approach this kind of situation gradually. Slowly become more involved with your parent's life and choices. (See page 6 in this chapter for more information on how to discuss this with your parent.)

Professional Assessments

If your parent is experiencing definite difficulties with ADLs or IADLs, it is a good idea to have a *professional assessment* done. There may be things you are missing that a professional will pick up on. A professional assessment is the first step to getting professional help and may allow you to access solutions you had not thought about or were not aware of. Also, if you try to tell your parent you think he or she needs assistance with something, you may meet with resistance. If you can have a third party professional tell him or her this, you may get a better response. A professional assessment is done by a *geriatrician*, a doctor who specializes in treating elderly patients. You can obtain a referral to a geriatrician from your parent's primary care doctor. While general practitioners do have some training and experience in treating the elderly, geriatricians have more. Another option is to see a *geriatric care manager*. This is not a doctor, but rather a social worker or nurse trained in assessing elderly people's needs and finding solutions for problems they face. Geriatric managers are more likely to come to your parent's home, whereas a geriatrician will not and will often focus on medical issues, not daily organizational issues.

It is important to remember that some challenges with ADLs and IADLs may be only temporary, as your parent recovers from an illness or injury. Talk with your parent's physician about his or her prognosis.

When you become involved in helping to make decisions for your elderly parent, it is always a good idea to have a complete medical evaluation done, even if you are using a geriatric care manager, so that you can provide a baseline to be used if future medical problems or needs develop. In this same vein, you can see the importance of continuing to have yearly checkups for yourself. A geriatric care manager can help you understand the day-to-day problems and needs your parent faces and can help you find solutions for managing them. A geriatric care manager can also help in finding, considering, and evaluating senior residences, assisted-living facilities, or other long-term care facilities. He or she can help you understand and assess the options you face. He or she can help arrange for in-home care and help you or your parent understand medical issues. Geriatric care managers can also completely manage all the needs an elderly person has by hiring and supervising care providers.

Talking to Your Parents about Needs and Choices

Finding a way to talk to your parent about his or her situation, changing needs and abilities, and future plans is difficult. In most cases, you cannot simply decide one day that you are now going to be in charge and barge into your parent's home announcing that you will be making some decisions and implementing some changes. You also cannot bluntly point out to your parent that he or she is no longer competent to handle some things. Remember to think about how you would feel in your parent's shoes in response to any possible action you are considering. Take this process one step at a time.

You also need to think about what kind of approach you will take. If you notice that your mother is having difficulty keeping the house clean, you can approach it in two kinds of ways.

1. "Mom, this place is really dirty. I don't even want to use the bathroom when I'm here. I'm going to hire someone to come in and clean once a week."

or

2. "Mom, I noticed that you might be having some trouble cleaning the bathroom. I know it's hard to reach around behind the toilet and inside the tub. I wiped it down for you while I was in there."

With the first approach, you put the person on the defensive. The approach is too direct, too accusatory, and it takes all control away from your parent. With the second approach, you are sympathetic and accepting while still allowing your parent to feel as if he or she is a respected adult. You can start to address a problem in this way, with gentle comments and observations, teamed with low-key assistance.

In the example at hand, the next step might be to offer to help vacuum since you know how heavy the vacuum is. After a few gentle interventions such as these, you could then suggest that having someone come and do housework once a week might make your parent's life easier. These kinds of gradual changes will help your parent adapt more easily and will allow him or her to feel as if he or she was part of the decision and is not a problem that is being solved.

Discussion Early On

At some point you will need to have a conversation with your parent about the future. It is almost always best to have this kind of conversation by first stating that you know it is a subject no one wants to talk about. State that you both know that he or she wants to remain at home and be independent for as long as possible, but you think it is a good idea to talk about some things that could happen so that you both can have a plan should the unthinkable ever happen. Talk about what your parent wants—what he or she envisions as an acceptable aging process and place in which to age. Many families never have these conversations (since they are difficult) and just deal with situations as they arise. But if you can manage to talk about what kinds of living options your parent wants for him- or herself, you have at least laid the groundwork for making these decisions together. Perhaps your parent has always planned on moving to an assisted-living facility, or maybe he or she just assumed you would make room in your own home. People make many assumptions and have lots of internal plans they never share with anyone. It is time to get it all out in the open and find out what everyone's expectations are.

When thinking about your own future, remember to have this type of conversation with your children. Do not assume that they know what you want or what your preferences are. You need to talk about your plans and lay the groundwork for them years in advance to allow for smooth transitions. *Wills, health care proxies* or *living wills*, and *powers of attorney* are documents that both you and your parent will need. (See Chapter 4 for an in-depth discussion.) Discuss the need for these with your parent. Don't approach him or her and say, "I think it is time you had a will drawn up." Find some reason to mention the topic—a newspaper article, a family member or friend's experience, or simply make something up if you have to. Then bring the discussion around and ask if he or she ever had a will drawn up. Some children of elderly parents are surprised to learn a will already exists. If this is the case, find out where it is kept. If there is no will, suggest that having one created is a good idea and that you are thinking of having one made for yourself since it is important to you that, should something happen, your belongings go to the people you choose.

Understanding How Your Parent Feels

Put yourself in your parent's shoes. You are getting older and you may feel as if the prime of your life has passed. You want to stay in your own home but are worried that someone will notice you are having trouble with some things. You do not want to be dependent on anyone. You are afraid that your family will put you in a nursing home where old people wander around looking confused, it smells bad, there is no privacy, and no one comes to visit you. You worry about becoming ill or disabled and about dying. You do not want your children telling you what to do, but you do want their help and support. Experiencing these feelings is difficult for your parent. But you must also remember that your parent probably also simultaneously sees him- or herself as having a lot of living left to do. He or she probably has friends, hobbies, and activities that mean a lot to him or her. Life is pleasurable when the worries about the future do not weigh in.

Coping with Your Emotions

At different points in your life you have probably noticed your parent or parents aging. It has probably taken you by surprise at times. As your parents become elderly and start to require assistance, you may be surprised, but you will certainly find that you have lots of emotions to deal with.

Children of aging parents often experience grief, sadness, anger, frustration, exhaustion, fear, helplessness, avoidance, relief, and a sense of loss. Noticing that your parents need some kind of help living their lives often feels like a big red flag that the end of life is approaching. All of these emotions are valid and you should not berate yourself for feeling any of them. What you do need to do is learn to live with and manage them. Your emotions will change as your parent's situation changes. Helping your parent age can be a tremendous burden on you, but it can also be very rewarding. Adults who take on an important role in assisting their parents while still being very involved in their children's lives are part of what is called the *sandwich generation*. You have lots of people and lots of needs pulling you in every direction. None of it is easy and it is difficult to find a way to manage it all. Make sure to read *Tips for Coping with Stress* at the end of this chapter on page 17 for information on how to deal with emotions while caring for an aging parent.

At some point you have to accept that your parent is aging and that his or her needs are changing. You should not necessarily interpret this to mean that he or she will die soon. This is often the greatest fear caregivers have. You do not know when that will happen and you cannot control it. You can, however, help your parent enjoy life, live safely and comfortably, and plan for the future. You must learn to accept your parent for who he or she is and make room to accept who he or she will become. You must also find a way to live with your new role in your parent's life. There are many support organizations available to help caregivers for elderly people. (See Appendix B for an organization that can help you.) You will also find that there are many local support groups. Ask your parent's doctor, other caregivers, personnel at the local senior citizen's center, or contact your state department for the aging (see Appendix A) for information about local groups, and use the worksheet at the end of this chapter on page 15 to help you assess the support organizations you find.

Respect your parent's feelings and remember that he or she is still your parent, is still an adult, and deserves your support and help.

Developing a New Attitude and Relationship with Your Parent

You may have spent a great portion of your life trying to remain independent from your parents. Now you find that you may need to become more involved with their lives than you have been previously. You may also find that the way you are used to dealing with your parents may not be the best way to continue dealing with them. As your parent changes, you will have to make some changes yourself if you want to be involved with his or her care and help him or her make choices.

Perhaps the most important attitude to develop is one of patience. Elderly people move slower. Your parent may move more slowly mentally as well. And you may also find that it takes time to help your parent make important decisions. Be patient. Learn to take a step back and not be so rushed when you are with your parent. The entire aging process is itself a gradual process, so it is important to remember that your reaction and approach to dealing with it should be gradual as well.

You may also find that because of physical or mental changes your parent is experiencing, you can identify problems and solutions much more quickly than he or she can. Give your parent time to reach the same conclusions you do, if possible. Take the time to explain things and take the time to express your concerns in gentle ways. There are certainly times when this approach will not work. If your parent needs assistance or medical care immediately, you have to step up to the plate and be the one who makes the call—even if it is over your parent's objections. You may also observe dangerous conditions in your parent's home that need immediate attention. You may find that you reach a point where it is simply no longer reasonable or feasible for your parent to remain at home or in the type of facility he or she is currently in. In those situations, you need to act to help keep your parent safe and healthy. Being a caretaker means taking on this responsibility. In most other situations, you have to take a respectful and easy approach. You will gain cooperation much easier if you are sweet and convincing rather than authoritative and demanding.

As you age, you will also have to cope with the emotions you experience. The resources in the appendixes can help you cope with the feelings and situations that may come up in your own life, as well as those you deal with in helping your parent.

Involving Other Family Members

In most families, one child or relative falls into the role of primary caregiver for a parent. This may be because of location, professional training, or simply because of relationships within the family. If you find that you are "the chosen one," either by circumstance, through your own choosing, or by default, expect to experience some difficulty dealing with other family members. The best way to handle other family members is to have a family meeting. Other members of the family may not be as aware as you are of the changes and difficulties facing your parent. If you have an assessment done, it is very helpful to share it with other family members. It is also a good idea to have the other family members speak to doctors or the geriatric care manager to get a firsthand account of the situation. It is best to lay everything on the line and make some hard and fast rules about who is going to be responsible for what. Maybe your brother can help your parent manage the upkeep of the home. Maybe your sister can take Dad grocery shopping. Spell out who is going to do what. Use the HOME LIVING PLAN (form 6, p.385) as a guide. If your family members really do not want to be involved, there isn't much you can do to force them to be. However, you may want to be firm that those who do not help do not get to criticize the decisions you make.

There can frequently be resentment and anger when the other family members feel left out of the loop. When large, important decisions must be made (moving Mom to an assisted-living facility, hiring a private nurse for Dad, etc.), get the rest of the family involved, or at the very least make sure they are informed of the situation, the choices, and the best solution to the problem. See *Tips for Working with Family Members* at the end of this chapter on page 18 for more suggestions on how to avoid family conflict when dealing with an aging parent.

It makes sense to have one person take primary responsibility for managing medical care. One person needs to have all the paperwork, arrange all the appointments, and stay in touch with health care workers. Continuity is very important and if you divide these duties up, important information can be over-looked. (See Chapter 2 for more information about managing medical care.). It is also important to have one person who is in charge of finances; otherwise, bills may not get paid on time.

Dealing with Resistance from Your Parent

This book discusses all the different levels of care and assistance available to your parent as he or she grows older. Your parent may be completely opposed to the idea of accepting help from anyone or opposed to changing his or her lifestyle. In all likelihood, some changes will have to be made as he or she ages. Do not expect your parent to gleefully agree to move to an assisted-living facility or to go from an assisted-living to a skilled-nursing facility. These kinds of changes are difficult to accept. Anticipate that your parent will be resistant to change. Expect your parent to be initially resistant to your advice, intervention, and assistance.

Overcoming this resistance takes patience, love, and understanding. Explain things to your parent. Share your concerns. Explain his or her medical conditions or physical limitations.

Fulfilling Your Role

Adult caregivers often feel resentful when the mantle of responsibility falls on their shoulders. In most families it is clear who will be the main caregiver, simply because of the way things in the family are always handled. You may feel this is unfair and want your siblings or other relatives to be more involved. If you find you are the one the burden falls most heavily on, you can first be somewhat relieved to know that at least you can make the decisions you feel are best and handle things as you want them to be handled. However, this is a lot of responsibility and takes a lot of your time and energy. Don't be afraid to ask for help from other family members. Just because the main burden has fallen to you does not mean everyone else can heave a sigh of relief and return to their normal lives. If you all love and care about your parent, then it is important that all of you be involved to some extent.

Primary caregivers often worry that the other family members will blame them if something goes wrong. It is easy to be plagued by this worry and it is easy to let guilt become overwhelming when you make choices other family members disagree with. You must remember, though, that you can only make the best decisions possible at the time. No one can see into the future and fully anticipate what will happen. Do the best you can and try to keep other people involved so that everything does not fall on your shoulders. Remember that your parent plays an active and important role in making decisions.

As you become more involved in your role as caregiver, you will find it may place a strain on other aspects of your life. You can't do everything yourself, and this is the time when you must ask your spouse, children, coworkers, and other people in your life for support and assistance.

Support Organization Evaluation Worksheet

Name of Organization: _____

Date: _____

- Does the group meet at a convenient time and location? (Rushing to get to a meeting is not going to decrease your stress.)

  _____

- Are the meetings informational or supportive?

  _____

- Which type of meeting (informational or supportive) are you really looking for?

  _____

- Do you feel comfortable with the other group members?

  _____

- Are there membership fees?

  _____

- If there are membership fees, are they reasonable?

  _____

- Does the group meet too frequently, just enough, or not frequently enough?

  _____

- Does the organization provide you with ways to get more information, resources, or help should you need it?

  _____

- Is the group leader friendly, welcoming, and receptive?

  _____

- Do you feel as if the organization or group has an agenda or approach that you do not agree with?

  _____

Tips for Coping with Stress

- Get organized! Keep a calendar, lists, and clear notes about what you need to do and when you need to do it.

- Enlist your spouse or partner. Get him or her to help as much as possible with the kids and your parent. Make sure household tasks are being shared.

- Keep in mind that you can take unpaid time off from work to care for an ill parent, spouse, or child under the *Family and Medical Leave Act.*

- Do not expect yourself to be perfect or to do everything.

- Make time to do things for yourself, even if it means leaving other things undone.

- Talk to your kids about the responsibilities you have and get them to pitch in or at least start to take more responsibility for their own activities, laundry, messes, and projects.

- Join a support group so that you can meet others in your situation and find out how they cope.

- Get siblings or other relatives to help out with your parent.

- Find community organizations that can provide your parent with support and assistance.

- Remember that the situation is stressful for your parent as well as you.

Tips for Working with Family Members

- Try to talk to everyone at once at a family meeting to discuss important issues.

- Set ground rules for your meeting, which may include no shouting, no emotional attacks, no discussion of other family problems or disputes, etc.

- Know your allies. In some families, there are defined "camps"—the brothers who insist an elderly parent be cared for at home by the sisters; the older siblings who believe assisted living is the best option, and so on. Evaluate who is going to be on your side and get their support. Work as a team to get support from other family members.

- Realize that everyone isn't always going to agree. Try to get everyone to agree to pitch in, even if they do not agree with the final decision.

- Do not expect old family differences to go away or be put completely aside. They will always be a part of interactions you have, but you can at least overlook them as you make these important decisions together.

- Try to make decisions that take your parent's needs and wants into consideration. Do not let this become a process that is completely removed from your parent and what he or she needs.

- Take time to make important decisions. Often other family members who are not as involved with your parent will need time to adjust to the changes and decisions.

- Try not to let this erupt into a traditional family squabble with old arguments resurfacing.

- Although money is an important consideration, do not let the entire process focus completely on money.

- Stress that the most important thing is keeping your parent healthy and happy. This is the goal that you are all working toward.

Understanding the Medical World | 2

When you become involved in helping your elderly parent cope with medical and lifestyle concerns, you may find that there are lots of things you simply do not know and do not understand. Looking ahead to your own future, you probably have a lot of questions and concerns about these topics as well. Dealing with medical personnel and caregiving personnel can be confusing, frustrating, and time-consuming. Dealing with insurance, financial, and legal issues can be equally difficult. The best way to cope with these situations is to arm yourself with knowledge and have a resource that can help answer your questions. This chapter will help you understand the medical world. Come back to this chapter as you face new problems and new situations dealing with medical care.

The Medical World

You probably already know that there are lots of things about the world of medicine that seem strange and confusing to those who are not medical professionals. Doctors, nurses, and other medical personnel seek to prolong life, follow the patient's wishes when possible, and reduce pain. They are also trained to keep medical information confidential. Remember that they are trained to prolong life and do not always take personal and lifestyle issues into consideration. They also may not see your parent as a priority. It is up to the patient and his or her family to insist on detailed explanations, creative options, and superior care.

Getting Involved

For most of your parent's life, he or she handled his or her own medical care alone or with the input of a spouse. When you feel that you want or need to be involved with your parent's medical care, it can be difficult to figure out just how you will do so. There are lots of different situations that bring you to this decision—perhaps Mom is receiving treatment for diabetes and you would like to understand the disease and treatment so you can help her manage medications and finger pricks; maybe Dad seems frail to you but insists nothing is wrong and you really want to have him checked out; or, maybe one of your parents has suddenly been hospitalized and you need to make decisions when he or she is unable to.

You should first understand that the medical personnel must allow your parent to make decisions if he or she is capable. Patients are truly at the helm of their medical care. Each patient has the final say about refusing or accepting medical care. Another important point to remember is that medical personnel usually cannot tell family members anything unless they are authorized to do so. For this reason, it is very important that you and your parent have a conversation about this. He or she should have an *advance directive* (see Chapter 4) that will authorize you (or someone else) to make decisions if he or she is unable to do so.

At some point you may also need to begin accompanying your parent on medical appointments and get firsthand information from the doctor. The best way to accomplish this is to go with your parent on an office visit. At the front desk, ask for a form your parent can complete that will give you permission to access his or her medical records. If your parent does not sign this, you will not have access to his or her medical records. The *Health Insurance Portability and Accountability Act*

(HIPAA) sets out very specific rules physicians must follow to preserve medical privacy. Your parent needs to authorize you to access his or her records.

Go into the exam room (allowing your parent privacy to change if your assistance is not needed). Be present during the exam unless it requires privacy (step into the hall if needed). Ask questions and listen to what the doctor says. Have your parent tell the doctor that you are part of the decision-making team now. A written release is essential since it will remain in the file and you can refer any medical personnel in the office to it should there be a problem. You can use a form provided by the office or use the MEDICAL RELEASE (form 1, p.376) in Appendix F. The form gives permission for the office to share all information with you and also allows the option of directing the office to contact you as well as your parent by phone and mail or to contact only you (useful if your parent cannot hear well on the phone or loses mail correspondence). It is a good idea to give one of these forms to each doctor or medical office your parent visits.

Dealing with Medical Personnel

To be able to deal effectively with medical personnel, you need to understand how they work and what their normal reactions to situations are.

In dealing with medical personnel it is always best to be pleasant and nice whenever possible. There are times when it is necessary to be pushy and insistent, but if you are always this way, it will have far less impact. Save it for when you need it. Keep these tips in mind not only to help you manage your parent's care, but also to help you manage your own medical care.

Use the evaluation questions and read *Tips to Get Medical Personnel to Listen to You* at the end of the chapter on page 59 to help you deal effectively with the medical personnel. Keep the authorization form in mind so that you can complete one yourself should you find you want a child, friend, or family member to help you with your medical care in the future.

Choosing and Evaluating a Doctor

The most important part of evaluating a doctor is finding one that you or your parent trusts and can communicate with. The best educated and most experienced doctor in the world is not the one for you if you find that you simply cannot connect to him or her or if he or she does not take the time to answer your questions. Many people find a good doctor by asking friends and family whom they use; however, you or your parent may be limited by insurance as to whom you can choose.

If you need a referral to a doctor in your area and friends and family cannot help, ask another doctor you trust for a referral. You can also look in the *Directory of Medical Specialists*, a reference book your local library should have.

You can use the worksheet at the end of this chapter on page 47 to evaluate various doctors.

Informed Consent

An important legal concept involved in medical care is *informed consent*. A patient has the right to have the doctor completely explain the proposed medical treatment in an understandable way before agreeing to it. Doctors must explain the risks and benefits of treatment to patients and cannot hold back information. In practice, many doctors do not give full explanations of treatments because time does not allow for it. Ask as many questions as you like to get all the information you can. Once you or your parent agrees to treatment, you can change your mind and withdraw consent at any time. You can also change your mind and agree to treatment you previously refused. Patients have the absolute right to control what is happening to their bodies. Insist on getting all the information you need to make choices and to manage your own or your parent's care.

Unfortunately, it can be difficult sometimes to get a doctor to completely and thoroughly answer all your questions. If you feel you are or your parent is being rushed, make an appointment for a consultation when you, your parent, and the doctor can sit face to face in his or her office and talk. When making the appointment, ask for at least fifteen minutes of the doctor's time. Often when doctors don't have the pressure of trying to squeeze you into a ten-minute slot, they can answer questions more thoughtfully and completely.

Today, many people do their own research online to find answers to their medical questions. The Internet is an important tool available to you, but it is also important to consult with your parent's doctor to be certain. When using the Internet to get information, be sure you rely on reputable sites, such as those associated with a hospital, research facility, or government entity. Never try to self-diagnose or self-treat, but feel free to bring information you've gathered online to the doctor to discuss it.

Second Opinions

It is your parent's right to seek a second opinion at any time. When seeking a second opinion, do not be afraid to tell the doctor you are doing so. You're not doing anything wrong, and in fact, many physicians welcome this. It is important to remember that there can be many approaches to one problem and you should help your parent explore these options. Insurance will usually pay for a second opinion.

Doctors

Doctors are on a tight schedule. They have approximately ten to fifteen minutes to spend with each patient during office visits. Don't let this make you or your parent afraid to ask questions, ask the doctor to repeat things, or request more information. Remember that you (or your parent) are paying for this doctor. You have probably spent time in a waiting room while the doctor spent time with other patients. Do not be afraid to insist on the amount of time you or your parent needs. (See *Tips for Having a Good Conversation with a Doctor* at the end of this chapter on page 56.)

Remember that doctors can help not only with acute medical problems, but also with problems such as sleep disturbances, eating difficulties, problems concentrating, difficulties walking, problems communicating, and so on. When you or your parent visits a doctor for the first time, bring a file with you that contains:

- a list of current medications with dosages;

- a list of all allergies;

- a complete medical history and family medical history;

- copies of relevant tests, procedures, and medical records;

- date of birth and Social Security number; and,

- insurance information.

Doctors are difficult to access by phone. If you feel you do need to speak to a doctor by phone, you will need to be insistent. Get detailed information as to when he or she can call you so that you can be certain to be available. Be persistent without being obnoxious.

This file is also something you should bring along to planned or unplanned hospital visits, visits to specialists, appointments for tests (such as CT scans or colonoscopies) and when meeting with nursing home or assisted-living facilities. Keep these documents in a folder or manila envelope, so that they are all together and can easily be grabbed and brought along. You might also find a small accordion file with dividers or a three-ring notebook to be a convenient way to get organized.

If you are accompanying your parent, you may need to remind the doctor that your parent has given permission for you to receive all medical information. Some doctors automatically ask everyone but the patient to leave the room. Insist on staying if this is what you and your parent want.

Nurses

In a doctor's office, you may have little contact with nurses in person. However, they are generally the people you will speak to if you call with medical concerns or questions by phone. If you are calling about your parent, remind them that you have permission to obtain information. If you are not satisfied with information given to you by a nurse, do not hesitate to ask to speak to the doctor. It can be difficult to deal with nurses in a doctor's office since you may feel that they do not really know you or your parent. Try to get to know the nurses you speak to by phone and write down their names. Understand that usually they cannot make decisions and often must consult with the doctor before they can get back to you with medication changes or orders for tests.

Physician Assistants, Nurse Practitioners, and Aides

You may see a *physician assistant* or *nurse practitioner* if you come in for an unscheduled (or sick) office visit. Many doctors employ these professionals to help handle sick or unplanned visits. Nurse practitioners and physician assistants have medical training and are able to diagnose and treat illnesses, including writing prescriptions.

They do not, however, have the extensive training that doctors do. If your parent is seen by a physician assistant or nurse practitioner and you feel that all your questions have not been adequately answered or that the care your parent has received is not adequate, ask to see the doctor. Be aware that you may be in for a long wait, and it is also possible the doctor may not even be in the building at the time you are there. If your doctor is part of a practice made up of a group of doctors, the other doctors in the practice can treat you or your parent, so remember to request this if your or your parent's doctor is not available.

Aides or *licensed practical nurses* (LPNs) are the personnel who weigh patients and take their blood pressure and temperatures. They can explain the results of these procedures and give you a comparison from the chart to compare past readings, but they will most likely be unable to interpret them.

Hospital Care

At some point, you may have to deal with yourself or your parent going to or staying in a hospital. This section will help you learn your way around and help you cope with this stressful event.

Entering the Hospital

When a person enters a hospital, he or she is asked to sign a *consent form*, giving permission to the hospital to treat him or her. It is important to read this form carefully. You have the right to alter the form to indicate that you are consenting only to specific treatments or to being treated by a specific physician and those under his or her direction. When entering the hospital, be sure that you or your parent brings insurance cards along. Other information that will be requested includes your or your parent's Social Security number, date of birth, address, medication allergies, medications currently being taken, and a medical history. If you or your parent will be staying in the hospital overnight, you can request a private room (if one is desired and if you are able to pay for this expense, which is usually not covered by insurance) as soon as you have decided to stay. You should also request telephone and television service immediately since it can take some time to get these items turned on. (Remember that insurance does not cover the cost of these items.)

When entering a hospital, the patient should also be given a statement of his or her rights while hospitalized. Hospitals usually give patients a brochure prepared by the American Hospital Association. You can read this online at **www.aha.org/ aha/content/2003/pdf/pcp_english_030730.pdf**. Hospitals also usually ask if the patient has a *health care directive* or *proxy* and can provide forms to execute one at the time of entry. If one already exists, the hospital should be given a copy of it.

Doctors

When dealing with doctors in the hospital, you may be baffled trying to figure out when you can actually see the doctor. Doctors are good about speaking to family members after a surgery or procedure, but then can be difficult to locate. Tell a nurse at the station that you would like to speak to the doctor. Ask if he or she can be paged or if you can leave a message asking him or her to call you. You have the absolute right to insist on speaking to a doctor from the practice that cares for you. It is also important to remember that when you or your parent is in the hospital, the primary care doctor or geriatric specialist may never visit the hospital. All care may be provided by a specialist or the doctor's practice may have designated doctors who only work in the hospital (called *hospitalists*). Call the primary doctor's office and ask that he or she contact the specialist to obtain current information. You will need to sign a release.

The primary care physician should be the one who is coordinating the care you or your parent receives and should be in contact with every specialist involved. Unfortunately, this may not happen unless you specifically request that it happen. He or she may be able to answer many of your questions, particularly if you need some basic information about a disease or illness. Many primary care doctors do not follow up and monitor a patient's care in the hospital, and you should insist that yours does. It is best to speak directly with the specialist about treatment options, recovery periods, and special care needed, but the primary care doctor can help you understand the big picture.

While in the hospital, you or your parent may be seen by interns, medical students, or residents. These are doctors in training. You have every right to refuse treatment by anyone. It is especially important to insist on speaking to your own doctor before consenting to any procedure or treatment.

Nurses

In the hospital, you will see nurses more than anyone else. The nurses are the ones who are responsible for dispensing medication, overseeing personal care, and monitoring patients' conditions.

Nurses work in shifts and sometimes these shifts may rotate or change often, so you may see many different faces. When you or your parent is hospitalized, getting to know the nurses is one of the best things you can do. Stop at the nurses' station and introduce yourself. Speak to nurses who come into the room when you are there. Ask them questions about your own or your parent's care. Ask anything you want to know. Ask to see your own or your parent's chart if you feel this would help you. Find out what kind of care you or your parent is supposed to be receiving and then track it to make sure it is actually happening.

There are nursing shortages in almost all hospitals. Registered nurses (RNs) are in short supply. Thus they are very busy and may be rushed in speaking to you. If you have questions and no one has taken the time to answer them, go to the station or call for a nurse and politely explain that you have some medical questions and would appreciate if someone could take a few minutes to speak with you.

If your parent is difficult to deal with, it is particularly important that you get to know the nurses. Your friendliness can make up for your parent's rudeness and may help ensure he or she gets better care. It also lets the staff know that there are family members looking out for this patient's well-being, which may help influence them to provide better care.

Aides, Orderlies, and LPNS

All of these medical personnel have some medical training and each type is authorized and permitted to do different things. In general, these kinds of health care workers do the routine work—the personal hygiene, basic monitoring, application of medications and procedures, and walking assistance your parent may require while in the hospital. They are unable to answer medical questions, but they can answer questions about basic care. Do not be afraid to ask someone who he or she is and what role he or she plays. It is hard to tell who is who in a hospital.

Dealing with Hospital Visits

When you or your parent goes to the hospital, you may feel scared and confused by this place that is somehow otherworldly. Understanding how to get information and how to direct your or your parent's care will help you manage in this environment.

Emergency Room

If you or your parent is taken to the emergency room (ER), an assessment will be made upon arrival and treatment will be given according to *triage standards*, which allow the most seriously injured or ill patients to be seen first. If you feel you or your parent has been waiting too long, go up to the nurse's desk and ask about when you or your parent will be seen. Notify the medical personnel immediately if you or your parent becomes worse or develops new symptoms while waiting. Patients who arrive by ambulance are usually seen more quickly than walk-ins; however, ambulance rides are costly.

ER personnel normally ask that all family members remain in the waiting room. Your parent can, however, insist that you accompany him or her to the exam room and if you are the patient, you can insist on a family member accompanying you. The medical personnel cannot stop a family member from coming along, but they can request that you step outside the room at certain times and may insist that family members stay outside during an emergency. Having a family member stay with the patient can help speed things up or allow the family member to gather information. If a patient is stuck in bed with an IV, he or she can't walk down the hall easily to ask when his or her CT scan will be done or to remind someone that he or she still needs pain medication. When a patient has a person with him or her, he or she can help make sure the patient is being treated properly. It also sends a clear message to the medical personnel that the patient is being watched over carefully by family members. It makes the team more accountable and more likely to provide better care.

It can be difficult to get a handle on what is happening in the ER. Talk to the nurse who is assigned to you or your parent as much as possible. He or she will have more time than the ER doctors to explain things and answer questions. Be certain you are present when the ER doctor visits your parent. Ask as many questions as you can.

Many people are surprised by the long waits in ER waiting rooms, but are even more surprised by the long waits they face once they are taken back to an exam room. Once you or your parent is taken to an exam room, a nurse will get in-depth information about symptoms and medical history. If treatment is needed immediately, it will be given. Most of the time, unless you are in a very urgent situation, it will take a while to receive any treatment. Part of the reason for this is the understaffing problems, but other reasons are that it often takes time to schedule tests or x-rays, get results, have blood tested, and so on. Once these tests are done, it then takes time for the results to be given to the ER doctor and for him or her to read them and decide on a course of treatment. If an overnight stay will be needed, it takes time for an open bed to be located in the hospital and for the paperwork for the transfer to be completed.

Hospital Stays

When you or your parent must stay in a hospital, try to gather as much information in advance as possible. Find out how long the stay will be, what the recovery will be like, and get details about the procedures and medications planned. Ask for second opinions whenever you want them and understand that most insurance does pay for them. Use the *Hospital Care Evaluation* worksheet at the end of this chapter to help you ask the right questions.

Most hospitals have set visiting hours; however, if you make it clear to the doctors and nurses that you are in charge of your parent's care and need to be able to have access to him or her (as long as your visits do not disrupt his or her sleeping or resting), most will not give you trouble about it. Because hospital staff is overworked and understaffed, it is a very good idea to make arrangements with family members so that someone is with the patient on a regular basis. Having people there for a majority of the time will ensure that the care is monitored. Emphasize to those who take turns visiting that they should not be afraid to ask questions. It is also a good idea to make sure family members have a sense as to what medication is being administered and what treatments are planned. If something does not seem right, they should ask. If your parent needs several medications, it may make sense to keep your own log of what is being administered because mistakes do happen with medication in hospitals. If you find that you are not getting the information you need, you or your parent is not receiving the level of care you expect, or you have other problems, ask to speak to a *patient advocate* or *patient representative*. These are hospital employees trained to help patients resolve problems. They can help you understand hospital routines, procedures, and administration. They can also help when you cannot seem to get anyone else to help you.

If you can afford it, hiring a private duty nurse can provide peace of mind and excellent care. Because the nursing staff is usually overworked, hiring a nurse who can meet your parent's needs is an excellent idea. He or she can provide immediate and personal care, monitor medication, get you in touch with the doctor, and access the chart. Costs can start at $25 per hour. (See Chapter 6 for more information about hiring private nurses.) When you or your parent is getting ready to be discharged from the hospital, ask to speak to a *discharge planner*. These are hospital employees who can help you understand the type of care you or your parent will need at home (or at a facility) and help arrange for this type of care.

Being Proactive

The best thing you can do when you or your parent is in the hospital is to view yourself as a participant. You should not be a bystander. Ask questions, gather information, help your parent cope with things, and be involved (see *Tips to Finding Medical Information* at the end of this chapter on page 60). The more involved you are, the more control you will have over the treatment you or your parent receives and the way decisions are made. If your parent is supposed to receive pain medication every three hours and the medication is late, do not wait and assume the medical staff will take care of it. Push the call button or go down to the nurse's station and remind them it is due.

Helping Your Parent Cope

Helping your parent cope with hospital stays can be difficult. Older people can sometimes become confused in the hospital even if they are generally clear-minded at home. Don't be alarmed by this, but do talk with the medical personnel about it to make sure it is not related to medication. Remain calm and reassuring with your parent throughout the entire hospital stay.

If you have a parent who becomes unpleasant or cranky when in the hospital, remind yourself that he or she truly needs you now more than ever. It can be tempting to walk out if you feel insulted, harangued, or blamed, but remember that this is your parent's way of reacting to the stress of the situation. The best thing you can do is take a mental and emotional step back. Don't get involved in quarrels or problems. Be pleasant and helpful. Think of all your parent has done for you in your lifetime and view this as your way of giving back to him or her. (See *Tips for Helping Your Parent Cope* at the end of this chapter on page 58.)

Managing Your Emotions

If you are the one in the hospital, expect to feel helpless, confused, and frightened at times. When you are ill or recovering from surgery or treatment, it is difficult to think clearly, to ask all the right questions, control your emotions, and feel as if you are in control of your body.

Gather as much information as you can from as many medical people as you can. Ask questions and make yourself known to anyone who is dealing with you or your parent.

Feel free to express your frustration or fear to the nurses and doctors caring for you, but do it in a nonconfrontational way. Hospitals have social workers and therapists on staff who can assist you with emotions and fears. Making sure your care providers remember you are human is a good thing. Forgive yourself for outbursts, confusion, or things that are out of character. When you are ill, you cannot possibly be yourself. Surround yourself with family members and friends who lift your spirits, help you understand your options, and help manage your care.

Having a parent in the hospital is an incredibly emotional situation. You are worried about his or her recovery, stressed out from all the time you are spending there and the disruption it is causing in your life, afraid he or she could die or suffer complications, annoyed at the demands that are made on you, and probably feeling guilty for not spending even more time at the hospital. Everything you are feeling is normal and fine. There is no way to make this situation easy for you. It is going to be hard and you have to find a way to cope with that.

Some people become very emotional when in the hospital visiting an ill parent. It is wonderful to let your parent know you are concerned, but crying and speaking your worries aloud to him or her will not help you or your parent cope. You have to pull yourself together and get through this. Cry in the bathroom or when you are home. View this as a job you have to do. You have to help your parent get better. You have to help manage the medical care he or she is receiving. You have to be there and be involved no matter how hard it is.

Making Decisions in a Hospital

You and your parent are not at the mercy of the hospital staff. You have the right to refuse treatment, inquire about alternative treatments, and control the care that you or your parent receives. When you or your parent enters the hospital, it is important to inform the staff if you or your parent has an *advance directive* (a combination of a living will and health care proxy—see Chapter 4 for more information about this). Make sure this information is included in the medical chart. Be aware that you or your parent has the right to leave the hospital at any time. This is called *leaving against medical advice* (AMA). No one can force you or your parent to remain in a hospital and receive treatment. However, if you or your parent leaves AMA, you will need to sign a form absolving the hospital of liability, and you should also be aware that some insurance will not cover treatment for conditions or worsening of illnesses that are the result of leaving AMA.

When you or your parent is hospitalized, you have the option of authorizing a *do not resuscitate* (DNR) *order*. This is a request by the patient or his or her relatives that the patient not be given cardio or pulmonary resuscitation. This means that if you or your parent has a heart attack, for example, the staff will not attempt to keep the heart beating or the lungs breathing. A DNR order does not mean the staff will withhold other treatment such as pain medication, antibiotics, physical therapy, and so on. To deal with other kinds of treatment, you or your parent may wish to refuse them in writing. (See Chapter 4 about advance directives.)

DNR orders are normally used when a person is quite ill and reviving him or her would result in unnecessary suffering and pain. Remember that medical workers must preserve life and must respond to a person in cardiac or pulmonary arrest even if it seems cruel to prolong the person's life because he or she is suffering so much. A DNR order will allow you to avoid this situation.

If a patient does not have an advance directive, state law allows *next of kin* to make a decision. *Next of kin* normally means a spouse or children, or parents or siblings if there is no spouse or child. It is important to understand, however, that these laws do not give family members as much decision-making power as an advance directive does. An advance directive can permit a family member to choose to remove a feeding tube, while next of kin laws would not permit this.

You may confront a situation at some point where you or your parent wishes to refuse treatment or wishes to follow a course of treatment that is different than that recommended by the supervising physician. If you cannot reach a resolution with the doctor, ask for a *patient advocate* to become involved. If the situation is not resolved, the issue will go before a hospital committee. If a resolution is still not reached that you agree with, you can ask that the issue go before a *peer review organization*. (Contact your local *agency on aging* for the name and contact information of your local peer review board.)

Coping with Long-Term Medical Problems

Whether you or your parent has a long-term illness or minor ongoing medical problems, you are going to be dealing with and managing medical care for the long haul. This is yet another one of the hats you must wear if you are to ensure that you or your parent remains healthy and as independent as possible. Coping with your parent's health problems is difficult since you must, in essence, wear two hats. You are, on the one hand, a sympathetic listener and helper. On the other hand, you must be a careful and thorough record keeper and manager. Facing a long-term illness or ongoing medical issue is emotionally draining for you and your parent. The best way to cope with the situation is to gather as much information as you can, ask as many questions as you can, and develop a plan for managing the problem. It takes time to absorb information and think of the right questions to ask. Also, as you or your parent lives with a chronic illness, it becomes more routine and easier to manage. The crisis aspect of the situation does pass.

Facing an illness or medical problem does mean that your or your parent's lifestyle may have to change. The rest of this book will help you decide how best to do this and how to make these kinds of choices.

Becoming a Medical Care Manager

When you step into the role of caretaker for your parent, you probably will find that you are in the position of managing his or her medical care. Your parent may be emotionally unable to do so, physically impaired in some way that makes it difficult to manage things, or both of you may just feel more comfortable knowing that you are overseeing all the care. You will need to keep track of all appointments, records, and insurance information, and make the commitment to be at every appointment (or arrange for some other family member or friend to be there if you cannot). You also must take the time to understand your parent's medical problems and the treatments and medications being used. If your parent is in a residential facility of some kind, you need to become familiar with the contract he or she has with the facility, the kinds of care provided, and what the limits are. All of this can seem a bit overwhelming—kind of like a second job. It is a big responsibility, but you have taken on this role to ensure that your parent is receiving the care he or she needs, and the only way to be sure this is happening is to become involved.

Record Keeping

First you must obtain the needed consents or releases that will allow your parent's health care workers to speak with you and share information with you. Once you have done that, you need to create a system for how you will manage your parent's medical care.

List of Providers. Create a complete list of doctors, therapists, vision or hearing care providers, dentists, drugstores, and test facilities that your parent uses regularly now or has used regularly in the past. Use the *List of Medical Contacts* in Appendix

F on page 377 to organize this information. Finding this information may require some digging. First write down the providers you are aware of. If your parent has kept medical receipts, look through those. Ask the primary care doctor's office for the names of specialists and other medical personnel your parent has seen. Look through your parent's address book. It works best if you can alphabetize the list, but it is not necessary.

Appointments. Next you need to get a handle on when appointments are. Look on your parent's calendar. If he or she does not know when appointments are or whom they are with, contact the primary care doctor to ask if there are any current referrals. Call the dental, vision, and hearing care offices to check if there are any upcoming appointments scheduled. Put all appointments on your own calendar and keep a calendar at your parent's home with these appointments clearly written in.

Insurance. Make copies of your parent's insurance cards for you to carry in your wallet. Make sure that you have all his or her insurance information—he or she may have private insurance as well as Medicare or Medicaid. There may be separate dental insurance as well. You may need to submit information to insurance if the doctor's office has not done so. You also will need to track payment by insurance. If your parent gets a bill, do not assume it has to be paid. Find out if it has been submitted to insurance, if any insurance payment is pending, or if payment has been made.

Medical records. Many people do not keep an independent set of medical records for themselves or the parent they are caring for. It is always a good idea to ask for a copy of all reports, lab work, referrals, and test results. Make it a policy that you always ask that you be given a copy of every document. This can be useful for insurance purposes, to help you and your parent understand the type of care being provided, and also so that you can provide copies to new doctors that you or your parent may see. Start by obtaining a copy of your parent's file from his or her primary care doctor. If he or she is seeing a specialist, ask for a copy of that file as well. There may be a small copying fee charged by the office, which is permitted by law.

Use an accordion-style folder or several different file folders to organize the information. Create a separate section or folder for information from the primary doctor, one for each specialist or therapist, one for referrals, one for insurance paperwork, and separate folders for dental, vision, and hearing care. Organize the information in the folders or section in chronological order, with the most current information on top.

Familiarize yourself with your parent's situation. If there are diagnoses, medications, or results that you do not understand, call and speak to the nurse. You can also do some research yourself to understand these things.

Drugs. Managing medications is a very important aspect of the assistance with which you are providing your parent. Start by gathering up all the prescription bottles in the house. Go into the medicine cabinet and get out everything you can find. You may find things that are several years old that need to be discarded to prevent confusion. (It is also a good idea to look at the nonprescription items in the home, throw out those that have expired, and place all the rest together, leaving out only those that your parent needs on a regular basis.) If you do not know what medications your parent is supposed to be taking, contact the primary care doctor's office and ask them to tell you. Another good source is the pharmacy. Ask to speak to the pharmacist and get a complete list. If you do not understand dosage instructions, ask (you may need to provide the pharmacist with a release signed by your parent for you to obtain this information).

Sit down with the information you have gathered from the doctors and pharmacists, with all the bottles in the house in front of you. Figure out what each bottle is and what it is for. Make sure you understand the dosage instructions. If you find bottles that you have no information on, call the pharmacy that filled it or the doctor's office that prescribed it (this will be on the bottle) and find out if it is a current medication and what it is for. You may find it helpful to look each drug up in a prescription reference guide.

Complete the PRESCRIPTION DRUG DOSAGE LIST (form 4, p.379) so that you have all the information written in one place and can easily access it. Make sure to fill in the exact dosage instructions and any special instructions, such as medication that must be taken with food. Fill in the date by which the prescription needs to be refilled in pencil so that you can keep this portion updated. Keep a copy for yourself, leave one copy at your parent's house, and have a copy your parent will keep in his or her wallet or purse, so that it always travels with him or her. It is important to have this information readily accessible in case of an emergency. If your parent lives in an assisted-living facility or nursing home, the facility will have this information readily available. It is still a good idea to keep a copy that you can carry if you take your parent on outings, so that if an emergency arises, you have this information available.

Many people find it is convenient to keep pills in a weekly or daily plastic drug organizer. You can place the correct dosage for each day or each time period in the plastic squares and will not have to worry about your parent taking the wrong pill or the wrong dosage. You can also color-code the bottles—put red, blue, yellow, or black stickers on the bottle (not the lids since they can be interchanged) and create a large color-coded chart that tells your parent when to take each color. If your parent lives in an assisted-living or skilled-nursing facility, drugs will be managed for him or her.

When a new drug is prescribed, use the *Medication Evaluation Worksheet* on page 49 to help you gather information about it. Keep one of these blank forms in the medical file so that if a new medication is prescribed at a doctor visit, you have this as your guideline for asking questions about it.

Part of managing medical care is ensuring that prescriptions are taken properly. Many elderly people become ill or die each year because of improper use of prescription medication. Therefore, you will need to carefully monitor the drugs and make sure they are taken in the appropriate amounts at the appropriate times. If your parent is unable to do so, then you will need to consider some kind of assistance—either an in-home aide or some kind of residential living situation as described later in this book. (See Chapter 6.) If you have questions or concerns about side effects, do not hesitate to consult with the pharmacist or prescribing doctor. If you feel the medication is not doing what it is meant to do, if it is causing other problems, or if it is affecting your parent's sleeping habits or mental functioning, contact the doctor immediately.

> Buy a book that provides information about side effects, interactions, and benefits of prescription and over-the-counter drugs. Look up every medication your parent takes.

Managing Lifestyle

When you become involved in assisting your parent with medical matters, you will probably find that this is more encompassing than you imagined. Part of ensuring that your parent remains in good health is making sure he or she is eating well, getting enough exercise, sleeping well, and maintaining personal hygiene. If he or she is in an assisted-living facility or nursing home, this will be monitored to some extent by the staff, but it is a good idea to remain involved.

To remain healthy, your parent needs to eat a complete diet. He or she may have dietary restrictions or requirements. If this information is unclear to you or your parent, it is a good idea to meet with a nutritionist (ask the primary doctor for a referral). You will need to monitor the quality and amount of food in your parent's home. This can easily be done if you or another family member (or hired aide) assists him or her with grocery shopping.

Elderly people need to remain active. This does not mean running a mile every day, but it does mean remaining mobile. Many doctors now recommend that elderly people do strength training (light weight lifting) to maintain bone mass and muscle strength. Your parent may need a cane or walker if he or she feels unsteady on his or her feet. Talk to your parent's doctor about this. Many elderly people can benefit from a short course of physical therapy, to help them learn how to maneuver themselves as their body and abilities change. Make sure your parent does not sit in a chair all day (unless this is medically necessary). Encourage him or her to move about.

You will have to find for yourself just how involved you need to be in all of these aspects of your parent's life. Becoming involved in all of these areas will take a gradual approach. If it seems your parent has things in one area under control, simply keep an eye out for any changes in his or her needs.

An important part of remaining healthy is being mentally stimulated, so consider if your parent has enough things to do at home and if he or she is getting enough social interaction. Research has shown that crossword puzzles, Sudoku, and other mentally stimulating activities can improve and prolong health.

Dealing with Disabilities

If your parent is disabled or becomes disabled, it is important that you and your parent have a clear understanding of the disability. Speak with the doctor and with physical therapists or other health care workers to gain an understanding of the disability. If your parent is still living at home, you will need to do a careful analysis of the home and add features that will assist with the abilities that are limited.

Being diagnosed with a disability can be devastating at first, so be prepared to help your parent cope with this. You will also find that it may be difficult for you to adjust as well. Gathering information will help and may ease many of your worst fears.

Remember to obtain a handicapped parking tag from your state Department of Motor Vehicles if your parent qualifies. Ask your parent's doctor about this.

Mental Health Issues

Two of the most common and dreaded mental health issues facing the elderly are *Alzheimer's disease* and *dementia*. Both are attributed to physical changes in the brain and both can be difficult to live with. Dementia encompasses all kinds of memory loss, impairment of judgment, inability to learn, and inability to focus or pay attention. Alzheimer's is a progressive disease that impairs memory. It may start as small losses of memory and can progress to a complete loss of reality. Your parent's doctor can perform assessments and tests and diagnose Alzheimer's disease and dementia. (Read Chapter 15 for more information.)

Be aware that elderly people are not immune to other types of mental illness. *Depression* is not uncommon among the elderly. If you feel you or your parent may be depressed, contact a doctor. Depression is treatable, as are many other kinds of mental illnesses. Be aware also that depression is common in adult caretakers of elderly parents. (For more information about taking care of yourself as you care for your parent, see Chapter 16.)

Dental, Vision, and Hearing

When managing your parent's health care, do not forget to include dental, vision, and hearing. It is a good idea to have teeth cleaned twice a year and have vision and hearing tested yearly. You might be surprised to learn that it is not uncommon to find that a parent who is believed to be suffering mental difficulties is actually experiencing hearing or vision loss. Additionally, problems with eating can be caused by dental problems.

Sleep Problems

Sleep problems are a common complaint of the elderly and are usually physical in nature. As people age, they need less sleep and the type of sleep they get changes. Elderly people experience less deep sleep, *rapid eye movement* (R.E.M.) stages, and often awaken feeling as if they haven't slept well. Seniors often find that they need to take short light naps during the day and may have periods of wakefulness at night. These changes in sleeping patterns can be upsetting for your parent and for you if you are worried about him or her prowling around the house or facility at night.

To help improve your parent's sleep, encourage him or her to:

- avoid caffeine or alcohol in the evening;

- develop a bedtime routine that is always followed;

- pull down shades or close curtains to darken the room;

- talk to his or her doctor, as some prescriptions can cause or contribute to sleep difficulties;

- play soothing music or white noise to help drown out household or neighborhood noise;

- exercise regularly but not right before bedtime;

- avoid naps late in the day; and,

- eat light meals or snacks in the evening.

Remember that sleeping pills are not a long-term solution to sleeping problems. If your parent has ongoing sleeping problems, you may wish to have him or her seen by a sleep specialist.

Doctor Evaluation Worksheet

Name: _____

Date: _____

- Is he or she board certified?

  _____

- How many years of experience does he or she have in this field?

  _____

- Are you comfortable with the office staff?

  _____

- Is the office clean, pleasant, and cheerful?

  _____

- Are appointments easy to obtain or are there long waits?

  _____

- Can you make appointments at times convenient for you?

  _____

- Are you seen promptly or do you have to wait?

  _____

- Is the doctor rushed?

  _____

- Is the doctor easy to understand?

  _____

- Is the doctor condescending or friendly?

  _____

- Are you encouraged to ask questions and does the doctor make time to answer them thoroughly?

  _____

- Are you encouraged to take the time to make decisions that work for you and your parent?

  _____

- Are you informed of risks and benefits of any procedure, treatment, or medication?

  _____

- Do you have confidence in the doctor's treatment plan?

  _____

- Can the office handle questions by phone or email?

  _____

- Does the doctor have experience with the problems or illnesses you need help with?

  _____

- Which hospitals does the doctor go to?

  _____

- Who covers for this doctor when he or she is not available?

  _____

- Are you treated with respect, courtesy, and kindness?

  _____

Medication Evaluation Worksheet

Doctor or Pharmacist Name: _____

Medication Name: _____

Date: _____

- What condition is it for?

  _____

- What is it supposed to do?

  _____

- How can we tell if it is working?

  _____

- What are the alternatives?

  _____

- Is it available in generic form?

  _____

- How much does it cost and what will insurance cover?

  _____

- How long must it be taken?

  _____

- How often must it be taken?

  _____

- Does it interact with other prescription, over-the-counter, or herbal/
  alternative medications?

  _____

- Is it habit-forming?

  _____

- Must it be taken with food?

  _____

- What happens if a dose is skipped?

  _____

- How long will it take to work?

  _____

- Are there any common side effects, and if so, what are they?

  _____

HOSPITAL CARE EVALUATION WORKSHEET

- What is the short-term outcome going to be for my parent?

  _____

- What is the long-term outcome going to be for my parent?

  _____

- Can you explain how this disease or illness functions?

  _____

- What are the treatment options and alternatives? Are there less invasive alternatives?

  _____

- Which one do you recommend?

  _____

- What are the side effects?

  _____

- What are the risks of this treatment?

  _____

- What is the length of time involved in treatment and recovery?

  _____

- How will pain and discomfort be managed?

  _____

- What would you choose if it were you or your parent?

  _____

- What medications are prescribed and why?

  _____

- What kind of care will be required after discharge?

_____

- Please describe the recovery period.

_____

- Are there other medical problems that need to be addressed or evaluated by you or other doctors?

_____

- What will the result be if we choose not to accept this treatment?

_____

_____

- Are you experienced in performing this procedure or treatment?

_____

- Can you provide me with statistics?

_____

- How often is this treatment or procedure performed in this hospital?

_____

- Are there other hospitals better equipped to handle this?

_____

- What are the costs of this treatment?

_____

Notes: _____

_____

_____

_____

_____

_____

_____

_____

_____

_____

_____

_____

_____

_____

_____

_____

_____

_____

_____

_____

Questions to Ask Other Medical Personnel

- Can you tell me your name?

  _____

- What is your role in my or my parent's care?

  _____

- What is the prescribed medication and what does it do? How often will it be administered?

  _____

  _____

- What kinds of things should I watch for that would indicate that I am or my parent is having a problem or is not responding to treatment?

  _____

- What procedure are you going to be doing?

  _____

- Can you describe what you will be doing so I understand?

  _____

- Where are you taking him/her/me?

  _____

- Why are you taking him/her/me there?

  _____

- When will he/she/I be back?

  _____

- I am/my parent is a little nervous. Can you explain to me exactly what will be happening?

  _____

Notes: _____

_____

_____

_____

_____

_____

_____

_____

_____

_____

_____

_____

_____

_____

_____

_____

_____

_____

_____

Tips for Having a Good Conversation with a Doctor

- Try to have the conversation in an area where it is somewhat quiet. Avoid hallways if in a hospital.

- If you are the patient, insist on meeting in an office instead of an examining room where you and the doctor can be dressed and you can be seated, if possible, in front of each other.

- Have some idea of what you are discussing beforehand. Try to gather some preliminary medical information yourself so you are starting off with some knowledge.

- Prepare a list of questions, if possible, beforehand.

- Speak somewhere out of the hearing of your parent if you are going to discuss things you would rather not have him or her hear.

- Look into the doctor's face when he or she is talking.

- Ask a friend or relative to be with you. Often there are things you forget that another person can remember.

- Have the doctor give you the update or information first. Then ask questions once you have the basic information.

- Ask the doctor to explain terms or words you are unfamiliar with.

- Ask any question you have, even if you are afraid it is a stupid question.

- Ask what the best way is to get in touch with him or her if you have more questions.

- Take notes or ask the doctor if he or she minds if you tape-record the conversation (a small handheld recorder is good for this). This can help you understand and comprehend details of the conversation afterward. Be aware that some doctors will be uncomfortable with this.

• Ask about short-term recovery as well as long-term recovery.

• Make yourself ask questions about life expectancy and quality of life.

• Ask about side effects and risks. Get actual percentages and numbers.

• Ask if he or she can recommend some reading material about the medical issue you are discussing.

• Ask what the alternatives are to what the doctor is recommending.

• Do not let the doctor leave until you feel that all your questions and concerns have been answered.

TIPS FOR HELPING YOUR PARENT COPE

- Let your parent know you are present.

- Encourage other family members to visit.

- Take steps to ensure your parent is physically comfortable and also has things to keep his or her mind occupied, like TV, books, magazines, knitting, or any other favorite activity that can still be done in the hospital.

- Be positive in your attitude.

- Encourage your parent to eat, walk, sleep, and speak (if medically possible).

- Keep your parent up to date with his or her diagnosis, planned treatment, and general outlook without dwelling on negative things.

- Encourage your parent to ask questions of the doctor and medical staff.

- Find out what kinds of concerns or questions your parent has, so you can ask if he or she cannot or will not do something.

- Make your parent an active participant in decisions so he or she feels in control.

- Reassure your parent that his or her home, pets, finances, and other matters are being taken care of.

- Allow him or her plenty of time to rest undisturbed by visitors.

- Try to create a schedule of visitors, so you do not have three people visiting on Monday and nobody on Tuesday or Wednesday.

TIPS TO GET MEDICAL PERSONNEL TO LISTEN TO YOU

- Speak calmly and clearly.

- Be involved and visible when your parent is being cared for or calm when you are being treated.

- Repeat your question, statement, or concern if it is not responded to.

- Do not personally criticize the person you are speaking to.

- Emphasize that you want the best for your parent and feel it is up to you to make sure he or she receives the best care possible. Or emphasize that you are in charge of your own body and want to make sure your questions and concerns are answered completely.

- Politely point out treatment or care that is unacceptable or inappropriate and ask how it will be remedied.

- Refuse to consent to treatment until it is adequately explained to you.

- If a problem is not taken care of, repeat your concerns the next time you speak with the person.

- Point out symptoms or problems you have noticed with your parent that the doctors or nurses may not have.

- Be consistent and firm.

- Thank people who go out of their way to help you or your parent.

- Try to control your emotions when dealing with medical personnel. While they are trained to understand a patient's family's reactions, their job is easier if they do not have to. You will get more information from them if you are not upset.

TIPS TO FINDING MEDICAL INFORMATION

At the library or bookstore:

- *The Merck Manual*

- *Taber's Cyclopedic Medical Dictionary*

- *The Cornell Illustrated Encyclopedia of Health: The Definitive Home Medical Reference*

- *Mayo Clinic Family Health Book*

- *Complete Guide to Prescription & Nonprescription Drugs*

Online:

- www.nih.gov

- www.medline.com

- www.ama-assn.org

- www.MayoClinic.com

- www.merck.com

Also check research websites run by disease-specific organizations, such as the American Cancer Society. (Visit your area hospital's website. It may contain medical information.)

By phone:

Contact the organization for your parent's disease or condition, such as the American Heart Association, the National Digestive Diseases Clearinghouse, etc. Contact the National Health Information Center (800-336-4797) for names and contact information.

Financial Issues   3

Becoming involved in your parent's finances can be a sticky situation. Your parent may be reluctant to share information or authority with you; other family members may be resentful, angry, or uncooperative; and, you yourself may feel uncomfortable with the entire situation.

Many people find that they start to become involved in their parent's finances when they become involved with managing health care or with decisions about where the parent will live. Finances are often an integral part of both topics. In planning ahead for your *own* future, try to follow the tips in this chapter so that your finances are already organized and can be easily under-stood and managed by a family member should you need assistance when you are older. Give some advance thought to whom you would like to step in should it become necessary.

When to Become Involved

It is often hard to know when a parent needs assistance managing money and paying bills. Money management is often one of the most private parts of a person's life. If you do not know if your parent needs help, but you are wondering if he or she might, look for these signs:

- overdue notices arriving in your parent's mail or turned off utilities;

- your parent is worried or concerned about finances;

- your parent is generally disorganized or confused about keeping paper-work;

- he or she makes references to limited funds or financial difficulties; or,

- he or she noticeably cuts back spending.

If you do not see any of these signs, you can always ask your parent if he or she is having money problems. Some of the following questions can help you determine if help might be needed.

- "Mom, are you getting your bills paid on time or is there something I can help you with?"

- "Dad, has the economic downturn made it hard for you to meet your expenses?"

- "Mom, are you having trouble paying for your new prescription? I noticed it was quite expensive."

- "Dad, have you talked to your financial advisor lately about where you should be keeping your money?"

Getting a Handle on Finances

Whether your parent has asked for your assistance or you (or your family together) have decided that your parent needs some assistance, you will need to manage your parent's finances in a careful and organized manner. You do not want your parent to suddenly feel out of the loop, and you want to be careful to manage money and assets in a way that will protect him or her.

Before you can manage anything, you have to know your parent's financial situation. Use the Basic Information Organization Sheet (form 5, p. 380) in Appendix F to help you discover and list all of your parent's assets and income. This form will help you organize not only all of your parent's bank accounts, property, and investments, but it will also help you obtain and organize all the other information you may need to assist your parent with all types of insurance, banking, nursing home applications, home management, and so on. This form will be one of the most important tools you will have at your disposal as you help your parent manage money, make life decisions, and manage health care. To find the information needed to complete the form, you may need to use the following methods.

- Obtain information directly from your parent, his or her spouse, or other family members.

- Locate birth, marriage, and death certificates in the home or get them directly from the record keeping agency.

- Locate insurance policies in the home or get them from the insurance companies.

- Find automobile titles and registration in the home or car or get them from the state.

- Locate deeds and mortgages in the home or get them from the lawyer who handled purchases.

- Find bank statements in the home or obtain them from the bank.

- Find investment or retirement fund statements in the home or obtain them from the financial institution.

- Check safe-deposit boxes and home safes for documents and valuables.

- Check computer files.

- Locate bills in the home or call the creditors to obtain copies.

- Determine what income your parent has by checking with the Social Security Administration, pension plan administrator, Veterans Affairs, and so on.

It is a good idea to prepare one of these master organizational lists for your own affairs as well. Make a second copy of the form in Appendix F on page 380 or create a file on your computer where you can keep and update all this information.

There are some elderly people who distrust banks and other financial institutions. If your parent is one of these people, you probably already know that he or she keeps money under the mattress, jewelry inside the flour bin, or bonds behind the canning jars in the basement.

> If you hide things in this way, tell someone or create specific instructions so your family members can find them. Consider moving your money and valuables to safe-deposit boxes or home safes.

Whether you believe your parent does this or not, it is worth your time to ask your parent (and other family members) if there are things hidden, buried, or concealed in the home or on the property. Assure your parent you are not going to remove them, but that you feel it is important that someone knows the location of these items in case he or she suddenly becomes incapacitated and cannot communicate where they are. Imagine if your parent began to show signs of Alzheimer's disease and one day could not remember where these items were hidden.

Helping Your Parent Think about Finances

In the course of organizing all this information, you will come to have a good sense as to how well your parent is managing his or her affairs. Maybe he or she just needs some help writing checks due to arthritis. Perhaps things just need to be organized in a way that makes it easier for him or her to find them. Another option may be for you to check in with your parent once a month or so to be sure bills are being paid, checks are being deposited, and so on. Setting up automatic bill pay from the bank account is another way to make things easier for everyone.

Retaining control of financial affairs is very important to some seniors, and you want to be careful not to overstep your bounds unless it is really necessary. If you feel it is important for you to have some input or control, talk to your parent about this and explain your concerns. Formulate a plan that will allow your parent to still maintain some kind of supervision or control of finances so he or she can still maintain a feeling of independence and self-control.

Talk with your parent about the future. There may come a time when he or she is truly unable to manage finances. Suggest to him or her that it is best to plan for this kind of future now. If your parent does not take the necessary steps now, there could come a time when he or she is ill and unable to pay bills and no one else has the legal authority to do so. In this kind of situation, property taxes can go unpaid, resulting in a lien on your parent's home, and finance charges can mount quickly. Planning for a future when your parent cannot manage his or her affairs is nobody's idea of a fun time, but it is a necessary step to take to make sure his or her assets and home are protected.

Legal Authority

Once you have organized all the information, you need to obtain the legal authority to manage or help manage your parent's affairs. There are several ways to do this. One way is to create a *joint checking account* with your parent's name and your name on the account. You can then use this account to write checks to pay your parent's bills. You must be aware, however, that such an account can affect Medicare eligibility (see Chapter 5), so it is important to discuss this with your attorney first. Both people who are *signatories* (or owners of the account) on a joint account have the right to withdraw all the funds at any time. When your parent passes away, the amount in the account automatically becomes yours. You will also need a power of attorney (see Chapter 4), which will give you legal authority to manage your parent's financial affairs.

Organizing Records

Develop an organizational system to help manage all the paperwork associated with your parent's home or financial affairs. Create a separate folder for each creditor, bank account, investment, insurance policy, and so on. Place the documents in the folder with the most current item on top and oldest at the bottom. Keep all the files together in a drawer, box, or file cabinet. Keep a checkbook register or use a computer program to balance bank accounts.

Bill Paying

Create a system for dealing with bills. It is a good idea to place unpaid bills in a box or separate pile. Write the due date on the envelope or highlight it on the bill itself. Organize the bills in chronological order by due date so you can easily see which one needs to be paid next. This system is one that helps your parent continue to pay the bills if he or she wishes to.

Budgeting

Once you have all of your parent's paperwork organized, you will need to work out a monthly budget so that you can be sure that your parent's expenses can be met. A budget is simply a plan for how money will be spent. If the total monthly expenses exceed his or her income, then you will either have to dip into savings on a regular basis (which is fine to do if there is enough and this is how your parent wishes to spend his or her savings) or find ways to cut back expenses. Be aware that as your parent ages, his or her expenses will probably increase, as he or she will need more services, more medical care, and possibly need to pay for a residential facility. Talking with a financial planner is a good idea.

Planning for the Future

A big part of financial management and record keeping is planning for the future. Planning for an elder's future (and for your own future as you age) means considering and planning for Medicaid and possible nursing home stays. It is very important that you consult with an attorney who handles Medicaid planning. As you will read in Chapter 5, Medicaid eligibility laws are quite strict and require careful planning to ensure that your parent's future health care needs will be met without draining all his or her assets.

You will have an advantage if you begin to plan for your own elderly years now, since many of the things that can be done to protect assets from spending down to Medicaid must be done far in advance.

LEGAL MATTERS | 4

Helping your parent plan for the future or planning for your own future involves not only a lot of thought and arrangement of daily life, but also some legal steps. To be fully prepared for all possibilities, it is necessary to have a *will*, *powers of attorney*, and a *living will* or *health care proxy*. All of these are documents that should be prepared by an attorney. There are forms available in stores and on the Internet that you can fill out yourself. Some of them are good and some are not—to be fully protected, it is best to consult with an attorney. You should also be thinking about Medicaid planning, and an attorney can help you do this as well.

As you learn about wills, powers of attorney, and health care directives and proxies, you need to think about your own wishes and your own plans. You can meet with the same attorney you select for your parent and create these documents for yourself as well. Because you are a younger age than your parent, you will have the opportunity to do some long-range planning that can help arrange your estate and assets in a way that will benefit both you and your heirs.

Finding an Attorney

It is important that you locate an attorney who is experienced in estate and elder law. General practitioners often prepare wills and health care directives, but since you need to at least discuss Medicaid and estate planning, it is best to find an attorney who specializes in these matters.

If you have an attorney you have used in the past, call his or her office and ask for a referral to an elder law specialist. Call your city or county bar association and ask for a referral to an attorney experienced in this type of law in your area. You can also contact your state bar association. The *American Bar Association* (ABA) can help you locate a lawyer referral program in your area (**www.abanet. org** or 800-285-2221). The *American Association of Retired Persons* (AARP) has a legal assistance program (**www.aarp.org** or 866-330-0753) that can assist you in locating an attorney in your area and accessing free or low-cost legal assistance for those who qualify. The *National Academy of Elder Law Attorneys* (**www.naela.com** or 520-881-4005) can give you a referral to a member attorney in your area. You can use the worksheets at the end of this chapter on pages 78–80 to help evaluate the attorneys you find.

> When visiting the attorney, it is a good idea for you to have a separate appointment to discuss your own legal documents. You can have your parent remain in the room if you wish.

Knowing Who the Client Is

When you go to see an attorney with your parent so your parent can prepare a will, health care directive, and powers of attorney, it is important to understand that the attorney is employed by and works for your *parent*. These documents will only be valid if they are signed by your parent when he or she is fully cognizant and able to make informed decisions. You can accompany your parent and attend the meeting if this is acceptable to your parent, but you cannot make any of the decisions. You can, of course, make suggestions and give your input.

Wills

A *will* is a legal document that disposes of a person's belongings after death. A will allows you to express your wishes about how you would like to divide your belongings among your family, friends, and favorite charities. The attorney will probably ask both you and your parent to complete a worksheet listing all your assets. You can give him or her a copy of the BASIC INFORMATION ORGANIZATION SHEET you've completed or you can transfer the information to the worksheet he or she gives you.

Writing a will is a part of what is called *estate planning*. Estate planning involves the arrangement and disposal of all your assets to maximize them. For example, when there was an estate tax (it is currently being phased out), attorneys could help you find ways to avoid or minimize the effects of it. It is still important to do estate planning even though we may no longer have an estate tax (at the time this book was published, the estate tax was being phased out, but it is up in the air as to whether it will be reenacted when the current legislation expires).

The attorney can assist you in planning for Medicaid and can also help you deal with your assets so as to minimize *capital gains* taxes (taxes paid on the increase in value of items like stocks). The attorney can set up trusts, arrange for charitable gifts, and help you understand the *probate* process (the process through which the court approves a will and allows property to be divided). The attorney can explain to you and your parent what would happen to your belongings if you died without a will (legally known as *intestate*). This differs from state to state, but in general your assets would be divided between your spouse and children. You and your parent should discuss your wishes with the attorney and have wills drawn up that reflect them.

It is also a good idea to create a letter with instructions about how small items of personal property should be divided. A will usually does not get into detail about who will get the books, dishes, and towels—things that are not of great value, but may have particular meaning or may be needed by one family member more than another. Pets are another item that should be included, with instructions as to who will become the pet's new owner. A will can also include charitable gifts or set up trust funds.

> If you have minor children, you should name guardians for them in your will, so that you have a plan for who will care for them should you pass away.

Trusts

Trusts are a way to give money or property away while maintaining some control over them. Usually a trust holds the asset or money and pays *income* to the *beneficiary* (person who benefits from the trust). A *testamentary trust* is one that is set up after a person's death, through instructions in a will.

Many people have heard of a *living trust*, which most people see as a way to avoid probate. The owner of the property creates the trust and acts as *trustee*, controlling everything in the trust. If he or she dies or becomes unable to manage it, a secondary trustee steps in. The creator of the trust can terminate the trust at any point.

The advantages of a living trust are that you can completely control the assets you place in it and end it at any point. A living trust also cannot be *contested* (or challenged) in court. The assets in the trust remain in the trust after the creator's death and do not pass through probate, but they are taxable. Many people favor these kinds of arrangements because there is no court involvement. If you are considering a trust of any kind, you need to speak to an attorney who specializes in estate law.

An *irrevocable trust* is one that cannot be changed once it is created. This can also be a useful tool in estate planning.

Powers of Attorney

Powers of attorney are another way for you to gain legal authority to help with your parent's affairs. A power of attorney is a legal document signed by your parent that names you as the person who has the authority to manage certain kinds of affairs for him or her. Each state has its own power of attorney form, so it is best to consult with an attorney who can create one for you.

There are two main types of powers of attorney.

Springing. This type of power of attorney can be signed today, but does not take effect until some event occurs, such as your parent becoming incapacitated, a specific date, and so on.

Durable. This type becomes valid once it is signed and continues indefinitely. The power of attorney will give you the right to manage your parent's bank accounts, taxes, investments, and bills. A power of attorney does *not* deal with health care decisions.

Once you are going to begin acting under the power of attorney, you will need to provide copies of it to *all* the institutions you will be dealing with so that they know you have the authority to manage your parent's affairs. It is a good idea to execute a power of attorney and keep it on hand for when it is needed. Situations can arise unexpectedly and it is best to be prepared. If you feel that you do not want the responsibility of managing your parent's affairs, then your parent can choose someone else he or she trusts.

Some states have what is called a *short form power of attorney*, which is a shortened version of the state's regular form, designed to be easier for seniors to understand and complete.

You may wish to think about executing a power of attorney yourself, for your own affairs, so that an adult child or close relative could step in and handle your affairs should you suddenly become unable to. You can execute one now and keep it in a safe place should it ever become needed.

Health Care Directives and Proxies

Often older people believe that there is no reason to create *health care directives* or *proxies* because their family members will make decisions for them if they become unable to. In most states, family members are allowed to make decisions for a patient who is not cognizant. However, if family members disagree or do not know what the patient's desires are, the situation can become difficult, confusing, and legally complicated.

Other times, seniors see no reason to create a health care directive since they believe the medical staff will care for them appropriately. It is important to remember that doctors and hospitals focus on maintaining and preserving life. They try to take care that pain is managed, but they will not and cannot decide to stop medical care and allow a patient to die. For many people, the thought of being kept alive by machines when they have no hope of recovery and when they would not be conscious is horrendous. To prevent this, you and your parent need health care directives to ensure that you are cared for in ways that meet your own personal wishes. These types of documents have different names and vary from state to state.

A *living will* is a document that describes a patient's wishes about life-saving or life-sustaining medical care when he or she is terminally ill or in a permanent vegetative state. The document can specify the types of treatments and procedures that the patient does not want to receive. It can also dictate the type of pain management a patient wishes to receive.

A *health care proxy* is similar to a power of attorney. It appoints a proxy who will make health care decisions for the patient when he or she is unable to do so.

An *advance directive* is usually a living will and health care proxy combined into one. Some states specifically recognize one document or another, but all states are bound to respect a person's wishes (based on the famous Cruzan Supreme Court Case, where Nancy Cruzan's parents sought the ability to turn off her life support).

Each state has different requirements and forms. It is always best to have an attorney prepare these documents, since he or she will understand what type of document is best accepted in your state. *Caring Connections* (**www.caringinfo.org** or 800-989-9455) is an organization that provides state-specific forms.

Once you or your parent has signed the appropriate form(s), it is important to give copies of them to your doctors and to provide copies to hospitals when either of you is admitted. You may also wish to register your living will with the *U.S. Living Will Registry* (**www.uslivingwillregistry.com**), a free service that places your advance directive in a secure site so that medical workers can access it from anywhere.

Guardianship

Guardianship is an option you should not have to deal with if you and your parent have executed all the documents described in this chapter. If, however, your parent is not mentally able to knowingly sign the documents, *guardianship* (also sometimes called *conservatorship*) is an option you may need to face. A guardianship is a legal decree by a court that a person is unable to manage his or her affairs.

The court selects a *guardian* (also sometimes called a *conservator*) who has legal authority to manage the person's affairs. To obtain a guardianship for your parent, you will need to hire an attorney and appear in court. The court will need evidence that your parent is legally incompetent. The court can appoint one person to handle all of your parent's affairs or different people to manage different aspects of the affairs.

ATTORNEY OBSERVATIONS EVALUATION WORKSHEET

Attorney's Name: _____

Date: _____

- Is the office staff friendly?

  _____

- Is the office comfortable and fairly orderly?

  _____

- Does the staff seem frantic or calm?

  _____

- Is the office accessible for your parent?

  _____

- Do you feel comfortable with and trust the attorney?

  _____

- Are you or your parent given enough time to make decisions?

  _____

- Are appointments able to be made at times convenient for you?

  _____

- If your parent is homebound, can the attorney come to him or her?

  _____

- Is the attorney easy to understand? Does he or she explain legal termi-
  nology in way that makes sense?

  _____

  _____

Notes: _____

_____

_____

_____

_____

_____

_____

_____

_____

_____

_____

_____

_____

_____

_____

_____

_____

_____

_____

_____

ATTORNEY INTERVIEW EVALUATION WORKSHEET

Attorney's Name: _____

Date: _____

- Is a large portion of your practice involved with elder law, wills, and estate planning?

  _____

- How many years have you been in practice?

  _____

- What is your fee?

  _____

- Are you experienced in Medicaid planning?

  _____

- What kind of estate planning package do you recommend?

  _____

- Can you explain how to avoid probate and if you recommend doing so?

  _____

  _____

- How quickly can you prepare the documents we need?

  _____

- Will you give me copies of the completed documents?

  _____

Notes: _____

_____

_____

_____

_____

_____

_____

_____

_____

_____

_____

_____

_____

_____

_____

_____

_____

_____

Paying for Health Care | 5

Dealing with insurance issues is probably the most complicated part of assisting your parent or dealing with your own care. The regulations are a bit complex, but if you take things step-by-step, you can get a handle on understanding and working with your insurance.

This chapter will also help you understand and plan your own insurance needs for your future. Many people assume that Medicare will take care of their health needs when they get older. This simply is not true, unfortunately, so read this chapter with an eye to understanding what your options are.

Health Insurance

There are different types of health insurance and it is important to understand the different kinds and keep them separate in your mind.

Medicare is a federally funded health insurance program designed to help pay seniors' health care costs. It has several parts: Part A, which covers hospitalization; Part B, which covers doctor visits; and Part D, which covers prescription drugs.

Medicaid is a health insurance program run by the individual states for low-income people and is supposed to be an insurance of last resort. You may have heard of someone having to "spend down to Medicaid," which means a person must use up most of their assets in order to qualify.

> It is easy to mix up these two types of insurance. An easy way to remember is that we care about seniors (Medicare is just for seniors) and give aid to those in need (Medicaid is for people who meet income requirements).

Private health insurance policies are the kind provided by employers or purchased by individuals. These policies are offered through private health insurance companies and the premiums are paid for by employers or by the insured people themselves. Some of these policies are called *Medigap*, which means they are designed to specifically cover things Medicare does not. *Long-term care insurance* is private insurance purchased specifically to cover the cost of assisted living and nursing home care.

Medicare

Medicare is health insurance available to seniors and is a program that is funded by the federal government. Medicare has been in the news a lot recently with the addition of controversial prescription coverage and ongoing discussions about how to improve the program. Medicare will probably continue to be a point of dispute with politicians, so keep an eye out for proposed and approved changes in the coming years.

Eligibility. Medicare is a federal benefit that accrues in the same way Social Security benefits accrue, according to earnings. For every year you work, your eligibility increases. A person is eligible for Medicare at age 65 and can apply three months prior to his or her 65th birthday and up to three months after the birthday for the initial enrollment period.

People already receiving Social Security benefits are automatically enrolled one month before their 65th birthday. You are also eligible if you are under 65 and have been permanently and totally disabled for at least twenty-four months. You can make changes to your Medicare subscription each year between November 15 and December 31. If you are eligible, you can purchase Medicare and you cannot be denied coverage because of your medical history. To enroll for Social Security or Medicare, call 800-772-1213 or visit your local Social Security Office.

Administration. What can make Medicare confusing is that the federal government contracts Medicare out to private health insurance programs, which then administer the benefits. So your or your parent's Medicare plan may be handled by Blue Cross or some other local health insurance company. Health maintenance organizations (HMOs) also handle Medicare. If you obtain your Medicaid coverage in this way, Part A and Part B are combined for you in what is called Part C. Some Part C plans do include prescription coverage. If it is not available, your prescription coverage is available through Part D. If you or your parent is covered by an HMO for Medicare, you or your parent will need to select a primary care doctor and follow the HMO's rules for referrals to specialists as well as dealing with Medicare rules.

> **Make sure you obtain a copy of your own or your parent's HMO's patient handbook or user guide.**

Coverage. Medicare has strict regulations about what types of care it covers and how much it pays. Medicare decides how much your doctor is paid for the treatment you receive—not the doctor. The doctor cannot charge you more than Medicare will pay if you are covered by Medicare and the doctor accepts Medicare. Because of this, many doctors will not accept Medicare patients. To find doctors who participate in Medicare, you can use the online search tool at

www.medicare.gov/Physician/Home.asp or contact your local Medicare office for assistance.

There are many things Medicare does not cover—extended nursing home stays (stays of up to one hundred days are covered in part), glasses, hearing aids, routine yearly checkups, private nursing care, or dental care. Be aware that the list of covered items changes yearly and is often increased.

Check with your local Medicare office or with your doctor to find out if treatment will be covered. There is a co-pay for almost everything covered under Medicare.

Part A covers:

- hospital stays;

- limited-skilled nursing home stays (up to one hundred days after a three-day hospital stay);

- hospice;

- home health services; and,

- blood work.

Part A is a benefit that is usually free of charge.

Part B covers:

- doctor visits;

- tests;

- lab work;

- medical equipment;

- outpatient care and outpatient surgery;

- ambulance trips;

- limited chiropractic care;

- shots;

- preventive care;

- outpatient mental health care; and,

- physical therapy.

A *premium* (payment) is required to receive Part B benefits (if you participate in Part C, you pay a premium as well). There may be state funds available to help pay this cost. The premium can be deducted from Social Security benefits. The premium is affected by your income if you earn more than $80,000 per year. There is also an annual deductible and a co-payment for most services.

Subscribing to Part B is optional and a person can choose not to accept the coverage at the time he or she signs up for Part A. However, the premium can go up 10% each year and if a person chooses to sign up for Part B later, he or she will have to pay the premium increases. Additionally, Part B open enrollment is only available from January 1 through April 1 of each year.

If you or your parent has a low income and few assets, he, she, or you may qualify for a special state program (*Qualified Medicare Beneficiary Program*) that pays Medicare premiums, co-pays, and prescription costs. In order to determine if qualification requirements are met, read the Medicare brochure "If You Need Help Paying Medicare Costs, There Are Programs That Can Help You," available at your local Social Security office or online at **www.medicare.gov/Library/PDF Navigation/PDFInterim.asp?Language=English&Type=Pub&PubID=10126**.

Medicare does not automatically cover all your expenses, even if they are on the list of Medicare-approved services. If your doctor agrees to accept Medicare payment as payment in full, you owe nothing. Many doctors do not agree to this, however, leaving you to pay out of pocket. The most you can be charged is 15% over the Medicare-approved amount.

Part D covers prescription drugs. This is the most recent change to Medicare and it has been very controversial. It can also be difficult to understand and manage your benefits under this plan. Medicare drug programs are available from a wide variety of companies that offer a wide variety of plans. Each plan covers different drugs. The selection can be confusing. The best thing to do is talk to your pharmacist about the drugs you take and then get some advice about which plan to choose, since different pharmacies contract with different plans. You should also use the online formulary finder, provided by Medicare, which will allow you to find and consider various plans:

http://formularyfinder.medicare.gov/formularyfinder/selectstate.asp

Find a listing of state-by-state pharmacy assistance programs at: **http://bulletin. aarp. org/states**.

You will pay a monthly premium for prescription coverage and then will also have a yearly deductible (capped at $250) as well as co-insurance costs. You can pay the premium out of pocket, have it deducted from Social Security benefits, or have it deducted from your savings account. You pay the first $250 per year in prescription costs yourself as a deductible. Once that has been paid, you pay 25% of costs totaling up to $2,400 and the plan pays 75%. Once you reach this level, you pay 100% of your drug costs up to $3,051. After this threshold, you pay 5% of your prescription costs for the rest of the year.

Although the prescription plan is optional, you should select one whether you need it or not. If you wait to join at a later date, your premiums will go up 1%

each month. If you currently have other prescription coverage, you are eligible to get Medicare prescription coverage without penalty should that coverage end, as long as you join within sixty-three days of the coverage ending. Before signing up for Medicare prescription coverage in addition to your current prescription plan, you should contact your plan administrator. In some cases, signing up for the Medicare plan may make you ineligible for your current drug plan, so always check.

Use the Medicare Drug Benefit Calculator online at: **http://sites.stockpoint.com/AARP/drugbenefit.asp.**

Medicare Advantage Plans comprise Part C, combining parts A and B into one plan, serviced by an HMO. These plans generally offer more benefits than regular Medicare, but require you to follow the rules of the HMO, which usually include getting referrals to see specialists. You can switch your plan each year between November 15 and December 31, if you choose.

Appeals. Although there are certain types of care Medicare will not cover, a patient has the right to *appeal* a denial of coverage by Medicare for either Part A or B. The claim must be submitted (this is done by the participating doctor) and denied before it can be appealed. The denial forms include instructions for how to appeal the decision. Your doctor will submit paperwork to Medicare if you decide to appeal.

Part B claims may then be reviewed. They must be submitted within six months of the denial and are decided within eight weeks of submission. If the review denies coverage, then you are entitled to a *fair hearing*. A fair hearing is an informal hearing where you can appear in person and present your position. You have six months to request a hearing after a denial. This is held at an office and is *not* in front of a judge. The hearing is recorded and *transcribed* (written down).

Part A claims for inpatient hospital care that have been denied are heard by a *peer review organization* (a group of doctors who determine if the claim should be covered). You have sixty days to request this review and a decision is made within thirty days, or ten days for nursing home care.

Both Part A and Part B denials that have gone through the previously explained appeals process without being resolved end up at an administrative hearing before an *administrative law judge* (called an ALJ). You have sixty days to request this. Your claim must be for a minimum of $500 for Part B or $200 for Part A to reach this point. If the ALJ denies the claim, it goes to the Social Security Appeals Council Review where sworn testimony and evidence is used in a formal proceeding. If this is denied, it can be appealed to federal court. If you are in a hospital and Medicare denies a claim allowing you to stay in the hospital, you must request a review of the decision by noon of the day of your planned discharge. The claim is then heard by a peer review organization.

> Your local Social Security Office can help you appeal a decision. You can find an attorney experienced in handling these matters through the *National Organization of Social Security Claimants' Representatives* (NOSSCR) at 800-431-2804 or **www.nosscr.org**. It is a very good idea to use an attorney to help you navigate this appeals process.

Medicaid

Medicaid is an insurance program designed to provide health insurance to people with low incomes. Most people who receive *Supplemental Security Income* (SSI) are also eligible for and automatically receive Medicaid. Medicaid receives funding from states and the federal government but is administered by each state individually, which means that each state has its own plans, rules, and regulations.

Eligibility. Medicaid eligibility is determined by looking at a person's income and assets. When considering eligibility, a person's home, wedding rings, burial plot, car, personal and household belongings (up to about $2,000), and life insurance policies with cash values under $5,000 are not considered. Everything is evaluated by your state's standards to determine eligibility. In general, to qualify you must receive only a few hundred dollars of income per month and have a small amount of savings—no more than a few thousand dollars. You need to check your state's rules for eligibility since they vary from state to state. In some states you may be required to pay co-pays for the care you receive under this plan. Some states allow you to apply for Medicaid online, by telephone, or in person, in addition to a written application. When you apply, bring the following information with you:

- proof of who you are (such as a birth certificate);

- proof of where you live (such as a lease or utility bills);

- proof of your income (such as pay stubs or a letter from Social Security);

- proof of what you own (such as bank account statements or a car registration); and,

- your medical bills.

In some states there is no limit on income, but those states require that income over a certain amount be paid directly to the nursing home with Medicaid paying whatever balance remains on the bill. Medicaid recipients can keep some income for their personal use and to care for their homes. Medicaid calculates income by using the name on the check. If a check is payable to you, it is your income, and if it is payable to your spouse, it is not your income, according to Medicaid.

To apply for Medicaid, you must provide financial records and proof of assets and expenses. Financial records for the previous thirty-six months before applying are considered (this is known as the *look-back* period, and is sixty months for transfers to irrevocable trusts). Decisions are made within forty-five days of application. To apply for Medicaid, contact your local agency on aging listed in Appendix A, or speak to the patient advocate or social worker at the hospital or facility where you or your parent is being cared for. You may want to consider using a professional *Medicaid planner* to help you apply.

Many people become eligible for Medicaid by *spending down* to it—in other words, using up their own assets to pay health care bills until they have so little left that they qualify for Medicaid. Becoming eligible for Medicaid is quite tricky and cannot be done simply by giving things away to family members. Medicaid planning is a big business these days and you should talk to the attorney who is handling your parent's or your own estate planning.

> You can find more information about Medicaid at the *Centers for Medicare and Medicaid Services* at **www.cms.hhs.gov**.

Medicaid transfers. Because Medicaid is designed to provide coverage for people with low incomes, there are rules in place to make sure people do not just give away their assets to become eligible. If the program did not discourage people from doing so with these rules, even a millionaire could transfer all his or her assets to his or her child today and become eligible tomorrow, even though he or she would have had enough money to pay for his or her own health care.

Be aware that transferring assets that are not exempt from Medicaid will create a period of ineligibility. To calculate this, you must take the amount of the transfer and divide it by the average monthly cost of nursing home care in your area. The result is the number of months you are ineligible from the date of the transfer. For example, if you transfer a mutual fund worth $20,000 to your son in January and then apply for Medicaid, the $20,000 is divided by the average nursing home cost per month in your area (we will use $2,000 in this example). Twenty thousand dollars divided by $2,000 is 10. So you would be ineligible for Medicaid for ten months—or until November of that year, even though you currently do not own the money anymore.

Make sure you write down the name and phone number of the Medicaid application counselor you meet with. It may take several visits or phone calls for you to provide him or her with all the necessary information.

You can always transfer the assets that are exempt (listed on pages 92–93) whenever you want without affecting your eligibility. There are rules restricting when homes or nonexempt assets may be transferred. An unmarried person can transfer his or her home to a minor or disabled child or to an adult child if the purpose of the transfer was other than to qualify for Medicaid (such as providing a disabled child with a home to live in, since he or she would be unable to afford one on his or her own). The home can also be transferred to a child who lived in it the previous two years to care for the parent or if the child has an ownership interest in the home and lived there one year prior. A married person can transfer the home to his or her spouse (who can then transfer it to the children without affecting eligibility).

A married person can also transfer any nonexempt asset to his or her spouse, but the spouse receiving it cannot transfer it within thirty-six months for less than its full value (it can be sold at any time for its full fair market value).

Transfers can be planned in a way so as to maximize eligibility yet minimize the amount a person must spend in order to become eligible. It is important to consult an attorney who specializes in this area to be sure you are making the best choices and following the law. Some examples of things that can be done include investing money in the home (such as paying off the mortgage or improving it), taking a *life estate* in the home and giving a remainder interest to a child (which means you have control over it as long as you live but your child automatically owns it when you die), and transferring assets while there are still two spouses alive. It is also possible to place assets in an irrevocable trust to protect them.

Some people actually get divorced to protect assets from Medicaid. The spouse who does not need Medicaid coverage takes all the nonexempt assets in the divorce settlement, protecting them from Medicaid. Being divorced does not mean you cannot live together, so some couples divorce in name only to protect their assets from Medicaid.

Medicaid programs have *estate recovery plans*, which mean that, even though a person is permitted to keep his or her home and still be eligible for Medicaid, the state will place a lien in the amount of the person's medical costs against the home and require a sale or a cash payment by the person who inherits the home to satisfy the lien after the person dies. The state cannot force a sale of the home while the spouse or minor or disabled child still lives there. The state can also seek reimbursement from the deceased's estate for the amount owed.

Spouses. The spouse of a person receiving Medicaid is permitted to keep some assets without applying them toward the other spouse's medical care. He or she may keep:

- all income in his or her name;

- $2,100 month's worth of income in the other spouse's name, if more than half of the couple's income is in the other spouse's name;

- the home;

- the Community Spouse Resource Amount (one half of all *liquid* assets (those that are in cash or cash equivalents like bank accounts and CDs, up to $84,000 in some states);

- his or her car;

- furniture and household goods;

- wedding rings;

- life insurance with a face value of up to $1,500; and,

- two burial plots with a savings account for burial up to $1,500.

Coverage. Medicaid coverage is broader than Medicare; however, receiving care can sometimes be more difficult. Medicaid covers prescriptions, nursing home care, home health care, doctor visits, and hospitalization. Some state plans cover dental care, eye care, hospice care, and therapy. The problem with Medicaid is that it can be difficult to find a provider. All hospitals are required to accept Medicaid, but nursing homes that choose to accept Medicaid have a certain number of available beds for Medicaid patients.

> The key behind this is to get into a nursing home using private pay or Medicare and then become eligible for Medicaid, because the nursing home is required to keep you even if all Medicaid beds are full. Many doctors will not accept Medicaid patients, forcing Medicaid patients to use busy clinics with long waiting times.

Medicaid provides retroactive coverage for nursing homes for up to three months before you applied, if you would have been eligible then. The facility must accept Medicaid payment as payment in full if it accepts Medicaid; however, all facilities do not have to accept Medicaid. Only *certified providers* (providers who choose to accept Medicaid and have been approved by Medicaid) must accept Medicaid payment. Medicaid provides unlimited coverage for nursing home stays and for assisted living (if assisted living is covered by the state Medicaid program).

Check the Medicaid website at **www.cms.hhs.gov** for more information about exactly what kind of coverage your state plan offers.

To receive federal matching funds, state Medicaid programs are required to pay for the following:

- inpatient and outpatient hospital services;

- physician, midwife, and nurse practitioner services;

- nursing home services for persons aged 21 and older;

- home health services for persons who qualify for nursing home care;

- pregnancy-related services;

- family planning services and supplies;

- laboratory and x-ray services;

- federally qualified health center and rural health clinic services;

- emergency services for noncitizens; and,

- early and periodic screening, diagnosis, and treatment (EPSDT) services for individuals under age 21.

States may also receive federal funds to cover optional services for eligible participants. Some of these include:

- eye glasses and eye exams;

- hearing aids;

- durable medical equipment;

- clinic services;

- nursing home services for persons under age 21;

- intermediate care facility services for persons with mental retardation;

- home- and community-based services; and,

- dental, optometry, prosthetic, and tuberculosis services.

If you aren't sure what programs you qualify for, visit *Benefits QuickLink* for an online tool that will help determine eligibility at **www.aarp.org/money/lowincomehelp/quicklink**.

Appeals. You must receive a notice of a reduction in benefits and have ten days to respond to it. You are entitled to a fair hearing in front of a hearing officer within ninety days of your request. Your benefits must be continued during this time. This is an informal proceeding. The government must show that it followed the law in denying coverage. You have the right to appear, have an attorney, and call witnesses. A detailed letter from your doctor is an important asset to bring to a hearing. If you are denied coverage in the fair hearing, you need to follow your state's individual procedures for appeals, which vary from state to state. For more information on dealing with appeals, see *Tips for Handling a Medicaid or Medicare Hearing or Appeal* at the end of this chapter on page 108.

Appendix B provides contact information for Medicare and Medicaid programs.

Private Insurance

Private insurance is usually the preferred method of paying for health care. You are not limited in your choice of care providers (unless you are in an HMO) and your coverage is fairly wide and understandable. Private health insurance can be expensive, however, which is why so many seniors rely on Medicare and Medicaid.

Medigap

Many people choose private insurance as a way to protect their assets since Medicaid coverage is not available until assets are spent down to a certain amount. Because there are so many things not covered by Medicare, many people purchase *Medigap* policies. Medigap policies may pay Medicare premiums, co-pays, and deductibles, and some policies cover other costs that are not covered by Medicare. It is best to purchase a Medigap policy no later than six months after enrolling in Medicare. After this time period, insurers can deny coverage based on *preexisting conditions* (illnesses or conditions you have already been diagnosed with, like diabetes or Parkinson's). Additionally, many people carry private insurance policies as part of retirement plans.

There are twelve standard Medigap plans, but all twelve are not offered in all states. They offer varying levels of coverage. All must include at a minimum:

- 60–90 days of hospital coverage with a lifetime reserve of 91–150 days;

- 365 days of hospital coverage after Medicare reimbursements;

- Part B physician coinsurance; and,

- 3 pints of blood per year.

Plans may include skilled nursing care, Part A and Part B deductible, parts of bills not covered by Medicare, and preventive care. There are no new policies offered at the time of this book's publication that cover prescription drugs. The premiums vary.

Ask which plan you or your parent is being offered. Note that Medigap policies only work with Part A and Part B and are not offered for those with Part

C Medicare. Complete all applications carefully and include all information requested. Read the policy carefully and understand what it covers exactly.

> Use the worksheet at the end of this chapter to help you evaluate a Medigap plan. You can also read the booklet "Choosing a Medigap Policy: A Guide to Health Insurance for People with Medicare," available at **www.medicare.gov/Publications**.

Remember that you or your parent has thirty days to review a policy, choose not to accept it, and get a full refund. The Medicare site has a free personal Medicare health care plan finder that helps you compare Medigap policies and evaluate your Medicare coverage. Go to **www.medicare.gov/MPPF/Home.asp**.

> A rule of thumb that is often used is that if the premiums are 5% or less of your income, then the policy is a good investment. Be aware that premiums rise over time, so you must be sure that they will never be more than 5% of your income.

There are private insurance policies that are not Medigap policies, so be clear on what you are buying. You can also evaluate private insurance companies by looking them up at **www.ambest.com**, an insurance rating website that offers ratings and analysis.

Long-Term Care Insurance

Since nursing home care can cost over $70,000 per year, long-term care insurance is an important tool for those who do not qualify for Medicaid and do not wish to have to spend down to meet its requirements. If a person is close to being eligible for Medicaid, it does not make much sense to purchase a long-term care policy. As a general rule, the younger a person is when he or she purchases long-term care insurance, the more sense it makes. However, you will want to discuss this with an elder law attorney. It may make more sense for you to invest the amount of the premiums and then use these funds to pay your health care expenses.

Plans are usually not available to those over age 80 and may be quite expensive for those in their 70s—the younger you are when you buy the policy, the lower the premiums. For some people it may make more sense to save the amount premiums would cost and use them to save for home care. Remember also that long-term care policies only remain in effect as long as premiums are paid, although most contain a waiver for premiums due while the insured is receiving long-term care. There is a worksheet at the end of this chapter on page 105 that you can use to help evaluate long-term care insurance policies.

You have thirty days to review the policy and return it for a full refund. Find out if your state has a state-certified long-term care insurance program. These special state-sponsored programs allow you to purchase long-term care insurance and qualify for Medicaid with a larger amount of assets than is normally permitted. Contact your local agency on aging for information on this or see the list of program contacts information in Appendix A.

> Check on the financial stability of the company (go to **www.ambest.com** to do this) because if the company goes bankrupt, the premiums you have paid will be worth nothing.

Veterans' Health Benefits

If you or your parent is an honorably discharged veteran, he, she, or you can apply for health benefits through the Department of Veterans Affairs (VA). There is now a tiered system used to provide some veterans with free care while others must pay premiums. You can apply online and get more information at **www.va.gov/onlineapps.htm**, or contact your local VA office.

Other Options

There are options other than insurance when it comes to paying for health care. You or your parent may be able to pay for health care out of savings. Most people do not have enough savings to do this and must consider other options.

Home Equity Conversion Loans

Home equity conversion mortgages (also known as *reverse mortgages*) are federally insured. The homeowner is allowed to continue living in the home and receives cash as a loan amount from the bank. After death, the bank will either own the entire home or own whatever portion of it has been paid out to the homeowner. Most states have limits on the amount that can be borrowed through this type of loan.

For more information, contact the *National Reverse Mortgage Lenders Association* (NRMLA) at **www.reversemortgage.org** or call 866-264-4466.

Living Benefits from Life Insurance

Some life insurance plans have *living benefits* (also called *accelerated benefits*), which allow the policyholder to begin collecting benefits while alive to pay for long-term care or other health care. Check with the insurer to see if this is available (riders can be added to existing policies that do not contain this provision).

No long-term care insurance policy will cover all your costs for the rest of your life. In many ways, buying a policy is a gamble. You may never use all the benefits you have available, or you may use them all up within a few years but continue to live a long time. You have to weigh the costs and benefits and choose which is right in your individual situation.

Viatical Settlements

Viatical settlements allow a senior to turn a life insurance policy into cash. They are usually only available when the person insured by the policy is terminally ill. A viatical company purchases the life insurance policy and pays a portion of the face value of the policy, and in return becomes the beneficiary of the policy, receiving the full death benefit at the time of death.

These kinds of settlements allow a senior to get immediate cash, which might be much needed. However, when you sell a life insurance policy it means that the people selected as beneficiaries will no longer receive the insurance payment upon your death. Many people rely on life insurance policies to pay funeral expenses, and if the policy is sold, then the family will have to pay the cost of the funeral.

Requirements for a viatical settlement usually include:

- that you are terminally ill;

- that you agree to allow the viatical company to access your medical records;

- that you have owned the policy for at least two years; and,

- that your beneficiary agrees to the viatical settlement.

Before choosing a viatical settlement, check to see if the life insurance policy contains an accelerated benefits clause, which allows the beneficiary to access some of the policy amount before death. There will usually be a fee for this.

If you or your parent is interested in a viatical settlement:

- shop around and compare at least two or three offers;

- check the company out with a call to your state attorney general's office;

- ask that the company place the purchase funds in escrow so you know they are waiting when you sign the papers;

- arrange for immediate payment upon signing; and,

- discuss it with your tax advisor and estate planning attorney before signing anything.

Annuities

You or your parent can sell the home and invest the proceeds in an *annuity*, which will pay out a set amount each month. This is sometimes called a *Medicaid annuity*. To qualify for Medicaid, a person has to have very few assets. By selling his or her home and receiving a set amount of cash in return each month, a person can qualify for Medicaid and still receive back the value of the home. This is different from a *reverse mortgage* because the entire home is being sold, and in exchange the senior owns an annuity. In the reverse mortgage situation, the senior holds the mortgage and thus retains a legal interest in the home. Compare the amount of the annuity with the amount of a reverse mortgage you or your parent could obtain.

Some states have placed restrictions on Medicaid annuities. Generally a Medicaid annuity is a poor investment, but if it works to legally shelter assets from Medicaid, it might be worth it. Discuss this option with your estate planning attorney carefully before making any decisions.

Getting Help

Talk to your financial planner for advice and information about all of these options. He or she can discuss your individual situation and recommend a plan that works best.

You will want to consider:

- how your choice will affect your Medicaid eligibility;

- how your choice will affect what you can leave to your beneficiaries;

- how your choice will impact estate tax considerations;

- whether you are getting a reasonable rate of return;

- if you would be better served to invest traditionally or purchase traditional insurance; and,

- what the ultimate cost to you will be.

Medigap Policy Evaluation Worksheet

Name of Insurance Company: _____

Name of Insurance Agent: _____

Type of Policy: _____

Date: _____

- What levels and types of care are covered and to what extent? (You want the most extensive policy possible.)

  _____

- How long is the waiting period before the policy begins to pay? (The longer the waiting period, the less valuable the policy.)

  _____

- Is there a requirement that Medicare approve the care before the policy will pay? (You do not want this.)

  _____

- What are the benefit limits?

  _____

- What conditions or treatments are excluded?

  _____

- Is the policy guaranteed renewable? (This is what you want.)

  _____

- Are the premiums set and cannot rise with time? (This is the ideal situation.)

  _____

- Are premiums waived once the policy begins to pay out? (This is the ideal situation.)

  _____

- Is a hospital stay required in order for benefits to kick in? (Avoid this if possible.)

  _____

LONG-TERM CARE INSURANCE EVALUATION WORKSHEET

Name of Insurance Company: _____

Name of Insurance Agent: _____

Type of Policy: _____

Date: _____

- What kind of care is covered?

  _____

- Is home care by nurses covered?

  _____

- Is home care by personal care aides covered?

  _____

- Are there restrictions and prerequisites for coverage (such as requiring a hospital stay before the policy kicks in)?

  _____

- What are the requirements for cognitive (mental) and physical impairment that activates the policy?

  _____

- Who determines when you qualify for benefits?

  _____

- If you qualify for benefits, is a case manager assigned to your case?

  _____

- Is there a waiting period (sometimes called an *elimination* or *reduction period*) after you purchase the policy before it will begin to pay out?

_____

- What are the reimbursement levels in the policy?

_____

- What are the maximum benefits? (Some policies will only cover two years of nursing home care total in a lifetime or one hundred days at a time.)

_____

- What is the daily maximum?

_____

- Are the reimbursement levels and maximum benefits enough to cover all nursing home or home care expenses you might incur?

_____

- Do benefit amounts increase with inflation?

_____

- What kinds of conditions are excluded from coverage?

_____

- How much are the premiums?

_____

- Are the premiums fixed (unchanging)?

_____

- Can the policy be canceled for reasons other than nonpayment? (You want a policy that cannot be canceled.)

_____

• Is there a *nonforfeiture clause* (allowing a partial refund of premiums if you cancel the policy)?

_____

• Is the policy guaranteed to be renewable?

_____

• Are preexisting conditions covered after the policy has been in effect six months?

_____

• Did the agent give you a sample policy to keep and read?

_____

Take some time to evaluate how much coverage you are getting, how much you think you might need, and how much this will cost you.

Notes: _____

_____

_____

_____

_____

_____

_____

_____

Tips for Handling a Medicaid or Medicare Hearing or Appeal

- Dress in a businesslike manner.

- Bring an attorney if you can afford one.

- Bring a family member or friend for support.

- Bring all of your or your parent's medical records with you.

- Have your medical records organized in an easy-to-access way.

- Bring a letter from your or your parent's doctor explaining the condition and the needed treatment.

- Speak calmly and politely.

- Be patient when waiting your turn.

- Obtain copies of all documents that are issued at or after the hearing.

- Do not be afraid to ask to have things explained or repeated to you—ask questions.

- Take notes and ask for copies of all documents that are part of the proceeding.

- Be aware that you can stop the proceeding at any time to obtain an attorney.

- Approach this seriously but remember it is not the end of the world.

Notes: _____

_____

_____

_____

_____

_____

_____

_____

_____

_____

_____

_____

_____

_____

_____

_____

_____

_____

_____

_____

_____

REMAINING AT HOME

Almost everyone who envisions their elderly years does so with the hope of being able to remain at home, known as *aging in place*. Continuing to live in your own home is the most comfortable option most people can imagine. It is not always possible to remain at home, but it is possible to plan so that your parent's home (and your home when you yourself reach this point) is as senior-friendly as possible, making remaining at home a feasible option. There are many things you can do to slightly alter your parent's home to make it safer and easier for him or her to move around and perform the activities of daily life.

Not all the suggestions in this chapter are needed for every person. It is a good idea to read the entire chapter so that you are familiar with the options you have should your or your parent's condition change. You should also read this chapter with an eye toward long-term planning for your own situation. For example, if you live in a two-story home now, you may wish to consider moving to a ranch at some point so that remaining in your own home will be a long-term possibility for you when you become older. Also keep in mind that there are specialists who can come and help you personalize a home to meet your parent's situation. There are many things you can do on your own, but if you need help, do not be afraid to seek out a geriatric care manager who can help you find a professional.

Evaluating the Situation

When considering whether it is appropriate for your parent to continue to remain at home on a long-term basis, you need to see the home with new eyes. There are many features of average homes that can make it difficult for an elderly person to manage. If you notice conditions around *your* home that are mere inconveniences *right now*, remember that what is a mere inconvenience now can become a danger when you are older. For example, a laundry room in the basement may just be a pain right now, but when you are older, navigating the stairs may become unsafe.

Modifying the Home

There are many products on the market designed to assist elderly people in modifying their homes. Once you begin to research the products available, you may be surprised at the sheer number of things available.

There is also some funding available to help cover the cost of home modifications. If you can obtain a prescription for the modification, it may be covered under Medicare or Medicaid. If the modification helps to weatherize the home, you or your parent may qualify for assistance from the U.S. Department of Energy. To locate the office in your state, visit its website at **www.eere.energy.gov/ weatherization/state_contacts.html** or call the number listed in your phone book's U.S. government section for "Department of Energy."

The U.S. Administration of Children and Families' Division of Energy Assistance in the Office of Community Services administers, the Low Income Home Energy Assistance Program (LIHEAP), which also has funding available. Contact it at **www.acf.hhs.gov/programs/liheap** or 866-674-6327. You or your parent may also qualify for a low-interest loan for home modification from the U.S. Department of Agriculture's Rural Development Office. Find your state office online at **www. rurdev.usda.gov/recd_map.html**. Contact your local agency on aging for information about local loans and financial assistance. (See Appendix A.)

Types of Modifications

There are solutions to many of the problems and difficulties facing elderly people who wish to remain in their own homes. What follows is a list of some of the common modifications that can be made to make a home safer and more accessible.

Bathrooms:

- handrails or grab bars by the toilet and bathtub

- seat in the bathtub or shower

- transfer seat to allow easy access to the bathtub or shower

- hand-held shower head

- nonslip rugs and decals on the floor and bathtub

- overhead heat lamp

- handles instead of knobs on faucets and drawers

- nightlight

- raised toilet seat

- remove lock on door

- shower dispenser for liquid soap and shampoo

- disposable wet wipes

Kitchen:

- rearrangement of items in kitchen cupboards so everything is within reach without bending or reaching (may require the addition of a free-standing cabinet)

- addition of bins that slide out from lower cabinets

- plastic plates and glasses to minimize breakage

- large letters and numbers for knobs on the stove

- handles instead of knobs on faucets and drawers

- placement of a fire extinguisher within reach of the stove

- nightlight

- jar opener

- potholders in easy reach of the stove and oven

- elevated dishwasher (instead of having it rest on the floor, build it a foot or two higher for easier access); there are also dishwasher drawers that are the perfect size for a person living alone

Laundry room:

- first-floor location

- top-loading dryer

- laundry chute from second floor

- smaller laundry baskets with grips on handles

- laundry cart on wheels

Bedroom:

- located on the first floor

- nightlight

- telephone next to the bed

- lamp next to bed

- chair or bench to make dressing easier

- hanging shoe rack

- remove lock on door

- hang as many things on hangers as possible instead of placing them in drawers

All areas of the home:

- higher-watt bulbs in lamps and light fixtures

- place electric cords out of the way and secure them against walls

- windows that can easily be opened

- ceiling fans instead of box fans

- electric appliances that automatically shut off (such as an iron)

- remove furniture that is low to the ground and difficult to get out of

- move tables with sharp edges away from high-traffic areas or remove from the home

- lock basement door, so he or she will not attempt to enter it

- brightly lit entrances to the home with handrails

- lock or remove any casters or rollers on chairs or furniture

- wall switches for lamps and overhead lighting

- carbon monoxide detector

- reflective tape on stairs

- plowing or shoveling service

- yard and garden service

- smoke detectors

- removal of area rugs that can cause tripping or catch on a walker

- ramps in place of short groups of stairs

- nightlights in hallways

- handles or levers instead of door knobs

- temperature controls on hot water heaters to prevent scalding

- digital clocks with large displays

- telephones with large number pads

- television remote with large buttons and numbers

- bulletin board or wipe-off marker board for important phone numbers or medication schedule

- handrails in hallways and near steps

- large digital number thermostat or air conditioning device

- medical alarm system

- medication dispenser or separator

- magnifying glass lamp for reading or delicate tasks

- doorways wide enough to accommodate a walker or wheelchair

- reflective decals on sliding glass doors and on stair risers

- extendable gripping tool, to enable access to items on high shelves or items that fall to the floor

- nonslip backing on area rugs

- cordless phone

- hearing aid compatible telephones

- wall calendar with large numbers

- magnifying glass with battery powered light

- remove all needed items from basement or attic storage

- stopper for car in garage

- reflectors at edge of driveway

- book stand

- card holder (for playing cards)

- large button and display calculator

- blood pressure monitor

- large-handle scissors

Even if your parent lives in a rental unit, he or she can still make modifications to make in-home aging possible. The *Fair Housing Amendments Act of 1988* Section 6(a) requires landlords to allow tenants to modify the unit if the tenant pays for the changes.

Websites for Elder Care Products:

- www.elderestore.com
- www.modernseniors.com
- www.123safe.com/seniors.html
- www.agelessdesign.com
- www.dynamic-living.com
- www.productsforseniors.com
- www.elderluxe.com

Creating a Plan

If your parent wishes to remain at home, it is essential that you develop a plan. Merely choosing to remain at home *is not* a plan. You need to think through all the possibilities and problems that may occur and find solutions. Use the HOME LIVING PLAN (form 6, p.385) in Appendix F.

Getting Help

You may wish to invite neighbors or friends to help keep an eye on your parent. Some communities have community watch programs or call-in programs where elders are contacted daily by watch volunteers. Neighbors are often willing to assist with bringing in mail and papers and checking in with an elderly person on a regular basis. *Meals on Wheels* programs may be available in your area and can provide your parent with one hot, balanced meal per day. You may also be able to hire an aide to come in once a day to assist your parent with bathing and cooking. Aides are not as expensive as nurses and provide just the right amount of assistance for a senior who still wants to be independent but needs some reliable daily help.

Coping with Emergencies

An important part of planning for your parent's in-home care is having a system to deal with emergencies. Make sure that a notepad or sticker next to the phone lists 911 so your parent can call for help. Also leave a list of family, friend, or neighbor phone numbers clearly visible by the phone. Keep your parent's doctor's phone number by the phone, too. Give neighbors phone numbers for family members so they know who to contact if there is a problem or they suspect there is a problem.

Contact your local post office for information about the *Mail Carrier Alert Program*, a program that has mail carriers notify family members if an elderly person does not retrieve his or her mail. Also, find out if there is a *Phone Assistance League* in your area. (See your local agency on aging in Appendix A.) This program will make daily calls to your parent, and if he or she does not answer or needs help, it will contact family members or emergency personnel.

Contact your local sheriff's department about the *Vial of Life Program*. The program provides a simple form to fill out, which contains an elderly person's name, medical information, doctor's number, and family contact information. This is then placed in an empty prescription pill container and attached to the top shelf of the refrigerator. Emergency workers automatically will check for this vial and have important information about your parent. Find out if your community has a special sticker or magnet to place on the refrigerator.

Emergency Systems

You may wish to consider installing an emergency alert system in your parent's home. These systems come with a phone or transmitter unit and a necklace or bracelet with a call button on them. If your parent needs emergency help, he or she just pushes the button and the company administering the system will try to contact the senior to see what assistance is needed, and then call relatives or friends and, if there is no answer or the senior makes it clear it is an emergency, calls 911. These systems are available on a monthly rental payment plan (usually under $50 per month) and can give both you and your parent peace of mind. Check with your local agency on aging for names of vendors near you.

Transportation

If your parent is still driving a car, you may wish to monitor this closely and make sure he or she is still able to drive dependably.

Drive with your parent once in a while and notice if he or she is:

- forgetting to signal;

- not noticing red lights or stop signs;

- weaving across lanes;

- driving much slower than the flow of traffic;

- having a hard time making turns;

- having trouble seeing over the dashboard;

- having difficulty reaching the pedals;

- stopping too quickly;

- not paying attention to traffic around him or her; or,

- reacting too slowly to driving situations.

Talk to your parent about his or her driving skills. Your parent's car or license is a symbol of independence to him or her, so you will want to help him or her maintain the ability to drive as long as possible. Maintaining a driver's license is important even if your parent stops driving—it is a necessary piece of identification that should be held for as long as possible. Talk to your parent about your concerns. Try some compromises, such as he or she will only drive during the day or only drive to the senior center and church. Perhaps talk about friends or family members who have stopped driving. Reduction in driving ability is a big change for older people and is also very symbolic of the loss of independence.

If your parent is not able to continue driving, transportation arrangements will need to be made. In some communities, the senior center can provide free transportation, so check into this. Find out if your parent can easily access public transportation. The *American Public Transportation Association* provides links to local public transportation at **www.APTA.com**. Make sure your parent always has someone he or she can call for a ride to doctor appointments, to get to the store, or for recreational outings. Create a list of relatives or friends available to drive and leave the list near the phone.

> The AARP, National Highway Traffic Safety Administration, and USA Educational Foundation offer a driving skills assessment at **www.NHTSA.dot.gov/people/injury/olddrive**.

Maintaining a Social Life

One of the main reasons people choose to age at home is to maintain their community connections. Even though your parent may experience difficulty walking or may have limited transportation available, he or she still needs contact with friends, acquaintances, and family. If your parent has a hobby or favorite activity, it is important that he or she still be able to participate in events, meetings, gatherings, and other happenings that interest him or her. Maintaining a social life will help your parent feel active, important, and mentally healthy. Remaining at home and never seeing anyone other than those who come to the house can be a lonely existence; therefore, it is important for your parent to continue to get out as he or she is able.

Many communities have special social gatherings, programs, and classes for elderly residents. Check with your local agency on aging or with your local senior citizen center to identify availability.

Spiritual Needs

Maintaining spiritual needs is also important in helping your parent remain active and healthy. If your parent likes to regularly attend church, mosque, or synagogue, see if a family member can provide transportation. The church or religious institution may be able to help provide transportation as well if you call and ask. Additionally, many clergy members are willing to make home visits to help seniors who are not comfortable leaving their homes maintain a spiritual life. You will also find that you can locate religious shows and services on television and radio and can provide your parent with reading material to help satisfy his or her spiritual needs.

Staying Active

Remember that staying active is one of the keys to continued good health. Encourage your parent to get up on a regular basis and walk through the home. Short outdoor walks, with or without assistance, can also be beneficial if your parent is able to manage them. Make sure your parent has things to read, things to see, things to do, things to think about, and people to talk to. Research shows that staying mentally active with puzzles, reading, and other intellectual activities can help maintain health.

In-Home Health Care

Perhaps your parent currently has medical needs that require daily or frequent medical attention. Even if your parent currently does not require medical assistance, it is important to understand the available options so that, should in-home care become necessary, you know where to turn.

Choosing In-Home Health Care

The most important thing to keep in mind about in-home health care workers is that your parent must be comfortable with them and able to accept the assistance they provide.

Throughout the entire process, put yourself in your parent's place. Imagine what it would be like to have strangers come into your home, manage your life, and do things to your body. You would want them to be people you feel comfortable with and can trust. You would be very concerned about the lack of privacy or amount of interference in your life. Keep these concerns in mind when you are selecting people.

Remember that the more skilled the provider, the more expensive the care. A registered nurse (RN) will cost much more than an aide, so make sure you closely match needs to qualifications. Many people feel that it makes more financial sense to have their parent enter a senior residence than to pay for in-home care. In actuality, it is less expensive for most seniors to remain at home, if they can afford the out-of-pocket costs involved. (Medicaid and Medicare do not pay much of these.) Expect home care to start at about $12 an hour (for an aide) and to top out near $100 an hour for the most skilled nursing care.

Remember that if you hire in-home health providers and you do not do so through an agency, you are supposed to treat the providers like employees and withhold taxes and provide W-2s. Many nurses and aides do home care part-time when they are not working for a hospital or facility and are willing to work off the books. Be aware that you are legally required to withhold taxes. Discuss this with an accountant. If you use an agency, you avoid this problem because the agency handles payroll and witholding.

You can use the worksheets at the end of this chapter to help evaluate both home care workers and home care agencies.

Check Appendix A for your state home care organizations. Contact your local organization for information and assistance.

The Choices

When you are selecting home health care workers, you will need to narrow down exactly what kind of care or assistance is needed so that you know whom you need to hire.

Registered nurse (RN). This is the most expensive choice. Depending on the level of care needed, you may be able to arrange for a visit once per day or once per week. An RN can perform a full range of medical care and administer medications. An RN can also be very helpful in making medical decisions and pinpointing when a doctor or hospital visit needs to be made.

Licensed practical nurse (LPN). A trained nurse who is not authorized to perform as many medical services as an RN, but can monitor blood pressure and do other medical tasks.

Aide. Performs personal hygiene care and some noninvasive medical care. An aide can do light housekeeping, prepare meals, and can be certified or uncertified.

Therapist. Licensed provider who assists patients in rehabilitating or improving physical abilities.

Housekeeping care. Unlicensed workers who perform household tasks.

Home health care agencies. These are agencies that employ home health care workers and provide you with the staff you need. You pay the agency directly and often have little say over who takes the shifts. However, all staff is bonded and if one worker calls in sick, there is another one to replace him or her. Make sure the agency is Medicare- or Medicaid-certified so that the care will be covered. Get the

Medicare survey report about the agency from your State Department of Health. (see Appendix A.)

Payment for Care

Medicare will pay for some in-home health care. Skilled nursing must be required and the person receiving care must be homebound (but not necessarily bedridden). The care needed must be prescribed by a physician. Coverage includes nursing, physical therapy, social services, aides, and medical supplies. Medicaid will also cover some home health care services. Check with your local agency on aging for details of what your state's plan covers. A private insurance policy will also provide some coverage for in-home health care. Check with your carrier.

Contact the following agencies for accreditation information on home health care agencies:

Community Health Accreditation Program
www.chapinc.org
800-656-9656

The Joint Commission
www.jcaho.org
630-792-5000

National Association for Home Care & Hospice
www.nahc.org
202-547-7424

Self-Provided Care

You may be able to provide some of the medical care your parent requires yourself. Other family members, your parent's spouse, and even your parent may be able to do so, as well. Your parent can learn to perform finger sticks for diabetes, colostomy bag care, and other routine procedures. A nurse or aide can teach family members how to monitor certain conditions, change bandages, help with exercises, and assist your parent with walking and bathing.

Your Role

If your parent chooses to remain at home, your role in his or her care will be quite involved and you will need to be the care manager. If your parent lives at a facility, you will not have as much responsibility, since the staff there will take on most of these duties.

Not only will you need to hire and manage home care staff, you will also need to manage your parent's overall condition. If your parent does not require in-home care workers, you may feel an even greater burden knowing there is no one there with him or her, and your reliance on neighbors, friends, and family may feel like an imposition.

As you assist your parent in remaining at home, you will probably think about your own senior years and how things will work out for you. Pay attention to what you like and what you do not like about the situation and file it away to help you plan for your own future.

Downsizing

Another option available to seniors who wish to remain in their own homes is *downsizing*. A home that was the right size to raise a family may be too large for a married senior couple or a single senior. A large home or yard can require too much maintenance and the utilities may be too costly for a person on a set income who has in-home health care costs. Many seniors choose to downsize—that is, sell the home and purchase a different one that is smaller, better equipped, and designed for an older person. This can be a good choice if the current home is getting to be too much to manage, has features that are not senior-friendly, or is too far away from family. Your parent should discuss this with his or her tax advisor first to make sure that he or she can take advantage of the capital gains rollover provision in the tax law. This essentially allows the homeowner to roll over profit from the sale of the home into the new home that is being purchased so that there are no tax increases due to the move. Some seniors find that a new manufactured, mobile, or modular home is a good choice for them. Some seniors find that their home is too large for them but is just the right size for a younger family member who is raising a family. Selling the home to a relative can be easier than selling it to a stranger and never seeing it again.

HOME CARE PROVIDER EVALUATION WORKSHEET

Name: _____

Degree or Certification: _____

Experience: _____

References: _____

Date: _____

- Is he or she dressed neatly?

  _____

- Does he or she appear confident?

  _____

- Is he or she friendly and cooperative?

  _____

- Is he or she patient and understanding with your parent?

  _____

- Is he or she bonded?

  _____

- Tasks he or she is able and willing to perform:

  _____

- Hours and days he or she is available:

  _____

- Can he or she recommend others in home health care work?

  _____

- Wage requirements:

  _____

- Will he or she work off the books?

  _____

- Does he or she have reliable transportation?

  _____

- What experience and training does this person have?

  _____

- Does he or she have references?

  _____

- Does your parent like him or her?

  _____

- Do you trust him or her?

  _____

Notes: _____

_____

_____

_____

_____

_____

_____

HOME CARE AGENCY EVALUATION WORKSHEET

Agency Name: _____

Name of Representative: _____

Types of Services Provided: _____

Types of Workers Employed: _____

Date: _____

- How are employees chosen and trained?

  _____

- Are you provided with a brochure or other written materials from the agency?

  _____

- Is there a contract for services?

  _____

- Is a case manager assigned?

  _____

- Will the agency evaluate your parent's needs and propose a plan of care?

  _____

- Does the agency communicate and consult with your parent's physician?

  _____

- How often will your parent be reevaluated?

  _____

- Is the agency certified?

  _____

• Is the quality of care monitored and inspected?

_____

• Does the agency accept Medicare?

_____

• How will you or your parent be billed?

_____

• Are references provided?

_____

• How long has the agency been in business?

_____

• What is their employee turnover rate?

_____

• Is the agency bonded?

_____

Notes: _____

_____

_____

_____

_____

_____

_____

CLOSING OR SELLING THE HOME | 7

If your parent has moved out of the home or is considering doing so, you will need to make some choices about maintaining the home or selling it. Your parent's eligibility for Medicaid and the need to pay nursing home or assisted-living facility bills will certainly play a large role in your decision whether to sell or simply close up the home. Whatever plans are made for the future of the home, moving out of it is a very emotional time for your parent, as well as for you and the rest of the family.

If your parent lives in a rental unit, you will need to decide whether or not to give up the lease. It makes little sense to pay rent on an apartment your parent will not return to. However, closing an apartment involves just as much emotion as closing a home, so it is important to read this chapter.

In reading this chapter, you should give thought to your own situation. Should the time come for you to leave your home and live elsewhere, which options seem as though they will make the most sense for you? Begin planning now for how you will handle the situation should you ever need to leave your home.

How to Make the Decision

Deciding whether to sell the home or simply close it is a difficult choice. In many situations, a sale will be necessary if your parent is paying the bills for the facility he or she has moved to. In other situations, such as a temporary rehabilitative stay or the decision to move in with a family member, it may be easier and better to simply close the home.

Making the decision to close or sell a home is one that needs to be done in close consultation with your Medicaid planning attorney. Even if you keep the home, the state is required to place a *lien* (essentially a debt that is filed against the home and must be paid when the home is sold) against it and recover the funds after the owner's death.

There are also emotional concerns involved. Selling the home will be a final step for your parent, and acknowledging that he or she will never return home is a difficult and painful realization for everyone involved. Homes are much more than places to live—they are symbols of independence and also in many ways hold memories of the time spent there. Choosing not to sell the home can also cause difficulties, as a parent may someday insist that he or she is moving back home, when he or she would be unable to care properly for himself or herself there. Use the *Deciding to Sell or Maintain a Home Worksheet* at the end of this chapter on page 144 to help make your decision.

Involving Your Parent

Your parent needs to be involved in this decision since the sale of one's home is an important and deeply personal event. As plans are being made or discussions are being had about your parent's decision to move to a facility or in with a relative, the topic of the home will certainly be a concern. If the finances dictate, it may be obvious that there is no choice and a sale must be made. However, if there is a choice, you must help your parent consider the options.

Selling the home will necessitate selling or giving away a large quantity of belongings since most probably will not be able to move with your parent. Your parent will need to decide or allow someone else to decide what will happen to these belongings. Your parent may hope that a family member will purchase the home. If this is the case, make sure it is discussed before a real estate agent is involved. The result of selling the home will be a lump sum that can be used to pay your parent's expenses.

> If a relative does purchase the home, make sure it is for fair market value to avoid Medicaid and tax problems.

Closing the home and keeping it will necessitate securing it, checking on it, repairing it, and paying taxes on it (unless your parent qualifies for a tax relief program allowing him or her to put off paying taxes—check with your town or city clerk's office about this). This can involve a lot of time, worry, and expense. An alternative may be allowing a relative or close friend to live in the home rent-free in exchange for handling maintenance and upkeep.

Coping with Emotions

As your parent faces moving out of the home, his or her emotions will be quite overwhelming. Even parents who are seemingly accepting of the situation can be hit quite hard when moving day approaches.

The best way to help your parent through this transition is to help him or her be prepared. Discuss everything that will happen. Find out what his or her worries and fears are and look for ways you can put him or her at ease.

No matter where your parent is moving, make sure he or she is familiar with it. Plan in advance what items will be packed and brought along. Discuss how he or she wants to deal with the rest of his or her possessions.

Your own emotions will be overwhelming at this time as well. Your parent's home holds a great deal of symbolism, whether he or she has lived there sixty years or six months. Saying goodbye to your parent's home is a bit of a grieving process, and you should allow yourself time to deal with this process. You should also expect that if you are managing the move, the sale, and the division of possessions you will be quite tired, frustrated at times, and perhaps resentful of your parent.

Remember that change can be good. You may have less worries about your parent now that he or she will be living elsewhere. Your parent may find that he or she feels more comfortable with the assistance that is now available. Try to look at this situation not as an ending, but as a change that can help make everyone more comfortable.

Dealing with Belongings

As your parent plans to move, you will both face the task of coping with the household belongings.

Things to Take

To cope, encourage your parent to make a list of items he or she will be taking along. Remember that if your parent is moving to a facility, there may be restrictions on the types of items that can be brought. Senior apartments have few restrictions, while nursing homes have the most restrictions. Make sure you ask what items can come along. If your parent is moving in with you or another relative, it will simply be impractical to bring everything, so you will still need to make decisions about what can be brought along. Remember that if your parent is moving to an assisted-living or skilled-nursing facility where staff will be in and out of his or her room, it is a good idea to leave items of value with family members because theft can happen.

The following is a list of common items elderly people wish to bring along. Make sure you talk to your parent about the items on this list. Many of these items are things that are commonly on the list of things people wish to bring along, or if they cannot bring them, on the list of items they want to personally give to specific family members or friends.

Commonly requested items include:

- family photos

- jewelry

- hobby or craft supplies

- radio

- TV

- blanket or quilt

- favorite chair

- reading lamp

- pillow

- side table

- bed

- framed artwork

- footstool

- financial records

- old letters and mementos

- favorite mug

- throw or area rug

- pets

- books

- personal care items

- sheets

- collections

- bible, rosary, religious symbols

- address book

- items with special meaning

- heirloom items

Things to Get Rid Of

As you and your parent sort through belongings, there will be things that can easily be thrown out, donated to charity, or sold at a garage sale. Try not to be too hasty in throwing things away—however, do not be a hoarder. For example, you may not see any use for the large unopened bottle of clam sauce in the cupboard, but a food pantry would be glad to receive it. There may be other household items that are not heirlooms that other family members can put to good use anyway.

Get some big boxes and label them "Garage Sale," "Charity," and "Garbage" and place things in the boxes as you come across them. You may also want to create a box for each family member and place items in them.

Storage

Putting some things in storage may be an option for your parent. Perhaps he or she is not ready to divide things up. A storage locker or larger space can be rented monthly at local facilities. Relatives may have space in attics or basements to store things. Be careful when considering this last option, because there can be confusion over what is being stored and what is being given.

Dividing Among Family

Since the items in the home belong to your parent, it is up to him or her to divide them among family, or whether to divide them at all. Some seniors feel strongly that their possessions belong to them and should only be divided when they die. Encourage your parent to try to be fair when dividing or making a plan for his or her belongings. Many long-standing family feuds begin over the division of a relative's possessions. Try to avoid allowing this to disrupt your family. Some seniors have strong wishes about certain pieces and prefer to allow family members to use a lottery system to divide the rest. You need to talk to your parent about what he or she is most comfortable with.

Selling

There may be many items that no one in the family really wants. You could sell them through the classified ads, on eBay, at a garage sale, to a secondhand store, or you could allow an estate sale to be conducted. (Be aware that estate sellers often do not provide very good value for the items they purchase. It may make more sense to donate the items or sell them in another way.)

Donating

Donating unwanted items to charity is another option. Discuss this with your parent. He or she may have a preference for a particular charity. Make sure that the charity is a nonprofit agency and get a receipt. Many charitable organizations will come and pick up items if you are donating a large number of things. There are some items they will not take, such as mattresses, furniture with tears or rips, air conditioning units, refrigerators, and so on. Check with the charity first if you think there may be some question about the items you are donating.

Disposing

After your parent and family members have taken everything they want and you have donated what you can, you will be left with some things that will have to be thrown out. For large items, find out if your parent's sanitation or garbage service has specific large item days or if you can dispose of them any time. Before throwing out a refrigerator, you must have the door removed and possibly have a certificate by a refrigeration specialist attached to it.

Check with your sanitation department or garbage service for specific requirements. To dispose of hazardous materials such as paint, oil, gasoline, and other chemicals, as well as tires, contact your town or county to determine if there is a hazardous waste drop-off center. Try to follow local recycling rules when sorting the garbage.

Pets

If your parent has a pet, this can be a source of great worry and sadness. If your parent is moving in with a family member or going to a senior residence, he or she may be able to bring the pet along. If pets are not permitted where your parent is moving, then arrangements will need to be made for the pet. Your parent will probably feel most comfortable having a family member or close friend adopt the pet so that your parent will still have the opportunity to see the pet. If this is not possible, you can place a classified ad in a local paper to find a loving home for the pet; this will allow your parent to select the person or family adopting the animal, and will give him or her a greater sense of peace and closure than taking the animal to an animal shelter will.

Securing the Home

After your parent leaves, whether the home is going to be sold and will only be empty for a short time or whether the home is not going to be sold and will instead remain closed, you will need to take precautions to make sure the home remains safe. See the list at the end of this chapter on page 145 for *Tips on Home Security*.

Utilities and Bills

When your parent moves, you will need to make sure that his or her mail is forwarded to the new address. That means that bills for the home utilities will also be forwarded to that address. You may wish to contact the utility companies and request that these bills be sent to your address if you will be managing your parent's finances. You will need to leave the electric and gas on, so that the home can be lit and minimally heated. The telephone can be disconnected and cable can be canceled.

Make sure your parent is receiving any senior property tax reductions that are available. (Contact the local town or city property tax office in the area for this information.)

The Selling Process

If the home is to be sold, you may first wish to inquire if any family members are interested in purchasing it. If they are, and are able to pay a fair price, your parent will save on the real estate agent's fees. If not, you will be best served to hire a real estate agent to handle the sale. If you decide to show the home yourself without an agent, you will need to advertise it, show it, and manage the initial contract. (See *Tips for Preparing a Home for Showings* at the end of this chapter on page 146.) Remember that you can act on your parent's behalf in these matters only if you have a power of attorney. (See Chapter 4.)

If you have a power of attorney, you will be able to handle the sale for your parent and sign all the necessary documents. If not, your parent will need to be the one to sign the documents. If the title for the home is in the name of your other parent who has passed away, you will need an attorney to first file a new title so that the home will officially be in the parent's name who is alive and selling the home.

When you work with a real estate agent, be aware that his or her job is to sell the home. Both the real estate agent who represents you or your parent and the agent who brings in buyers technically work for you or your parent. There are some buyer's agents who work exclusively for the buyer. If a buyer's agent will be coming, your real estate agent will let you know. Understand that the agent you list the home with will probably not be the person showing it to potential buyers. Most buyers are brought in by the agents they are working with.

When an offer is made on the home, you have the choice of accepting it, counter-offering, or turning it down. Consult with your real estate agent about this at the time. You will need to consider how close the offer is to your asking price, how much you need to get out of the sale, and how hard it has been to find a buyer. Once the home is sold, the commission will be split between the listing agent and the agent who brought the buyer in. Once the contract is signed, the sale is handled by attorneys and the agents' roles are done. Use an attorney experienced in real property law. Discuss the fees and costs that you or your parent will be responsible for with the attorney. Expect the sale to take between one and three months to close.

Letting Go

At some point, whether you sell the home or close it now for a future sale, both you and your parent need to let go of it. Both of you will have fond memories of the home and the time spent there, but you cannot allow yourself to wallow in grief over it. It is, after all, just a house and your memories will live on. Your parent has a future to live for and so do you. You must now turn your eyes to that. Your children and other family members must also let go and move on. Support each other through this difficult adjustment.

DECIDING TO SELL OR MAINTAIN A HOME WORKSHEET

- Has your parent already left the home?

  _____

- Is your parent away permanently or temporarily?

  _____

- How likely is it that he or she will return?

  _____

- What has your parent's attorney recommended you do?

  _____

- Is there a relative nearby who can and is willing to maintain the home?

  _____

- How much will it cost to maintain the home?

  _____

- Does your parent need cash from the home now?

  _____

- Are you able to divide, store, or give away the home furnishings?

  _____

- Is your parent willing to agree to a sale?

  _____

- Is there a relative who could live in the home?

  _____

- Are there neighbors who could help out?

  _____

Tips on Home Security

- Lock all the doors and place padlocks on doors that may not have had locks (such as a side garage door, tool shed, or backyard gate).

- Place indoor and outdoor lights on timers so that they will go on and off, making it appear as if someone is living there.

- Try to leave at least some furnishings in the home, so that if someone looks in a first-floor window, the home will appear inhabited.

- Arrange to have the driveway and sidewalk plowed or shoveled and the grass cut regularly (often neighbors will do this to help out or for a small fee).

- Arrange to have free local pennysaver-type papers brought in or disposed of so they do not pile up.

- Alert neighborhood watch committees that the home is now empty. You may also want to alert local law enforcement that the home is vacant.

- Stop by the home once in a while and change the timer settings on the lights to coincide with seasonal changes; alter the drapes and curtains that are closed and open.

- Check for maintenance work that needs to be done and have it repaired fairly quickly.

- Consider installing a home security system.

Tips for Preparing a Home for Showings

- Paint all interior walls and ceilings white.

- Air the house out completely.

- Clean the oven.

- Clean the carpets.

- Clean the windows.

- Mow the lawn and weed flower beds.

- Put away photos—you want the home to be a place in which the buyer can imagine him- or herself living, rather than a place the buyer sees as someone else's home.

- Remove or replace stained carpeting.

- Open drapes and curtains to make the home appear bright.

- Look at the house with a critical eye to determine if it is appealing to buyers. *Stage* the home as much as possible by removing huge pieces of furniture and arranging furniture to show off the possibilities a room holds.

- If the home is being sold after your parent's death and he or she died while in the home, do not mention this to real estate agents or buyers.

- Find out your state's rules about seller disclosure of problems with the home and follow them.

- Refresh the home as much as possible by hanging a fresh shower curtain, hanging clean towels, placing fresh flowers strategically, replacing very dated fixtures or window treatments, and so on.

- Do any obvious repairs if they are affordable.

- Clean countertops, sinks, tubs, and toilets.

- Box up or put away most of the clutter and knickknacks that might be out.

- Make sure there are working lightbulbs in all fixtures.

- Decide if appliances will be included in the sale.

- Wipe out cupboards and drawers.

- Leave the home at a comfortable temperature when a showing is planned.

- Make sure your parent will not be home during showings.

- Prepare a sheet with information about the age of the home, features, lot size, and other things you want potential buyers to know and leave copies of it out for buyers to take.

- Place items such as incontinence garments, medication, walkers, shower seats, and other things that scream "senior" in a closet or cupboard if possible.

FAMILY LIVING

8

An option that is often appealing to seniors and their family members is having the senior share a home with a family member. This option can seem quite attractive due to the cost savings and the reduction in guilt as well as the comfort level it provides for the senior. However, there are many things to consider before choosing this option. It may not be as simple as it seems on the surface. You may feel that when you are older you would rather live with a child or other relative than move to a facility, but living with a relative can be difficult. This chapter will give you insight into making this kind of decision for your parent or for yourself in the future.

Family Member Living at the Senior's Home

Sometimes there is a family member who is able to move into the senior's home and provide enough assistance to allow him or her to remain at home. Grandchildren who are college graduates, recently widowed family members, or recently divorced family members are the most common choices. This arrangement can be beneficial for both people involved. The senior can remain in his or her own home and the relative can do the cooking, cleaning, transportation, and other assistance that is needed as well as provide companionship. The family member gets a place to live and also feels good that he or she is enabling the senior to remain at home.

Sometimes two older people might choose to live together—two siblings, two friends, or a romantically involved couple. If two seniors decide to live together, make sure that the two can manage on their own. If one person is more highly functioning than the other, this can be a good choice, but if both need a lot of assistance, this probably is not the best choice. In general, stay away from adding a roommate your parent does not know well or feel comfortable with.

There can be problems with having a relative move in with your parent. The relative may find that the assistance needed goes beyond what he or she is able or willing to do or that it is more time-consuming than anticipated. There can be conflicts over who is really in charge in the household and arguments over things like meals, television, cleaning, laundry, and so on. Some seniors are very set in their ways and everything must be done in those ways. Bad feelings may result if the care the relative offers is criticized. If he or she is asked to leave or if he or she decides to move out, leaving the senior with no assistance can also be a problem.

If you are considering this kind of arrangement, you, your parent, and the relative need to sit down first and set some ground rules. Create a list of what the relative will be responsible for doing as far as personal care, cleaning, laundry, cooking, transportation, and so on. Determine what kind of assistance will continue to be provided by other family members. Also, determine up-front if the relative moving in will contribute to the household expenses, such as utilities and food costs. If he or she will be driving the senior's car, determine who will pay for gas (and make sure that this does not pose an insurance problem—if someone is regularly driving a car, he or she is supposed to be added to the policy as a driver). If there are problems, agree that the relative must give some kind of notice before packing up and leaving. Make yourself available to the relative by phone or through visits so you can discuss how things are going and any problems, so that you remain on top of the situation.

You can create a legally enforceable roommate agreement, but most of the time this is unnecessary when dealing with a family member. Instead, create a clear set of rules and financial guidelines so everyone knows what to expect and there can be no confusion.

Expect to have to deal with some feelings of discontent from your parent as he or she adjusts to living with another person. It will take time to make small adjustments so everyone is comfortable. You may wish to reevaluate the situation every six or twelve months. Your parent's needs may change and the relative living there may be unable to continue to meet growing needs. Some additional in-home assistance from other family members or home health care workers may be an answer.

Sharing Your Own Home with Your Parent

Many children opt to have their parent move in with them when the parent is no longer able to live independently.

First, you must consider if you have room in your home. Moving your parent in may mean rearranging your living space. If you have children living at home with separate bedrooms, you could have the children share a room and give the empty room to your parent. If you have an office in your home, perhaps you could move the items in it to your bedroom or family room. You may have an unfinished room in your home that could be completed. If you have both a family room and a living room, you may be willing to give one of them to your parent. Other options include building on a small addition or converting a garage or basement to a livable space.

If your parent is selling his or her home, he or she may be willing to contribute all or part of the profit from that to renovations. Another option is for you to sell your existing home when your parent sells his or hers and then pool the funds to purchase a home that will accommodate your parent and your family.

Be sure to discuss these options with your elder law attorney because they can affect Medicaid eligibility.

Privacy Issues

If your parent moves in with you, it may mean that you will share every meal (unless your parent's area has a separate kitchen), every morning, every evening, and every weekend with him or her. You may also be sharing a bathroom. If you like to be alone and do things your own way, this may not feel very comfortable to you. Your parent may also be uncomfortable with all the togetherness that will ensue. To make it work, you need to set boundaries and give each other space. Having two TVs may alleviate some problems. Arranging showering schedules may also help. Maybe you will want to put in a phone line just for your parent. Making sure your parent has his or her own space will help make everyone more comfortable.

Impact on Your Family

If you have a spouse or children at home, think about the impact the living arrangements may have on them. It is important to talk to your family members about the decision and to get their input. Be clear about the changes that will have to happen to the house and to the family's schedule. Your spouse may need to provide some of the transportation your parent needs. Your teenager may be asked to be home some weekend evenings so that your parent is not left alone. Listen to your family's feelings about the changes and decide if it really will work. For some families, having a senior move in with them brings added joy, closeness, and benefits for the whole family. For other families, the situation brings tension, stress, and confusion, which is not good for anyone in the family.

What Your Parent Brings Along

If you decide to go ahead and have your parent move in with you, talk to him or her about what items can be fit into your household. Some seniors have unrealistic expectations and think they can bring their dining room set, lawn mower, and pool table. Show your parent the room that will be his or hers and talk about what will fit. If you have room elsewhere in your house for other items, let your parent know. (See Chapter 7 for information about storing or selling the rest of the belongings.)

Constant Supervision

If your parent truly needs constant supervision, this will take a toll on your household. You will either need to make sure someone is home at all times or you will need to arrange for adult day care for your parent. Another option is to hire in-home care. (See Chapter 6 about supervision options.)

Coping

Even if you have a fantastic relationship with your parent, living together will not be easy. Expect to have conflicts and disagreements. It can be hard for your parent to adjust to living in a household where he or she is not in charge. The last time you lived together, your parent called all the shots and now you (or you and your spouse) are in charge.

There will be days when you will feel as if you will lose your mind if you do not get away from your parent. Your parent will feel the same way about you. To deal with this, make sure you can get away from each other. Arrange for other relatives or friends to take your parent on outings. Continue to make social plans for yourself. Give each other space.

Compromising will become an important skill for you. It is easy to get emotionally tied up in the conflicts that occur. You need to be able to take a step back and rationally look for a solution that will enable both of you to get what you need. Try to remain practical and deal with your emotions separately.

ECHO Housing

An alternative to living with a family member is living next to him or her. *Elder Cottage Housing Opportunities* (ECHO) are separate, small, temporary homes that can be placed in the backyard or side yard of a family member's property. These cottages can be leased for as long as they are needed and then removed when they are no longer needed. You will need to check with your local zoning laws to make sure this type of dwelling is permitted. ECHO homes allow an elderly person to live close to a family member, while giving everyone space and privacy. Contact your local agency on aging for information about resources for ECHO housing in your state.

In-Law Apartments

What is traditionally called an *in-law apartment* may be an alternative to consider in your parent's situation. An in-law apartment is a separate living space inside a family's home. Usually these units have a bedroom, bathroom, sitting area, and small kitchen. You might be able to convert part of your home into one of these units or you may wish to build an addition or convert garage space. An in-law apartment allows a senior to have his or her own separate living area within a family house, while still being close enough to have support and assistance at all times. Again, your community may have zoning ordinances about this, so check with your town or city before converting an area of your home or building out.

SENIOR LIVING 9

Once you and your parent have decided that he or she cannot or will not remain at home or with a family member, you must consider what kind of living arrangement will work best. This chapter will cover *senior-living residences*. *Assisted-living residences* are covered in the next chapter. *Nursing homes* are covered in Chapter 11 and *Continuing Care Retirement Communities* are covered in Chapter 12.

As you read the next chapters, note the benefits and detriments of the types of housing discussed. This is information you will want to have to make plans for your own future.

What Is Senior Living?

Senior-living residences can also be referred to as *independent living* or *senior apartments*. They offer the least restrictive type of away-from-home arrangement. Residents live in an apartment by themselves or with a spouse. Each unit contains at the very least a cooking area, living area, sleeping area, and bathroom so that the resident can live independently. Most senior-living units are handicap accessible and outfitted to provide conveniences that make the unit senior-friendly (such as the home safety or modification tips included in Chapter 6). There are usually common areas such as activity rooms where residents can socialize with one another. Organized activities and outings are planned by the facility. The apartment building as a whole often functions as a community in which everyone lives independently but bonds together for social activities.

Assistance

Senior-living units have some staff on the premises, but staff may not be available twenty-four hours a day. Most senior-living units have call buttons or emergency pull cords to contact staff should assistance be needed. They also often have expedited access to hospitals and nursing homes.

There are usually no services included in the price of a senior-living unit, but services can be arranged at extra costs. Cleaning services, personal care aides, meal preparation, visits by RNs, and other types of assistance can normally be provided at extra cost if requested. These services usually can be added on as they become necessary.

Costs

Seniors in residences normally pay a monthly rent. Some residences may adjust the rent with regard to income. There is no state or federal financial assistance available for senior-living rent. It is not covered by Medicaid, Medicare, or private insurance.

Who it Is Appropriate For

Senior residence living is appropriate for seniors who are mobile, require little assistance, and are able to cook and handle personal care for themselves. This type of arrangement offers freedom of independence coupled with the reassurance of knowing that assistance is close at hand should it be needed. It also offers a feeling of community, since residents spend time together, and can ease loneliness through group interaction. Often seniors who come to senior-living residences are moving out of their long-time home because they are no longer able to completely maintain it. A senior-living apartment completely removes the responsibility for maintenance and upkeep. Removing this burden can help many seniors relax and enjoy themselves.

Finding a Senior Residence

Contact your area agency on aging for a list of area senior residences. (See Appendix A for the listing in your state.) You or your parent may know friends or relatives who live in senior housing. If so, ask them about the place where they live and visit them there. You can also use your local phone book to compile a list of nearby senior residences.

Once you have a list of residences, call and make appointments to visit them. Be sure to get a brochure from each place when you are there since it will help you remember them. You can also bring a camera to take photos, or use a camera phone if you have one. Get the costs in writing. It may be a good idea to take notes while speaking with the staff since there will be many details explained and it will be impossible to remember them all. Start a file for each residence you visit.

Evaluating

You should also plan to make an unscheduled visit so that you can see what the residences look like when the staff does not know you are coming. Once you have done this, you need to evaluate what you have seen and compare the different residences you have visited. You will want to weigh cost against comfort. Perhaps your parent is willing to pay a bit more to have larger-sized rooms or a balcony. You can use the worksheets at the end of this chapter to help you evaluate senior residences and their specific staffs.

Consider the services and activities available at each residence. Think about the types of people you saw living there. You want to choose a place that your parent can afford and will feel comfortable in. You may also want to weigh in the distance to your home or to other relatives' homes. You will be apt to visit more often if it is close by. Some senior-living facilities are located within walking distance of stores or malls. Others provide regular transportation to certain stores or shopping centers. Weigh this convenience factor as well.

Involving Your Parent

While you will want to play a part in helping your parent visit residences, ask questions, and look around at places, you need to realize that this needs to be his or her choice. If your parent is not behind the decision to move to a particular residence, he or she will not be happy there. Give your opinions, point out things your parent may not be considering, and actively participate in helping your parent evaluate costs, but let him or her make up his or her own mind about the final decision. If you push for a certain place and it does not work out, it will forever be your fault. You do not want that responsibility.

Evaluating the Contract

Read the contract closely before your parent signs it. Make sure your parent is completely certain this is the right decision. The following are some contract provisions to avoid:

- restrictions on guests and visitors (long-term overnight guests might be prohibited, but you want your parent to have fairly free access to visitors);

- indications that fees might rise without warning;

- provisions that allow the residence to evict your parent without cause;

- nonrefundable application and initiation fees;

- required fees for services your parent does not currently need;

- failure to list services (and their costs) that have been agreed upon;

- no guarantee of a specific unit;

- complete disclaimers of liability;

- the residence's ability to move your parent to a different unit at any time; and,

- a requirement that a family member sign the contract in addition to the senior. (Only the senior's signature is required. If you sign the contract, you can be held financially responsible.)

Making the Move

Read Chapter 7 to help you decide what you will do with your parent's home when he or she moves. Your parent will need to make choices about what can be brought to the senior residence and what cannot. Make sure you are clear on what (if any) furnishings the residence will provide. At that time you can determine what your parent needs to bring.

Make sure that you make arrangements for your parent's phone, cable, and utilities to be turned on in the unit before the move occurs. (If the residence takes care of this, make sure it will be done before the move.) Remember to have mail forwarded and to change the address for magazines, newspapers, insurance companies, creditors, banks, and so on.

Moving can be very stressful for your parent, particularly if he or she has lived in one home for many years. There is a grieving process involved in leaving your long-time home, so be respectful of what your parent is feeling. Take the unpacking in stages. Your parent will feel very tired from the stress of the move, so do not feel that you need to get it all unpacked in one day. Do make sure that all essentials are unpacked and easy to find before you leave for the day. Suggest that your parent leave a nightlight on until he or she is familiar with the apartment enough to move around in the dark.

Adjusting

Because moving is so stressful and because this will be a big change for your parent, realize that it may take a while for him or her to adjust to life in a senior residence. You will want to check in on your parent frequently. Your assistance will probably be needed with unpacking and rearranging furniture. Make sure you give your parent time alone to adjust to the new place. Encourage him or her to get to know the other residents and to slowly begin participating in group activities.

Developing a Routine

Hopefully your parent will develop a routine and begin to feel comfortable in this new place. Encourage him or her to develop a routine and build a schedule to occupy the days.

Your Role

After your parent has settled in, you will want to observe the residence when you visit and make sure it is being kept safe and clean. You will also want to make sure your parent's needs are being met—that he or she can cook alone, bathe alone, and so on. Make sure your parent is receiving any services that were promised or separately contracted for. Check in at the staff office and ask how the staff thinks your parent is getting along. Get to know the staff members and encourage them to call you if they have concerns.

Dealing with Your Feelings

You will probably experience a variety of emotions as your parent moves to a senior residence. It may seem to you as if this is the first step toward a nursing home. It may or may not be. It is important to focus on who your parent is today and try not to worry too much about how he or she will change in the future. You may also feel a sense of relief in knowing your parent is in a safe and comfortable place.

Dealing with the Future

Once your parent is living in a senior residence, it will be important to think about how he or she is doing every few months. Take a few moments to reevaluate the situation. Is he or she requiring more and more assistance? Will he or she soon need more assistance than the residence can offer? Watch for changes in his or her abilities.

Senior Residence Staff Evaluation Worksheet

Name of Facility: _____

Name of Staff Contact: _____

Date: _____

- What are the costs?
  _____

- Do residents have to meet mobility or physical ability minimums?
  _____

- What do the costs include?
  _____

- Are there application fees?
  _____

- Are other services available at additional cost?
  _____

- Is staff available twenty-four hours?
  _____

- Are call buttons or cords part of the units, and if so, whom do they call?
  _____
  _____

- What kinds of activities are planned and how often?
  _____
  _____

- What kinds of outings are planned and how often?

  _____

  _____

- Are there extra costs for group activities?

  _____

- Where are the common areas?

  _____

- Is there a residence council?

  _____

- Are outer doors locked at night?

  _____

- How many residents do you have?

  _____

- How many openings do you have?

  _____

- Is there a waiting list, and if so, how long is it?

  _____

- Is rent adjusted according to income?

  _____

- What kind of proof of income is required?

  _____

- Are overnight guests permitted, including children?

  _____

- Are pets permitted?

  _____

- Are furnishings included, and if so, what kind?

  _____

- What kind of security is in place?

  _____

- Is transportation offered, and if so, is there a fee?

  _____

- Do staff member regularly check in on residents?

  _____

Notes: _____

_____

_____

_____

_____

_____

_____

_____

_____

_____

_____

Senior Residence Evaluation Worksheet

Name of Facility: _____

Date: _____

- Are the common areas clean and comfortable?

  _____

- Do residents interact with each other?

  _____

- Are activities posted, and if so, do they look interesting and frequent enough?

  _____

- Are you shown a resident unit?

  _____

- Is it bright and comfortable?

  _____

- Are home safety measures evident?

  _____

- Are the hallways brightly lit?

  _____

- Do residents seem happy and friendly?

  _____

- Are call buttons or cords evident?

  _____

- Are staff members friendly and helpful?

  _____

- Are the room sizes adequate?

  _____

- Does the place smell pleasant?

  _____

- Are exits clearly marked?

  _____

- Is everything handicap accessible?

  _____

Notes: _____

_____

_____

_____

_____

_____

_____

_____

_____

_____

_____

Assisted Living

10

Assisted-living facilities are also called *custodial care facilities, senior-living* or *intermediate care facilities*. They are designed for seniors who need help with the activities of daily life, but who do not require extensive medical or health care. *Assisted-living* residences allow seniors to remain independent, yet receive the assistance they need to function and remain safe.

Assistance

Assisted-living facilities usually offer one-room or small apartment units where a senior can live and receive assistance from the staff. Private or shared rooms are available. These kinds of facilities can vary greatly and are called different things, such as *domiciliary care, sheltered housing, residential care*, and so on. Sometimes these facilities are in converted buildings, new buildings, or large residences. The types of services that are available vary from place to place, but usually include help with dressing, bathing, housekeeping, laundry, transportation, and medications. Meals are usually offered in a group setting. Residents are monitored occasionally throughout the day. Rooms are normally furnished, but some facilities permit residents to bring their own furnishings.

Cost

Most facilities cost around $2,100–$3,000 per month, but many can cost much more. Most states allow for Medicaid coverage for assisted living, but Medicare does not offer coverage. Long-term care insurance policies may provide coverage. Check with your carrier for information.

Who it Is Appropriate For

Assisted living is a good choice for a parent who does not have any serious medical conditions that greatly impact his or her daily life, but who needs some assistance with daily living—such as managing medications or assistance with bathing or meals. Assisted-living facilities will accept couples as well as individuals and can be a good choice for any elderly person who just cannot continue to manage at home or in a senior residence. Pets are usually not permitted and overnight guests are not allowed.

Finding a Place

Start with facilities where friends or family live or have lived. Ask friends, neighbors, and colleagues for experiences they have had with these types of facilities. Contact your local agency on aging for a list of local care facilities. (See Appendix A in order to find the agency in your particular state.) Once you have a list of places you would like to consider, set up appointments. Allow your parent to see the facilities as well. Start a file for each facility you visit.

Evaluating

After you have asked your questions and looked around, come back unannounced at another time. Try to visit unannounced during the day and at night to see how the facility is run at both times. You may also wish to eat a meal or two at the facility with your parent to evaluate the food. Consider how convenient the facility is to you, other family and friends, and senior centers and churches.

Decide if you feel the facility is clean and the residents are treated well. Ask about programs that are run for the residents—craft programs, music programs, and visits by hair stylists. Find out if laundry is done for residents and if there are extra fees for this service. You can use the worksheets at the end of this chapter to help evaluate the assisted-living facilities and their staffs.

Involving Your Parent

Talk to your parent about his or her impressions of the facility. Ask what he or she liked and did not like. Encourage him or her to talk with residents while visiting the facility. Let him or her go into and spend a few minutes in a room similar to the one he or she would have there. Stay for a craft or music program that your parent can observe. Share your impressions of the facility with your parent. Try to reach a decision together.

Contracts

Once you and your parent select an assisted-living facility, you will be asked to sign a contract. Only your parent will be signing this. You should never sign a contract for your parent's care unless you do so using your power of attorney. Otherwise, you are the one financially responsible for the care. Look to make sure the following items are included in a contract your parent is considering signing:

- clearly stated fees;

- a complete listing of services provided;

- a description of the size and type of room your parent will have;

- a provision that the facility will provide care for your parent as long as it is able to meet his or her needs, with an explanation of what kind of care is outside its capabilities; and,

- eviction only for nonpayment, inability to meet the senior's needs, if the senior causes danger to him- or herself or others, or if the residence closes.

You can read a sample assisted living contract online at:

www.hss.state.ak.us/dph/CL/PDFs/Residential%20Services%20Contract.pdf.

Never sign a contract that releases the facility from all liability for harm to your parent or his or her belongings.

Your Role

You want your parent to find a facility that will take care of his or her needs, and you want him or her to be comfortable there. You also need to weigh cost versus amenities. The location of the facility should be important to you. If it is close to your home and to other relatives, your parent will be more likely to have frequent visitors.

When you visit your parent, you should take note of any problems you see or concerns you have and take them up with the staff and administrators. Make yourself known to the staff—become a common friendly face. If you are a frequent visitor, the staff will need to be sure your parent receives quality care since you will have many opportunities to complain if he or she does not.

You will need to help your parent adjust to the new facility. (See *Tips for Assisted Living* at the end of this chapter on page 178.) Accepting help with bathing and dressing may be difficult for your parent and he or she may also try not to be a burden and refuse to ask for things he or she needs. He or she may have a hard time adjusting to the meals prepared by the facility. Encourage your parent to ask for things, to communicate with the staff, and to try to become comfortable with the assistance he or she is receiving.

Your Feelings

It is difficult to move your parent into an assisted-living facility. It can be difficult to admit and to see that he or she needs that kind of assistance with daily living. You may feel sad that he or she has had to move out of the home and you may dislike the institutional feel of the facility he or she is in. Try to remember that your parent will be happier and safer once he or she is receiving the care that he or she requires. You can relax a bit knowing that there is staff available around the clock to assist him or her. Many elderly people become reclusive when they remain in their own homes and can no longer drive. Your parent will now have the opportunity to interact with peers, participate in group activities, and go on outings.

The Future

Your parent may be able to remain in assisted living for many years. The staff will tell you if he or she reaches a point where more extensive medical care is needed, but you will also want to monitor this yourself. Should you feel that your parent's needs can no longer be adequately met by the facility, you will need to begin to think about a move.

Assisted-Living Facility Staff Evaluation Worksheet

Name of Facility: _____

Name of Staff Member: _____

Date: _____

- What are the costs and what do they include?

  _____

- What are the fees for additional services?

  _____

- Is Medicaid accepted?

  _____

- Do units have kitchens?

  _____

- What is the staff-to-resident ratio?

  _____

- Is there an RN on duty at all times?

  _____

- Do residents' personal items need to be labeled?

  _____

- Is there a staff social worker?

  _____

- Is there a fee for laundry services?

  _____

- How often are rooms cleaned?

  _____

- How are medications dispensed?

  _____

- What types of activities are planned and how often?

  _____

- Are there residents with dementia or Alzheimer's?

  _____

- What kind of security is in place?

  _____

- Are friends and family encouraged to visit?

  _____

- How large are the rooms?

  _____

- How often are beds and linens changed?

  _____

- What items can residents bring with them?

  _____

- Are choices available for meals or is only one entrée prepared?

  _____

- When are meals scheduled?

  _____

- What happens if a resident misses a meal?

  _____

- What kind of transportation is available?

  _____

- How often is transportation available?

  _____

- Is there a fee for transportation?

  _____

- What kind of medical care is available on the premises?

  _____

- Is a physical exam or assessment required before admission?

  _____

- Are there minimum physical ability requirements residents must meet?

  _____

- Are both single and double rooms available?

  _____

- Are there unrestricted visiting hours?

  _____

Assisted-Living Facility Evaluation Worksheet

Name of Facility: _____

Date: _____

- Does it have a homey atmosphere that is not institutional?

  _____

- Is the facility a good size—not too large or small?

  _____

- Are the bathrooms clean?

  _____

- Are there any unpleasant odors?

  _____

- Is the staff friendly?

  _____

- Are the floor plans easy to understand?

  _____

- Is there good lighting?

  _____

- Are there nonskid floors?

  _____

- Is there handicap accessibility?

  _____

- Are there handrails in the halls?

  _____

- Are there clearly marked exits?

  _____

- Are there places residents can go for solitude?

  _____

- Is there an outdoor area, patio, or courtyard?

  _____

- Are there mobile, active residents?

  _____

- Are there emergency call systems in the rooms?

  _____

- Do the residents seem happy and well-cared for?

  _____

- Is there a list of activities for residents posted?

  _____

- Do you see family and friends visiting?

  _____

- Are there community rooms, activity rooms, and living rooms?

  _____

- Is there security?

  _____

- Are the rooms comfortably sized?

  _____

- Is there adequate closet and storage space?

  _____

Notes: _____

_____

_____

_____

_____

_____

_____

_____

_____

_____

_____

_____

_____

_____

_____

_____

_____

_____

_____

_____

Tips for Assisted Living

- Label all clothes if they will be laundered by the facility.

- Store out-of-season clothes at a relative's home.

- Store valuables with a relative or in a safe at the facility.

- Hang pictures or photographs to personalize the room if permitted.

- Leave some snacks in the room.

- Bring along or purchase a small TV, small sitting chair, and clock radio.

- Place personal care items in a small basket or plastic crate if there is no storage space in the bathroom.

- Help your parent get to know his or her roommate if he or she has one.

- Encourage your parent to walk around the facility.

- Try to interest your parent in planned activities.

- Bring small-sized holiday or seasonal decorations for your parent's room.

- Make sure your parent understands how to operate the phone, TV, radio, shower, and any other controls in the room.

Nursing Homes

11

Nursing homes are what everyone dreads when they think about senior care, although the facts are not always as bad as most conceptions people have. There are, however, some alarming statistics about nursing homes. According to the U.S. Department of Health and Human Services, 90% are inadequately staffed and more than half of the 17,000 nursing homes in the United States fail to properly care for residents by placing them at serious risk of infections, bedsores, dehydration, pneumonia, and malnutrition, while 30% of nursing homes are cited for instances of abuse.

This does not mean that all facilities are bad or that a parent in a nursing home is doomed to receive poor care. Whether you are looking for a facility for your parent or thinking about the possibility of nursing home care for yourself in the future, these statistics are scary; however, it is possible to find good, affordable nursing home care. You need to know what to look for and how to stay on top of the care that is being provided. It is also important to remember that nursing homes may become your only option at some point. It is best to prepare for that eventuality as far in advance as possible.

Understanding Nursing Homes

Nursing homes are also sometimes called *long-term care facilities* or *skilled-nursing facilities*. Whatever the name, these facilities provide nursing and medical care for elderly patients in a residential setting. It is important to realize that nursing home care does not have to be "the end of the line." Often, elderly people need to have short-term stays in nursing homes after hospitalizations or for rehabilitative purposes. Other patients do require constant long-term care, and for this they do need to become permanent nursing home residents.

If you or your parent is in need of nursing home care, you most likely will be told by a health care provider, hospital discharge planner, or assisted-living staff member. It is important to ask questions about exactly what kind of care is needed and whether it is possible to get this kind of care at home. Nursing homes are for seniors who need constant medical care and attention that cannot be provided at assisted-living facilities or at home.

The majority of nursing homes are chains—55% are owned by a parent company that operates one or more nursing homes—which can add a level of bureaucracy. The average size of a nursing home is 107 beds. Most nursing homes are run for profit, although 27% are nonprofit, and 7% are government-run. According to statistics from the Centers for Medicare and Medicaid Services, nursing home patients, on average, receive thirty minutes of care per day from a registered nurse, plus thirty-eight minutes from a licensed practical nurse, and two hours and eighteen minutes from a nurse's aide.

Costs

Medicare will provide coverage for nursing home care *only* if the resident was in the hospital for three days immediately prior to the nursing home stay. Medicare will only pay for a total of thirty days of nursing home care in every one hundred–day period. Coverage exists only as long as the patient needs skilled nursing care. If you or your parent qualifies for Medicaid, Medicaid will pay the costs of nursing home care once Medicare coverage ends.

Nursing homes are not required to accept Medicare or Medicaid. If a nursing home does accept Medicaid, it can limit the number of beds available for Medicaid residents. Thus, you or your parent may not be able to get into a facility if all the Medicaid beds are full. However, if a patient enters as a private pay or Medicare pay and then becomes Medicaid pay (by spending down to Medicaid), the nursing home cannot make him or her leave. The nursing home must accept Medicaid if it has other patients with Medicaid. A facility that does not accept Medicaid will not be required to keep this kind of patient and can require private payment.

> A patient who enters a nursing home under Medicare or Medicaid cannot be required to pay a security deposit or advance payment. Nursing homes also cannot require a family member to guarantee payment.

Nursing homes are expensive, with the average daily cost now at $194 per day (which is over $70,000 a year). If you or your parent has long-term care insurance or private insurance, some of the costs may be covered. You need to read the insurance policy closely to understand what is covered since you cannot assume the policy will provide complete coverage. Many have caps or percentages that apply to payment.

Finding a Nursing Home

Learn about the nursing homes in your area. Talk with friends and family about their impressions of local facilities. Ask your parent's doctor for information and impressions. If your parent is in a hospital, talk with hospital social workers and discharge planners. Your local agency on aging can provide you with a list of area nursing homes. You can view a list of nursing homes by locale online at **www.medicare.gov/NHCompare**. You may also want to contact your long-term care *ombudsman*. An ombudsman is a state employee who evaluates and inspects nursing homes. The *Elder Care Locator* is a free national directory that can help you find care in your area. You can reach it at:

800-677-1116

or

www.ltcombudsman.org/static_pages/ombudsmen.cfm

Nursing homes are governed by the *Nursing Home Reform Act,* which contains standards for nursing homes to follow. Once you have created a list of nursing homes to consider, make appointments to speak to an administrator and get a tour. Plan on returning unannounced once during the day and once in the evening so you can see what the facility is like at all times. Create a separate folder for each facility. You can use the worksheets at the end of this chapter to help you evaluate nursing home staffs.

When you meet with the administrator, ask to see the latest three *state surveys* (also called *inspections*) of the facility. Your local ombudsman can help you obtain these as well and can help you interpret their results. Nursing homes must be accredited to receive Medicare funds. These surveys will help you understand what kinds of problems exist at the facility. Be wary if you see the same problems year after year. A good nursing home will make improvements based on the survey. All nursing homes will have problems—the purpose of the report is to pinpoint problems so they can be fixed, not to praise facilities for the good work they do.

What to Look for

Use the Nursing Home Checklist in Appendix E on page 363 to help you evaluate what you see in the facility. In general, you want to be sure that:

- residents are treated with kindness and respect;

- the facility is clean and cheerful;

- the food is appealing;

- staff is available and friendly;

- residents seem well-cared for (talk to some to find out); and,

- the place is as homey as possible and does not feel like a cold institution.

Warning signs include restraints used on the residents, unpleasant odors, residents' calls for assistance being ignored or put off, listless residents, lack of privacy, and secrecy by the staff. Make sure you note handicapped access and clear markings on exits.

> Read an online guide to nursing home tours at www2.aahsa.org/consumer_info/ how_to_choose/tour_nursing_home.asp.

Evaluating

When evaluating a nursing home, you have to remember that its primary purpose is to provide medical and daily living care. If your parent needs to be in a nursing home, he or she is going to have reduced privacy and reduced independence. You want to make sure the care he or she receives is of a high quality and that he or she will live comfortably there while receiving it. Find out if your parent's doctor will visit him or her at the nursing home if needed. Consider how convenient the nursing home is for you and other family members. Your parent will want frequent visitors, and making sure the nursing home's location is convenient will make visits more likely. Look to see if a *Nursing Home Resident's Bill of Rights* is posted. If there is one, read it and ask for a copy of it.

Involving Your Parent

If your parent does not already know that he or she needs to receive nursing home care, you need to tell him or her. This can be a traumatic time for seniors, since many see it as the last step before death. You need to make sure your parent understands why he or she needs this kind of care, but you also want to reassure him or her that there is a lot of life left to live.

Emphasize activities that take place at the nursing home, the friendly staff, the other residents who will provide companionship, and the fact that you and other friends and family members will visit frequently. Assure your parent that he or she is still part of the family and will be able to come to family events (health permitting) and spend time with family members. Emphasize the hobbies or favorite activities that he or she will continue to be able to do while there.

At the same time that you emphasize the positives, you do need to be honest with your parent. Many patients in nursing homes are quite ill and your parent is going there because he or she requires skilled nursing care.

Understanding the Contract

When your parent enters a nursing home, he or she must sign a contract with the facility. It is important to read this closely and to do so before the day of admission. The contract sets out all of your parent's costs and all of the nursing home's responsibilities. You need to read and understand it. If you were promised something and it is not in the contract, you need to insist that it be added in writing. Look for contract clauses about:

- the basic daily or monthly charge and what it covers (optional services should have pricing listed as well);

- additional charges;

- your parent's right to apply for Medicare or Medicaid;

- when, how, and why your parent can be transferred to a different room at the home;

- any special diets your parent may need;

- the refund policy;

- the bedhold policy; and,

- reasons for discharge.

Avoid clauses that:

- limit the home's liability for injuries or damage or theft of your parent's belongings;

- require your parent to give all his or her income to the facility directly;

- have restricted visiting hours;

- require a consent form for unneeded medical procedures;

- require a living will or health care proxy; and,

- require your parent to pay even though he or she is eligible for Medicaid.

Your parent is the one who will be signing the documents. You will only be signing if you have power of attorney for him or her. In all other instances, you should not sign the contract. Sometimes a nursing home might tell you it needs you to sign as a guarantor or to indicate that you are next of kin or the responsible person to contact. This is unnecessary and you should not sign unless you are willing to take on financial responsibility for your parent's bills.

Be aware that the facility is always responsible for *negligence* (failing to use appropriate care to prevent harm) no matter what you sign. Some contracts may contain provisions asking your parent to limit his or her liability or to waive the right to sue. Do not sign or let your parent sign these types of contracts.

Nursing Home Reform Act

The *Nursing Home Reform Act* is a federal law that governs nursing homes. The law lists certain things that may not be included in a nursing home admission contract. One of the important things included in the law is a restriction on discharges from the home. Your parent can only be made to leave if:

- it is necessary for his or her welfare because the facility cannot meet his or her needs;

- your parent's health improves so that he or she no longer needs to remain there;

- your parent endangers the safety or health of other residents;

- he or she does not pay; or,

- the home closes.

Nursing Home Policies

Make sure you have a full understanding of the policies, procedures, and rules before your parent enters a nursing home.

Bedhold

Make sure the contract explains its *bedhold policy*. If your parent has to temporarily leave the nursing home (e.g., for a hospital stay), the facility can charge a fee to hold your parent's bed until he or she returns.

If a facility accepts Medicaid, it will have a set number of days Medicaid will pay for the bed to be held while the patient is away at a hospital or other facility. Ask what the bedhold policy is in terms of Medicaid.

Assessments

A nursing home must assess a new patient (determine what kind of care he or she needs) within fourteen days of admission. Assessments must be done once a year after the initial assessment, or when any significant change in the patient's health occurs.

Plan of Care

The plan of care specifies how the nursing home plans to care for and treat the patient. It is important for the patient and family members to get a copy of this and understand it. If you do not agree with something in the plan, say so. Ask questions if anything is unclear.

Staff

Nursing homes must have twenty-four-hour staffing, and an RN must be present at least once a day. If there are more than 120 beds, there must be a staff social worker. Dental care must be provided to patients as well as medical care. Residents are free to choose their own doctors.

These are the bare minimum requirements. Look for a nursing home that exceeds these basic requirements and has the highest staff-to-patient ratio.

Facilities

There can be no more than four beds per room and each room must have a bathroom with accessible bathing facilities. Again, this is the bare minimum requirement. There must be a system in place for residents to summon assistance.

Restraints (physical or drug-induced) are not permitted as a general policy, but are allowed by individual order when necessary. Restraints should be a red flag to you when visiting any nursing home.

Making the Move

Often the move to a nursing home happens unexpectedly and quickly. One of the most common scenarios is that your parent is hospitalized, recovers partially, but then needs skilled-nursing care either on a temporary or long-term basis. One of the reasons many people are dissatisfied with the nursing home care their parents receive is that the decision is made in a hasty manner. You find out your parent is going to be discharged in three days and you must scramble to find a home that has an open bed and is affordable and decent. This is hard to do even when you have the luxury of time. Doing it after coping with the stress of hospital care and under a tight timetable is next to impossible.

If your parent is in assisted living and you feel he or she is declining or if he or she is living at home and is declining, it is well worth your time to gather some preliminary information about nursing homes in your area. Contact your local ombudsman and speak with your parent's doctor if possible. Put together a list of places and then visit them at your leisure. Gather information. Find out about waiting lists. If you find a place you think is perfect, put your parent on the waiting list. Even if he or she needs more immediate care, you can always move him or her to the better facility when a bed opens up.

Once you do move your parent, expect there to be an adjustment period. He or she may hate everything in the beginning. Listen to the complaints and give them some time. It may be difficult for your parent to adjust to the schedule, staff, and types of care he or she is experiencing. If your parent is in pain, uncomfortable, or very upset, ask to speak to the *charge nurse* (head nurse on duty) immediately. Make sure you stop by at different times of the day so you can get a sense of how your parent is faring at all points in the day.

If your parent has never had a roommate before and is experiencing one for the first time now, realize that this will be a difficult adjustment. Sharing your private space with someone else can be quite upsetting, particularly when you do not get to choose the person yourself.

Visit your parent frequently during the adjustment period. Encourage him or her to get to know other residents and to participate in activities when possible. Try to speak to your parent by phone on days when you cannot visit. There is an online guide to coping during a family member's first thirty days in a nursing home available at **www.longtermcareliving.com/family_guide/1st30days/index.htm**.

Getting to Know Staff and Procedures

Before your parent moves in, become familiar with the facility. Learn where the nurses are stationed, where meals are served, where activity rooms are, and so on. Once your parent arrives at the facility, go to the nurses' desk and introduce yourself. Find out who is the charge nurse and meet the other staff who will be caring for your parent. Be friendly and courteous to them. If you have concerns about your parent, let them know.

Be aware that the staff members who will have the most contact with your parent will be aides who will handle personal care, meal assistance, and minor medical care. Nursing homes also have social workers on staff and doctors on call.

Nursing homes have a board of trustees that sets the overall policies of the facility. The administrative staff handles the day-to-day operations. In addition to nurses and aides, there are therapists, activity coordinators, dieticians, physical therapists, volunteers, and also pastoral staff. The more people you get to know on staff, the better position you will be in to know what is going on and to have changes made if any problems occur.

Settling In

After a few weeks have gone by, your parent should start to settle in. If you feel that your parent is not adjusting well, talk to the charge nurse and to the staff social worker. There are changes that can be made—a different roommate, a different room, medication adjustments, more independence, and so on—that can help your parent feel more comfortable.

Your Role

When your parent is in a nursing home, your role needs to be quite extensive. Not only do you (along with other family members) need to provide companionship, but you also need to carefully monitor your parent's care. The more active and involved you are in his or her care, the better care he or she will receive. If the staff sees you frequently, knows you care, and sees you asking for changes when things go wrong, they will make the effort to give your parent better care.

You will want to develop a pattern to your visits and coordinate with other family members if possible. If you and your three brothers all visit Mom on Sunday and no one comes the rest of the week, you are not spending your time wisely. Frequent short visits will help break up the days for your parent.

You can read an online guide with tips for nursing home visitors at:

www.longtermcareliving.com/family_guide/visit/visit1.htm

Dealing with Problems

The problems that occur in nursing homes have been well-publicized as of late. Unfortunately, our nursing home system does not always provide the kind of quality care we want our parents to have. Because of health problems or limitations, your parent is in a position where it is difficult to stand up for his or her rights. One of your biggest burdens is standing up for him or her. There are ways to solve problems and care deficits in nursing homes, and if you feel your parent is receiving substandard care or treatment, make your voice heard.

Your first approach must be to speak with the charge nurse on duty and with any aides involved. Going directly to the person who has created the problem or who can best resolve it is always your best course of action. Do not let loose the cannons and go over the caregivers' heads without a good reason. Politely and calmly let them know what the problem is and make sure they fix it. If you feel a problem is severe, a problem continues to happen despite your complaints, or if you feel there is simply an overwhelming number of problems, you should speak to the director of nursing, the administrator, or the staff social worker. If you still cannot get results, contact the board of trustees.

Nursing homes that accept Medicare must allow family members to form a *family council*, a group of residents' family members who meet to discuss problems, events, and solutions. The family council must be permitted to meet without staff present. Go to the family council with problems. If there is no family council, you can start one. Residents also have the right to form *resident councils* (if the facility accepts Medicare), so you might want to encourage your parent to become active in that respect.

If none of these approaches solves your problem, you need to go outside the nursing home for help. Contact your local ombudsman about your problem or concern. He or she will investigate your complaint and help you find ways to solve it. You may file a complaint with the state licensing agency (you can locate information about your local agency at **www.medicare.gov/NHCompare**) and request that the agency perform an inspection. If any problems are found, the facility must fix them or face license suspension. If your parent is in immediate danger, the inspection must happen within forty-eight hours. If a resident has been harmed, the state has ten days to get the inspection done.

> Nursing homes must have a formal complaint and grievance process. Check with your state ombudsman about this. See Appendix A for more information.

If you still do not feel your problem has been solved or feel that you have not been taken seriously, you can file a complaint with the federal Health Care Financing Administration, which oversees Medicare and Medicaid (visit **www.os.dhhs. gov/about/opdivs/hcfa.html** for more information about the organization). This option is only available if the facility accepts Medicare or Medicaid. If you want to file a complaint about Medicaid fraud, contact your state Medicaid fraud control unit. (Ask your local agency on aging for contact information.) For further advice on filing official complaints about nursing home facilities, see *Tips for Filing Complaints with Government Agencies* at the end of this chapter on page 197.

You may also wish to speak to a local nursing home advocacy group. These organizations support and help residents and their families. Contact your local agency on aging for information about a group near you or check online at **www.nccnhr.org**.

As a last resort, you can always hire an attorney. Your parent may be eligible for free legal services. (See Appendix B for referral services.) You or your parent can always hire an attorney to handle the problem for you. You may find that your attorney can get action just by sending a simple letter when you have been sending letters and making calls for weeks. A private attorney can also sue a nursing home for *damages* (monetary compensation) related to physical or emotional harm that your parent has suffered. See Appendix D for information on nursing home residents' rights.

Nursing Home Staff Evaluation Worksheet

Name of Facility: _____

Name of Staff Member: _____

Date: _____

- What are the costs?

  _____

- What services are included with these costs?

  _____

- Are there extra fees for additional services?

  _____

- Is Medicaid accepted?

  _____

- How many Medicaid beds are there and how many are currently available?

  _____

- What is the employee-to-resident ratio?

  _____

- Are there separate areas for patients with dementia and Alzheimer's?

  _____

- What is the daily schedule?

  _____

- How many RNs are on duty at a time?

  _____

- What is the total number of beds in the facility?

  _____

- Are activities planned for residents?

  _____

- Is there a family resident council?

  _____

- Are single rooms available?

  _____

- Are there set visiting hours?

  _____

- Is there a waiting list, and if so, how long is it?

  _____

- What items may patients bring with them?

  _____

- What is the ratio of RNs to other staff?

  _____

- What kind of security is in place?

  _____

- What is the bedhold policy?

  _____

Notes: _____

_____

_____

_____

_____

_____

_____

_____

_____

_____

_____

_____

_____

_____

_____

_____

_____

_____

Tips for Filing Complaints with Government Agencies

- Use dates and exact incidents whenever possible.

- Include your contact information.

- Indicate the length of an ongoing problem, with specific dates of incidents when possible.

- Include names of staff members if necessary.

- Include the complete name and address of the facility.

- Indicate your parent's name and that he or she is a resident if you are writing about him or her.

- Specify if the problem is an emergency and if your parent is in immediate danger.

- Keep copies of all correspondence that you send.

- Follow up by phone if you feel a response has not occurred in an adequate amount of time.

Continuing Care Retirement Communities

12

Continuing care retirement communities offer a variety of different kinds of care in the same facility. These are also sometimes called *life communities*. *Continuing care retirement communities* (CCRCs) provide senior living, assisted living, and nursing home care. Residents are simply moved up to the next level of care when needed. Often these different levels are housed in different buildings. Most states have regulations governing CCRCs.

CCRCs often focus on helping residents maintain healthy, active lifestyles and may have amenities such as swimming pools, tennis courts, and golf courses. Classes for activities such as yoga, tai chi, strength training, and stretching may be offered. There is an emphasis on disease and illness prevention.

U.S. Department of Health and Human Services (DHHS) studies show that continuing care retirement community residents have an expected lifespan of one to two years longer than other seniors.

How it Works

Usually a continuing care community requires its residents to sign long-term contracts. The contracts provide that the facility will care for the residents through any stage of care that is necessary. There is usually a large entrance fee ($20,000 and up) with monthly payments that can amount in the thousands. Residents can buy their spots outright or rent them. The contracts can vary greatly. Some communities offer unlimited care of any kind needed for the resident's life (known as an *extensive agreement*). Others include a certain amount of nursing home care and charge additional fees for any care provided above that limit (known as a *modified agreement*). Some do not include any nursing home care at all and bill for all of it separately (known as a *fee-for-services agreement*).

Some communities offer *equity ownership* (real estate ownership) in the community. This allows the community member to sell his or her equity interest, but resale is usually limited to people who meet the community's requirements. When equity ownerships exist, there is usually an owner's association.

You can read an online report about how to evaluate CCRC financial reports at:

www.carf.org/pdf/ccrc.pdf

Requirements

CCRCs usually screen residents for health requirements. Residents must be in good physical health when entering, and mental health is also an important component. Communities usually also have income requirements. U.S. Department of Health and Human Services (DHHS) studies show that 40% of CCRCs require that residents have a monthly income that is one and a half times the monthly fee, while 25% require a monthly income two times the monthly fee. In addition to health and income requirements, 80% evaluate potential members' assets.

If a senior sells his or her home to invest in a CCRC with an equity interest, the IRS does not allow rollover of capital gains.

Considering the CCRC Option

Continuing care is attractive because it relieves you and your parent of any further decision making and creates a long-term plan for your parent's care. Your parent will feel secure knowing where he or she will be living. There will be no last-minute crises in trying to find a good nursing home with an open bed. The downside is that it is very expensive and out of reach for most people. Once you are in a continuing care community and living in assisted-living or nursing home sections, you can spend down to Medicaid and have your care paid for that way. Medicare and Medicaid will cover some expenses, as will long-term care insurance.

Contracts

It is important to carefully read the contract for a CCRC. It is also a good idea to have it reviewed by an attorney, since the contracts tend to be long and complex. You should avoid contracts with these provisions:

- services can be reduced or cut back without warning;

- eviction for reasons other than nonpayment, failure to comply with facility rules, or causing danger to self or others;

- no guarantee of care if beds are full;

- indication that the facility is "sponsored" by a nonprofit group or religious organization (often there is no real involvement from the sponsoring agencies);

- waiver of all negligence by the facility; or,

- no refund of the entrance fee.

Problems

It is important to read a contract for continuing care very closely and make sure there are no hidden fees. You also need to consider what will happen to your parent if the continuing care community goes out of business. Your parent must pay a substantial amount of money to enter the community and does so assuming it will always be there to care for him or her. If the facility goes bankrupt, your parent will be out on the street and will have lost that investment. Talk to the continuing care community contact person about these concerns. Ask for information showing the corporation's financial well-being and stability. Speak to your local ombudsman about these concerns. (See Appendix A for contact information for your state ombudsman.)

Evaluating

If the nursing home or assisted-living facility sections accept Medicaid, they must be licensed and accredited by the state. Check with your local ombudsman for copies of the inspection reports. Facilities that do not accept Medicaid are not subject to any state monitoring. Check the refund policy. Refunds may be available in full, partial, or on a declining scale.

Use the worksheets on the following pages to evaluate the staff at a CCRC. Continuing care communities are accredited by the *Commission on Accreditation of Rehabilitation Facilities* (CARF). Contact CARF at 888-281-6531. You can also find a list of accredited facilities at **www.carf.org/Providers.aspx?content= content/Accreditation/Opportunities/AS/CCAC.htm**.

CCRC Staff Evaluation Worksheet

Name of Facility: _____

Name of Staff Member: _____

Date: _____

- What cost arrangements are available?

  _____

- Do fees change with care levels?

  _____

- What is the entry fee? Is it refundable?

  _____

- Is equity ownership possible?

  _____

- How many openings are there?

  _____

- Where are the buildings for the different levels of care?

  _____

- Who determines what type of care a resident needs?

  _____

- Is the facility or company accredited by any agency?

  _____

- What health requirements do you have?

  _____

- What income and asset requirements do you have?

  _____

- What amenities do you offer?

  _____

- What is the staff-to-resident ratio at each level of care?

  _____

- What are the staff qualifications?

  _____

- What kinds of staff are provided at each facility?

  _____

- Are married couples welcome?

  _____

- What happens when spouses require different levels of care?

  _____

- What happens if a spouse becomes divorced or widowed?

  _____

- What services are included in the monthly fees?

  _____

- What are the charges for additional services?

  _____

- Can services be cut back or reduced under the contract?

  _____

- What happens if a resident needs to move to the next level of care but there is no room there?

  _____

- Do you accept Medicare and Medicaid?

  _____

- Is there a resident council?

  _____

- What are the reasons for eviction? Is there a way to appeal?

  _____

- Are there set community rules that must be followed, and if so, may I have a copy of them?

  _____

- What are the consequences for breaking the rules?

  _____

- Are residents required to buy private health care?

  _____

- Can residents use their own doctors?

  _____

- Are pets permitted?

  _____

- Are overnight guests permitted?

  _____

- What kind of security is in place?

  _____

- Is the company financially sound?

  _____

- Can you offer me proof of the company's financial stability?

  _____

CCRC FACILITY EVALUATION WORKSHEET

Name of Facility: _____

Date: _____

- Did you view all the different levels of care facilities available?

  _____

- Are all facilities located in the same general area so that friendships can be maintained even if care changes?

  _____

- Do residents appear active and happy?

  _____

- Is the staff friendly and helpful?

  _____

- Are you comfortable with the kinds of amenities offered?

  _____

- Are the facilities pleasant, clean, cheerful, and well-maintained?

  _____

- Did you see information about group activities?

  _____

- Do the facilities smell pleasant?

  _____

- Are the community rules reasonable?

  _____

HOSPICE

13

Hospice (also called *palliative care*) is a type of in-home or residential care for patients with life-ending illnesses. Hospice care seeks to support the patient and family through this difficult time while keeping the patient comfortable and managing his or her pain. Hospice care is patient and family-oriented, and uses a different approach than traditional medical care. The goal of hospice care is to provide a pain-free and dignified death while minimizing symptoms of illness. Hospice care does not try to extend or shorten life, but to make what is left of it pleasant and liveable. Most hospices are not in favor of life support systems, feeding tubes, aggressive treatments, or other care designed to prolong life.

Getting Hospice Care

Hospice care is designed for patients who have six or fewer months to live. A patient must be referred to hospice by a doctor for the care to be covered by insurance. Once a referral is made, most hospice programs are able to make contact with the patient and family within one day and can begin to provide a full range of services within one week.

Care at Home

Hospice programs were originally created to allow patients to die at home, in comfort, with their family present. Hospice still mainly provides in-home care. Hospice workers visit the home on a regular basis and immediate support and advice is available by phone. Hospice programs maintain relationships with hospitals so that a patient who needs temporary hospital care can be transferred to a hospital and then returned home while under hospice care.

Care at Facilities

Hospice programs have expanded and now usually can provide care at a nursing home, hospital, or other facility. Some hospices maintain their own residential facilities for patients who cannot be cared for at home.

Team Support

Hospice works in a team-based approach to care. A family member is designated as the team leader and works with doctors, nurses, aides, therapists, dieticians, social workers, counselors, and other health care workers to provide well-rounded care and support. For information on what you can do to make hospice care as pleasant as possible for your parent, see *Tips for Keeping Your Parent Comfortable* at the end of this chapter.

Hospice workers seek to care for the patient and the family as one unit. Hospice care does not end with the death of the patient. Bereavement counseling is provided for at least one year after the death. Hospice programs also offer *respite care*, allowing family caregivers free time while the patient is cared for by other team members.

Payment for Hospice

Private insurance and Medicaid cover hospice care. Medicare offers some coverage. To be eligible for Medicare coverage, a patient must receive Medicare Part A (see Chapter 5 for more information about Medicare) and be certified as terminally ill with six or less months to live (a DNR order is not the same as this certification).

Care must be provided by a Medicare-approved hospice. The coverage includes medical staff care, medication, brief hospital stays, in-home health aides, social workers, and family therapists. While receiving hospice care, the patient cannot receive treatment for the disease. So if your parent has cancer and is receiving hospice care, he or she cannot receive chemotherapy or radiation—anything designed to treat the disease instead of the pain. Learn about Medicare coverage for hospice online at **www.eperc.mcw.edu/fastFact/ff_82.htm**.

What to Look for

There may be several hospice programs in your area, so you could end up having to select one. Your local agency on aging can put you in touch with local hospice programs. Use the worksheets at the end of this chapter to help you evaluate various hospice programs.

Contact the *National Hospice and Palliative Care Organization* at **www.nhpco.org** or 800-658-8898 for a list of hospice programs in your area.

Making the Decision

Making the decision to obtain hospice care can be a difficult one because it is an admission that the end of life is near. You and your parent need to come to this conclusion and decision together. You need to talk to your parent's doctor and find out what the choices are. For a doctor to recommend hospice care, he or she must believe that the patient's life is ending and that there is not much traditional medicine can offer to cure, hold back, or stop the illness. Hospice care can also come about when a patient decides he or she wishes to stop treating the disease.

You and your parent need to come to a decision that what he or she really needs is an emphasis on keeping him or her comfortable, as opposed to medical care that seeks to cure or hold back the illness. In a sense, you must decide to give up the fight.

Coming to this decision can be very emotional and painful but it often brings with it a sense of relief. Hospice care offers many patients the opportunity to relax and enjoy the days that remain without the stress of medical tests and aggressive treatment. Hospice workers are experts at managing pain while maintaining the patient's awareness.

Creating a Hospice in Your Parent's Home

If there is no hospice organization in your area, start by contacting one of the hospice organizations listed in Appendix B. There may be a hospice organization in your area that you are unaware of. If not, these organizations can also assist you with setting up your own hospice-type plan. Hospice is really an approach to dying, and you can incorporate this philosophy into your parent's care yourself.

Hire private nurses and aides to provide home care and learn how to provide some care yourself so you can become the team leader. Talk to doctors, nurses, and aides about the decision you and your parent have made to treat him or her with a hospice approach. Make sure you also contact a counselor, clergy member, or other mental or emotional support counselors to provide support for your parent and for you.

If your parent is in a nursing home, you can speak to the care providers there about taking a hospice approach to your parent's care.

Spiritual and Emotional Support

While part of what hospice does is provide spiritual and emotional support to patients and families, it is important to create your own support network as well. Invite family members and friends to spend time with your parent. Notify any clergy you or your parent would like to have support from. Clergy members are able to perform religious ceremonies at home or at the facility where your parent is staying. Ask friends and family to take over for you from time to time to give yourself a break. Invite them to bring photographs or other things to reminisce with your parent.

Hospice Program Staff Evaluation Worksheet

Program Name: _____

Staff Member: _____

Date: _____

- What kind of care does the program provide?

  _____

- Are home-based and facility-based care available?

  _____

- How do you decide which type of care approach to take?

  _____

- What requirements must be met to qualify for the program?

  _____

- What kind of evaluation will be performed?

  _____

- What kind of documentation is needed?

  _____

- What kind of care is recommended?

  _____

- What kinds of professionals will be involved in the care being provided?

  _____

- What kinds of credentials do staff members have?

  _____

- Who will be the team leader?

_____

- Will the team work with my parent's doctor?

_____

- How is a care plan developed?

_____

- How often is the care plan reevaluated or updated?

_____

- Who decides the amount of pain medication provided?

_____

- How often will hospice workers see my parent?

_____

- Is someone available by phone at all times?

_____

- What kind of emotional and spiritual support is provided?

_____

- Can referrals be made to a hospital if needed?

_____

- Is care offered if my parent is placed in a nursing home?

_____

- Is the program Medicare-certified?

_____

- How long has the program been in existence?

_____

- How many patients does the program care for at this time?

  _____

- What is the program's philosophy?

  _____

- What do the services cost? How much will insurance cover?

  _____

- Is there a time limit on the services provided?

  _____

- Is respite care offered?

  _____

- Is there someone in the program who can help us decide if we are ready for hospice care?

  _____

Notes: _____

_____

_____

_____

_____

_____

_____

_____

TIPS FOR KEEPING YOUR PARENT COMFORTABLE

- Have a medical professional experienced in pain management prescribe medication.

- Try to arrange for him or her to come home if possible.

- Surround your parent with items that have special meaning or memories.

- Make your parent's room cheerful and comfortable.

- Avoid foods or scents that bother your parent.

- Allow him or her to maintain personal privacy and dignity.

- Provide him or her with music, books, or television shows when wanted.

- Find out if he or she would like any special meals.

- Make temperature adjustments if possible to accommodate your parent's needs.

- Keep his or her mouth moist.

- Do not force food or drink.

- Move his or her body frequently to avoid stiffness.

- Spend time with him or her.

- Make friends and family welcome.

COPING WITH END-OF-LIFE ISSUES

14

Coping with the end of your parent's life is extremely difficult, whether you have little or no warning about it or whether you have months to prepare for it. No one is ever truly prepared to say goodbye to a loved one. And you cannot expect yourself to ever truly be ready.

What to Expect

When you face the end of a parent's life, you can expect to feel many competing emotions—grief, rage, resentment, denial, an urge to maximize the time you have, and overwhelming love. Since the death of a parent is an issue that looms larger and larger as your parent ages, you may spend years, months, or just days experiencing the full range of these feelings. One of the best ways to cope and to help your parent cope is to contact your local hospice program. See Chapter 13 for more information about hospice.

Expect your emotions to be overwhelming. Expect not to act like a rational person sometimes. Expect to be angry at your parent and at other people. But do not forget how your parent is feeling through all of this. There has been a lot of research conducted on the stages of dying. Read some of the books recommended in Appendix C to get a complete picture of the process. Remember that nothing about this process is easy and that everyone must cope with it in their own way.

Your Emotions

The best way to deal with your emotions as you face this process is to live with them. Do not try to suppress them, deny them, or ignore them. Everything you feel is real and all of it must be dealt with. You may find that you need time off from work or time alone to find your equilibrium and deal with everything you feel.

It is important to understand that although some of your feelings may seem inappropriate or wrong, this is probably not the case. Many people who are caring for dying parents feel resentful, find humor in odd ways, become angry at their parents because of the situation, or occasionally look with relief to the time when it will finally be over. These are all natural reactions. If you feel overwhelmed by your feelings and find you cannot function, seek assistance from a clergy member or a bereavement counselor. Rely on other loved ones and close friends to help you. Ask for help and do not be afraid to accept it. See *Tips for Coping with Your Emotions* at the end of this chapter on page 230 for further information on dealing with your feelings.

Helping Your Parent Cope

Most experts agree that if a person is mentally able to understand that he or she is dying, he or she deserves the right to be told. Sometimes children choose to hide this information from their parents, which can result in a difficult charade involving lies and deceptions. Let your parent have the dignity of understanding what lies ahead.

The Five Stages of Grief Experienced by the Dying

- shock and denial
- anger
- bargaining
- depression
- acceptance

Your parent will probably progress through the five stages of grief described by Elizabeth Kubler Ross at his or her own pace. You can help your parent cope by offering your time and attention, and by making sure your parent has all the information and support he or she needs. For further information on how to help your parent deal with his or her emotions, see *Tips for Helping Your Parent Cope* at the end of this chapter on page 231.

Finding Your Own Way to Say Goodbye

Sometimes people find that after a loved one dies there are things they feel they should have said or done. Remember that you cannot change the past or anything that has happened between you and your parent. What you can instead prepare for is how you leave each other. Consider if there are things you need to say to your parent while you still can. Asking yourself that question can be very difficult and painful, because in doing so you must accept that your parent is dying. Make the time you spend with your parent as pleasant as possible, but do not try to overdo it by filling every single moment with meaningful discussion. Say what you need or want to say. Do not expect too much from your parent. Give what you need to give and find peace in knowing that you have done what you needed to.

Pain Management

Pain management may be an important part of your parent's treatment at this point. Getting it right can be difficult—there must be a balance between reducing pain yet allowing the patient the ability to have conscious and clear thought. Speak to your parent's doctor about the pain management techniques that are being used. There are doctors who specialize in pain management and you may wish to request a consultation with one.

Quality of Life

Your parent's quality of life at the end of his or her life is probably of great concern to you. Talk with your parent's doctor about achieving some kind of meaningful quality of life. This may mean a move to a hospice facility or a move to a nursing home to live the final days there. People who are dying experience physical changes that may include increased sleep, confusion, chest congestion, bluish extremities, incontinence, loss of appetite, and more. Speak to your parent's doctor or care providers for information about what to expect and how to make sure your parent is comfortable.

Understanding the Procedures that Follow Death

If you are with your parent when he or she dies, realize that once the moment comes, there is nothing that you need to do immediately. You can take some time to sit with his or her body if you wish. If your parent dies in a hospital, you may be given the opportunity to view his or her body briefly there. If your family requests an autopsy (or if one is recommended for medical reasons or is required by law—note that this is rare), the body will be moved to the morgue. From there, the body can later be transported to the funeral home.

If your parent dies at home, it is necessary to have medical personnel verify the death. You will need to call your parent's doctor to have your parent declared legally dead. Discuss this with the doctor in advance to understand the procedure.

Taking Care of Yourself

It is easy to forget to take care of your own basic needs at times of great grief. Make sure you drink and eat and make time to rest even if you cannot sleep. Remember that only by keeping yourself physically well are you able to offer comfort and support to other loved ones. Remind yourself that it is important for you to go on with your life and that this is what your parent would have wanted.

Grief

Grief takes on many forms. Some people cannot stop crying. Some do not cry at all. Others direct their energy into other tasks or things to stay busy. Whatever works for you is okay. Do not feel as if you have to fit into someone else's definition of a grieving child. Be yourself through this and you will feel more comfortable. Keep in mind that you have to take care of your body's physical needs or you will get sick.

> Remember that as anxious as you are to have the details and arrangements made, it is important to take time to deal with your own grief and your own needs.

Funerals and Memorial Services

If you and your parent made previous arrangements for a funeral or memorial service, you will still need to contact the funeral home to notify them and set definite times. If no arrangements have been made prior to your parent's death, discuss with your family members how to proceed. If there is a funeral home other family members have used, perhaps you wish to consider it. Some families prefer to have a memorial service instead of a funeral.

Realize that you have a choice among burial, cremation, entombment, and full medical body donation. You are not required to have a funeral, viewing, or memorial service of any kind. You may choose what is called *simple disposition*—immediate burial or cremation. If you wish to have a printed program or mass card, plan out what you would like it to say before ordering it (the funeral home can assist you with this).

Speak with your clergy member about church or temple services and what kinds of decisions you must make about the service. If your parent did not choose to have a church service or if you have decided not to have one, you may wish to hold a memorial service instead. A memorial service can be held at a funeral home or anywhere you choose and may or may not include displaying the casket.

The funeral director will help you make decisions about caskets, cemeteries, cremation, services, and so on. It is difficult to make these kinds of decisions at a time when you are filled with grief. Try to take a few moments to be clear-headed in your choices and decisions. Do not be afraid to ask the funeral director questions, and always be sure to ask about costs. Remember that any additional services the funeral home arranges for (such as transportation for the family and so on) do have an added cost. Funeral homes must comply with the following *Federal Funeral Rule*.

- The funeral home must provide a general price list in writing or over the phone.

- The funeral home must inform you that embalming is not required in most cases, but if you do not select this then direct burial or cremation is required.

- The funeral home must inform you of fees for items it rents or purchases on your behalf and whether a service fee is included.

- A casket is not required for cremation—a container made of cardboard or canvas is all that is required and funeral homes must make this option available.

- Customers must be allowed to choose only the services or goods they want.

- The funeral home must disclose state law requirements.

- An itemized statement must be provided showing the individual and total prices.

- A funeral home cannot tell you that a procedure will indefinitely preserve a body unless it will, and it may not tell you a casket will keep out dirt, water, and so on unless it really will.

Many families host a meal after the funeral, so reservations and arrangements need to be made for this. You may choose not to have such a meal or you might prefer to have it at someone's home.

Burial generally takes place after the funeral or memorial. Each cemetery has its own requirements as to what kind of casket is required. Your funeral director will know this information. Be aware that burial can normally only occur at cemeteries. It is illegal in most places to bury a body anywhere other than a licensed cemetery. So, for example, you could not bury your parent in your backyard, in a favorite nature area, and so on without specific legal and zoning permission. Cemeteries also have requirements about containers for cremated remains. If you do not wish to bury your parent's cremated remains, you can request that the funeral home give the remains to you to scatter or keep.

Many people choose to *preplan* and *prepay* for their own funerals. This is an option you may wish to consider for yourself. In doing so, you relieve your family of the burden and cost of making these decisions. Some people leave instructions for their funerals in their wills. Be aware that this kind of instruction is not binding and may not even be read until after the funeral. To be sure your wishes are carried out, you should discuss them with family members or preplan your funeral.

Obituary

Someone in your family will need to call the obituary department of your local paper, or the funeral director may handle this. Information needed for an obituary includes:

- your parent's full name (and maiden name if applicable);

- date of birth;

- date of death;

- place of death;

- cause of death (if you wish to include it);

- name of your parent's spouse (and maiden name if applicable);

- names of your parent's children and their spouses;

- names of your parent's grandchildren if you wish to include them;

- date, place, and times of funeral home viewings, memorial service, and/ or funeral service;

- date, place, and time of burial if public;

- any important facts or information about your parent's life and achievements; and,

- where donations should be sent if they are preferred over flowers.

Notifying Friends and Family

You will probably want to let close friends and family know of your parent's death yourself. Ask these friends and family to make calls to other people for you. Give each person a list and ask him or her to add anyone to it you may have forgotten. Do not feel you have to spend a lot of time organizing this or working on it. Word does get around and almost everyone who needs to be notified will be notified.

Protecting Your Home

Unfortunately, there are people who read obituaries and then plan to rob the homes of the deceased's family members while they are at the funeral home or church service. Because of this, you may wish to limit the information you provide in the obituary, perhaps, for example, not naming adult grandchildren. It is a good idea to ask a friend, neighbor, or relative to watch your home for you while you are at the funeral services. If you cannot find anyone who can do so, leave lights on in your home as well as a television or radio. If you have a local neighborhood watch program, notify them and ask them to watch your home. Find someone to watch your parent's home as well if at all possible.

Caring for Your Other Parent

If your other parent is still with you, you will probably feel concerned about him or her and feel a sense of responsibility for him or her. Make sure that someone can be with him or her immediately after your other parent has passed away. Decide if you feel he or she needs to come and stay with you or another relative or have someone go and stay there for the first few days after the death.

Make sure your parent eats and drinks and rests. Help him or her to stay active if possible, with walks through the house or hallways. Help him or her make the funeral decisions. Arrange for someone to bring meals to him or her.

Realize that it will take your parent a long time to adjust to living without his or her spouse. Expect to spend extra time with him or her in the coming months. Be aware that after one spouse dies, the other is susceptible to illness, depression, and mental confusion. Try to help your parent remain healthy and mentally active in the coming months.

Finances

Once your parent dies, all his or her assets are supposed to be frozen temporarily. This means you will not be able to access your parent's bank account or pay his or her household expenses. All of this will be handled by your parent's estate. If your parent's home is receiving phone calls from bill collectors, explain that he or she has passed away and everything will be handled as soon as possible. Notify life insurance companies and provide certificates of death. Apply for survivor benefits for Social Security, veteran's benefits, and retirement programs (contact your local Social Security office, veteran's affairs office, or the administrator of retirement programs). Get at least ten copies of the certificate of death for these purposes.

Probate and Estates

If your parent left a will, the will must go through the court system and be *probated*, the process through which the terms of the will become legal. All of your parent's belongings, debts, and assets are part of his or her *estate*, a legal term for the grouping of your parent's items. If your parent dies without a will, this is called dying *intestate*, and if there are any items that do not automatically move to someone else (such as joint bank accounts), then the estate must still go through the court system to be divided, a process called *estate administration*.

You will need an attorney to handle your parent's estate. The probate process takes a few months in most cases, so this is not something you need to get started on immediately after the death of your parent.

Making Your Peace

Recovering from a parent's death is a very long process. Do not expect to be over it quickly, if ever. Grief is a gradual process. You will find that your grief changes over the months ahead and sometimes it seems harder to go on and other times it seems easier. Give yourself time and be patient with yourself.

At some point you will need to go through your parent's belongings. Doing so can be very difficult, so do not rush to get this task done. Approach it when you are ready. If other family members will be involved, remember that this is a very emotional process and sometimes people argue over the distribution of belongings because of the grief they feel. Do not let this kind of argument affect your relationships.

Remember the happy times you had with your parent and all that he or she gave you throughout your life. If you have children, share your memories with them. Some people find they are comforted by displaying a special photo of their parent in their home or by treasuring some of their belongings. Do whatever feels right to you.

Tips for Coping with Your Emotions

- Do not suppress your feelings.

- Realize that you may feel overwhelmed by your feelings.

- Expect your emotions to sometimes feel inappropriate.

- Know that there will be ups and downs.

- Take the time to enjoy the time you have with your parent now.

- Let go of the past and any regrets or bad feelings you hold about it.

- Get support from friends, family, and clergy.

- Take time for yourself and for things you enjoy.

- Say things that need to be said before it is too late.

- Be honest with yourself about what is happening to your parent.

Tips for Helping Your Parent Cope

- Be honest with your parent about the prognosis.

- Encourage him or her to talk about the prognosis with you and with doctors.

- Talk with him or her about death if he or she is ready to do so.

- Make any arrangements your parent decides he or she would like made after his or her death.

- Allow him or her to talk about the past.

- Share your feelings with your parent.

- Listen to him or her when he or she needs to talk.

- Get medical assistance to help with pain management.

- Encourage family and friends to spend time with your parent.

- Have patience with all of your parent's emotions and reactions.

ALZHEIMER'S AND DEMENTIA | 15

Alzheimer's disease is just one of the conditions that can affect elderly people, but it is one of the most feared since it results in memory loss. Many children of elderly parents are concerned about their parents developing or showing symptoms of Alzheimer's. Additionally, as people age, they themselves worry about developing this disease. These fears are not unfounded—the *Alzheimer's Association* reports that 13% of people over 65 and 42% of people over 85 develop it; at the time of this book's publication, 4.9 million people over the age of 65 have Alzheimer's. If you suspect your parent is developing Alzheimer's, it is essential that you speak to his or her doctor about it.

Understanding Alzheimer's and Dementia

Alzheimer's disease is a degenerative brain disease that destroys the nerve connections to memory cells in the brain, resulting in memory loss. The disease begins gradually and eventually causes personality changes, impaired judgment, and loss of the ability to communicate. The end result is a person who needs complete and total care.

Many people confuse Alzheimer's with other symptoms of aging. One common confusion is with *dementia*. Dementia can look like Alzheimer's when in reality it is a symptom of something else. Dementia is a loss of brain function that can be caused by drugs, thyroid disease, depression, oxygen deprivation, and diseases like Parkinson's. Because it is difficult to tell the difference between dementia and Alzheimer's, it is important to consult your parent's doctor. Dementia has many of the same symptoms as Alzheimer's, the most important of which is memory loss.

Diagnosis

There is no single test for Alzheimer's and it is usually diagnosed by ruling out other possibilities. The Alzheimer's Association has developed a list of warning signs that include common symptoms of Alzheimer's disease (some also apply to other dementias), which are listed under *Ten Warning Signs of Alzheimer's* at the end of this chapter on page 242. Individuals who exhibit several of the symptoms listed should see a physician for a complete examination.

Treatment

There is no cure for Alzheimer's, although research is progressing. There are several drugs that can be used to treat the symptoms of Alzheimer's. There are also therapy treatments to help relieve some of the behavioral changes that occur.

Development of the Disease

Alzheimer's generally begins gradually and its development speed differs with each patient. Your parent's doctor can give you a personal timeline. Some doctors classify patients as early, middle, or late, depending on how far the disease has progressed. A wide variety of tests may be needed to make the diagnosis. Ask your parent's doctor what tests he or she recommends. Because there is no sure way to diagnose Alzheimer's, your parent may be given a diagnosis of possible, probable, or definite Alzheimer's.

What to Expect

If your parent is diagnosed with Alzheimer's, you can expect him or her to eventually experience:

- memory loss (short-term at first, then long-term);

- confusion;

- difficulty reasoning;

- anxiety;

- delusions;

- hallucinations;

- depression;

- problems sleeping; or,

- disorientation.

Your parent may have a difficult time accepting the diagnosis and may also forget the diagnosis. He or she will probably be angry, depressed, and overwhelmed by the diagnosis. You may wish to ask your parent's doctor for a referral to a therapist or counselor experienced in dealing with Alzheimer's patients and their families.

You should also expect to have difficult emotions yourself over the diagnosis. Watching your parent's memory deteriorate is painful and also very frustrating. You will feel grief and anger at what is happening. Talk to a therapist or counselor to help yourself cope.

You may worry about developing Alzheimer's yourself. It is unclear if Alzheimer's is a genetic disease. Early onset Alzheimer's (striking people under age 65) does have a genetic component, but researchers are not yet sure if you will be predisposed to Alzheimer's if your parent has it. The best way to deal with the possibility of developing Alzheimer's is to try not to worry about it. There is nothing you can do to change what will happen.

Coping

The biggest and hardest part of dealing with a parent with Alzheimer's is having patience. There will be times when it feels as if your parent is just being stupid or is making things difficult on purpose. You need to remember that none of this is his or her fault and he or she has no control over the symptoms of the disease. It is natural to lose your temper or snap at your parent. You need to remember that this is part of your own coping process. Try to be as patient as you can. Take a deep breath and count to ten if you feel like you are going to lose control.

If you are your parent's primary caregiver, it is essential that you make arrangements to give yourself a break. Coping with Alzheimer's is extremely stressful. Make time for your own interests, friends, family, job, and so on. Consider joining an Alzheimer's support group. The Alzheimer's Association can provide you with contact information for the one closest to you. (See Appendix B.)

> Appendix B contains Alzheimer's support and information organizations. Appendix C lists books dealing with Alzheimer's and dementia.

Being Prepared

Once your parent receives a diagnosis of Alzheimer's, there are several things you should do. First, you should make sure your parent has a will, a living will or health care proxy, and a power of attorney. You need to speak with an elder care attorney to address Medicare eligibility. If your parent lives long enough, he or she will require full-time care at some point, and financial arrangements are going to be important.

You also need to begin thinking in terms of your parent's safety. If he or she lives alone, you will need to make plans to arrange for help around the house. Your parent's doctor can give you a sense as to how quickly you need to put a plan in place.

> There are home safety products designed specifically for Alzheimer patients. These include motion detectors, doorknob covers, oven locks, memory aids, and much more. Locate these products at area home safety or medical supply stores or at either **www.alzstore. com** or **www.caregivingsolutions.com**.

You will want to get information about the Alzheimer's Association's *Safe Return Program*. This program provides ID tags (to be worn as jewelry or on clothing) and a twenty-four-hour hotline and database. If your parent is found wandering, the person or agency who finds him or her calls the hotline, which then contacts his or her caregiver. If you discover your parent is missing, the program contacts local law enforcement and faxes a photo of your parent to them. Family support is provided by local Alzheimer Association support groups while the parent is missing. There is a small fee for the program ($40 at the time of this publication). See **www.alz.org/we_can_help_medicalert_safereturn.asp** or call 888-572-8566 for more information about the Safe Return Program. For more information on preparing your parent for Alzheimer's, see *Tips for Helping Your Parent Manage with Early Stage Alzheimer's* at the end of this chapter on page 241.

Leaving Home

You will want to include your parent's doctor and caregivers in the decision about when it is appropriate for your parent to move into a facility. You may find that your parent can move to assisted living at first and may later need to move to a nursing home.

The Alzheimer's Association has an online center filled with information about residential care at **www.alz.org/carefinder/index.asp**. In selecting a care facility, you will want to follow the suggestions given in Chapters 9–12. You can use the worksheets for assisted living and nursing home evaluations from the previous chapters, in addition to the *Alzheimer's Facility Evaluation Worksheet* on the following page, in researching residential care for your parent.

Moving Forward

It is important that you keep living your life and maintain your own physical and mental health even though your parent has Alzheimer's. Watching him or her progress through the disease is painful, but there is nothing you can do to stop it. You can make time to spend with your parent and take steps to make sure he or she is comfortable and receiving good care, but you cannot stop the progression of the disease. Grief and loss will be a constant part of your life, but your parent will have lots of good days ahead. You have a lot left to share. Even if your parent forgets who you are or what you do for him or her, you will know that you have done what was possible to make a difference in his or her life.

Alzheimer's Facility Evaluation Worksheet

Name of Facility: _____

Name of Staff Member: _____

Date: _____

- How experienced is the staff in working with Alzheimer and dementia patients?

  _____

- Does the staff have special training in this area?

  _____

- Is twenty-four-hour supervision offered?

  _____

- Are there other Alzheimer or dementia patients currently in residence? How many?

  _____

- Is the facility limited to Alzheimer and dementia patients?

  _____

- Are Alzheimer and dementia residents in a special care unit or are they mixed with other residents? Why do you feel this is the best arrangement?

  _____

  _____

- What particular safety measures are in place to prevent wandering, injury, and disorientation?

  _____

- What activities are available?

  _____

- Are there programs and activities designed to support memory retention?

  _____

- How do you deal with the progression of the disease among your residents?

  _____

- Do you have residents in all stages of the disease?

  _____

Notes: _____

_____

_____

_____

_____

_____

_____

_____

_____

_____

_____

_____

TIPS FOR HELPING YOUR PARENT MANAGE WITH EARLY STAGE ALZHEIMER'S

- Join the Safe Return program.

- Give him or her a small notebook with his or her name, address, phone number, directions home, names and phone numbers of family members, doctor's name and phone number, and an extra house key taped inside it, and make sure he or she carries it in a pocket or purse.

- Organize drawers and household items in a systematic way to make it easier for him or her to locate things.

- Label drawers and cupboards.

- Help your parent set up and follow a daily routine.

- Leave a list of phone numbers (including 911) by the telephone.

- Put together a small photo album with recent photographs of family members and label each one with the family member's name and the relationship he or she has to your parent.

- Leave a set of keys with a neighbor.

- Alert neighbors and friends to your parent's condition.

- Call your parent to remind him or her to take medication or eat.

- Post a calendar and mark off the days.

- Take your parent to Alzheimer's support group meetings.

- Suggest that your parent keep a journal.

- Arrange for in-home care and assistance.

- Have your parent execute a health care directive and general power of attorney while he or she is still competent.

Ten Warning Signs of Alzheimer's

1. *Memory loss that affects job skills.* It is normal to occasionally forget an assignment, deadline, or colleague's name, but frequent forgetfulness or unexplainable confusion at home or in the workplace may signal that something is wrong.

2. *Difficulty performing familiar tasks.* Busy people get distracted from time to time. For example, you might leave something on the stove too long or not remember to serve part of a meal. People with Alzheimer's might prepare a meal and not only forget to serve it, but also forget they made it.

3. *Problems with language.* Everyone has trouble finding the right word sometimes, but a person with Alzheimer's disease may forget simple words or substitute inappropriate words, making his or her sentences difficult to understand.

4. *Disorientation of time and place.* It is normal to momentarily forget the day of the week or what you need from the store. But people with Alzheimer's disease can become lost on their own street, not knowing where they are, how they got there, or how to get back home.

5. *Poor or decreased judgment.* Choosing not to bring a sweater or coat along on a chilly night is a common mistake. A person with Alzheimer's, however, may dress inappropriately in more noticeable ways, for example, wearing a bathrobe to the store or several blouses on a hot day.

6. *Problems with abstract thinking.* Balancing a checkbook can be challenging for many people, but for someone with Alzheimer's, recognizing numbers or performing basic calculations may be impossible.

7. *Misplacing things.* Everyone temporarily misplaces a wallet or keys from time to time. A person with Alzheimer's disease may put these and other items in inappropriate places—such as an iron in the freezer or a wristwatch in the sugar bowl—and then not recall how they got there.

8. *Changes in mood or behavior*. Everyone experiences a broad range of emotions—it is part of being human. People with Alzheimer's tend to exhibit more rapid mood swings for no apparent reason.

9. *Changes in personality*. People's personalities may change somewhat as they age. But a person with Alzheimer's can change dramatically, either suddenly or over a period of time. Someone who is generally easygoing may become angry, suspicious, or fearful.

10. *Loss of initiative*. It is normal to tire of housework, business activities, or social obligations, but most people retain or eventually regain their interest. A person with Alzheimer's disease may remain uninterested and uninvolved in many or all of his or her usual pursuits.

Reprinted with permission of the Alzheimer's Association.

KEEPING YOUR OWN LIFE ALIVE | 16

Much of this book has focused on the facts about elder care and information you need to help your parent make decisions or to make decisions for him or her. It is time to step back and think about yourself and how you can effectively manage all these responsibilities while continuing to have your own life.

Getting a Handle on What You Are Facing

The best way to deal with the decisions, conflicts, and problems you face as you help your parent or parents is to gather as much information as you can so that all your decisions can be informed. Gathering information can be time-consuming, but it will be time well spent. Use the resources in the appendixes at the end of this book as a starting point. If you are using a computer, read everything on the websites that are relevant and then follow the links on the pages to other sites. Keep following links as long as they lead you to useful information.

If you are not using the Internet, you can call the organizations listed in Appendix B and ask them to send you information. You can also speak to someone there on the phone and explain what kind of specific information you are looking for and he or she can most likely point you in the right direction.

Do not forget to use your local library to gather information. If you do not know where to look, the librarian can help you. You can start with some of the books listed in Appendix C. Additionally, you want to use the professionals who are involved in your parent's life to the fullest extent. Talk to your parent's lawyer, financial planner, physical therapist, nurse, doctor, aides, geriatric care manager, counselors, and anyone else who has professional knowledge. Do not be afraid to ask questions and challenge assumptions.

Make sure you organize the information you gather in some way so that you can easily come back to it or share it with your parent or other family members. Use folders, notebooks, and the worksheets provided in this book. Once you have gathered information and organized it, you will find that you have a sense of control. You know what your choices are, you can see the facts, and now you can work with them and with your parent to make decisions and arrangements.

Setting Priorities

You have a lot to deal with and you have to accept that you cannot do everything. What you can do is deal with one thing at a time, and the best way to do that is to deal with the most pressing and important things first. Decide what is a priority for you each day and each week. It may help to make lists. A "to do" list that is written in order of importance can help you get things done. You can also write your list and then go back and put stars next to those things that are high priority. If you can look at a list and see clearly the things that absolutely must get done, you can organize your time better to manage them. Part of setting priorities is finding a way to balance things. You cannot let your responsibilities with your parent take over your entire life. You have to make room for things that will keep your own life going as well.

Managing Your Time

With all that you are trying to manage, you probably feel overwhelmed and exhausted. Incorporate some basic time management skills into your life and you will find that you will have a little breathing room.

Do two things at once when possible. Talk to your parent on the phone while folding laundry or filing. Do all your errands in one trip in one afternoon.

Delegate things when possible. Ask your son to take the dog to the vet for you. Suggest that your sister visit your parent this weekend instead of you. Ask your spouse to do more things around the house.

Simplify. Make changes in your life that pare some things down. Buy take-out for dinner once a week. Use a dry cleaner that will pick up and deliver the clothes for you. Stop your volunteer work for now. Decide not to have the entire family for Thanksgiving dinner at your house. Mow the lawn once a week instead of twice.

Stay organized. It does take some time to get organized, but once you do you'll find that using a system saves you a tremendous amount of time. Placing bills to be paid in chronological order makes it much faster to pay them than having to hunt through the stack in a panic.

Accept that some things won't get done. So maybe your house hasn't been vacuumed in a week and a half, maybe you didn't have time for that drink with your friends, and maybe you didn't get the Christmas tree taken down in your parent's room at the nursing home yet. It's okay! You can't do everything, and some things will be delayed or just won't get done. As long as you are getting the things that matter done, do not waste your time worrying about the small things that slip past you.

Accepting Change

It is important to realize that nothing in life is static. Everyone and everything is changing. You are changing and so is your parent. Your parent is going to continue to change. Sometimes this change will be gradual and slow and other times events will happen that will mean things have radically changed in a short period of time. You have to be prepared to face these changes. Try to view changes not with a sense of loss or sadness, but with a practical look at what needs to be done and how you and your parent can continue to enjoy life. Remain optimistic and focus on happy things. Remember that you can handle any changes that come if you just take them one at a time. You can choose a nursing home if you look at one at a time. You can make decisions about medical care if you listen to what the doctor tells you word by word.

> There is nothing you can do to stop things in your life and your parent's life from changing, so don't fight it. Things will change and the best thing you can do is face it armed with information and the ability to be flexible.

Involving Your Family

Getting your spouse, children, and other relatives involved in helping your parent is the best thing you can do. You cannot carry the entire burden yourself. You need help with things because you cannot be with your parent at all times. You also need the emotional support and the laughter that your family provides. Lean on them, let them help, listen to them, and include them.

Having your family involved will benefit your parent as well. Think about what life will be like when you are your parent's age. What do you think will probably be the most important thing in your life—the thing you care the most about? It will most likely be your family. Getting family involved with your parent will give him or her something to think about, things to do, and lots of emotional support.

Managing Your Job

You may feel torn in two sometimes. You have a busy and full life of your own that could easily take up all your time, but you also need to spend time with and energy on your parent and his or her care. It can be especially difficult to manage a job and devote the time you need to your parent. Remember that your job is essential in your life and you have to give it priority. You need to have the energy to do it well.

Arrange for other people to be available to your parent when you are at work. You cannot do your job and constantly field phone calls from your parent. You can make time for emergencies and you should make it clear to all caregivers that you are to be contacted if there is a problem.

Maximize your time off so that you take some of it for yourself—to relax, catch up at home, take vacations, etc. But plan on using some of the time to spend with your parent.

Take a look at your schedule. If you really feel "maxed out" with all your responsibilities, is there any way to adjust your schedule? Some employers will allow you to telecommute some of the time, work four ten-hour days instead of five eight-hour days, or use flex time. If you work part-time, maybe you can change the days you are working to better mesh with other relatives' schedules so they can be with your parent when you cannot. Think creatively about your situation.

Family Medical Leave Act

The *Family Medical Leave Act* is a federal law that gives certain employees the right to take an unpaid leave from their jobs to care for family members. You are eligible for such a leave if you work for a public agency (federal, state, or local) or for an employer with fifty or more employees and if you have been employed there at least twelve months and worked at least 1,250 hours in the last twelve months.

You may take up to twelve weeks of unpaid leave in a twelve-month period to care for an immediate family member (which includes a parent) with a serious health condition. You can take this time off as one big block or you can cut your hours, take one day off a week, etc., to total twelve weeks of workdays within a twelve-month period.

Your employer must keep your health benefits in place (but you may have to pay premiums yourself) while you are gone and must restore you to your original job or to an equivalent job with equivalent pay when you return. Your employer cannot penalize you for taking the leave or allow it to affect any of your benefits.

If you and your spouse work for the same employer, you are entitled to a total of twelve weeks unpaid leave divided between the both of you in a twelve-month period.

Keeping a Social Life

It may seem like the first thing to jettison from your life is your social life. How can you justify a night out with friends when your parent is home alone or having a hard time adjusting to the new senior residence? You need to continue your social life because it is part of what gives you the strength to go on. It is important to do things that are fun and things that give you a release. You have to feed your own needs before you can help anyone else. If you are stressed out, cranky, and just plain miserable, you won't be of much help to your parent. Build time into your schedule for your social life. You may find you need to reduce the time you have available for this, but it is essential that you keep it in your schedule.

Battling Guilt

Guilt is something you are probably dealing with. You feel guilty that you do not do more for your parent, you feel guilty that he or she has to move to a facility, you feel guilty when you realize you do not want to go visit today, and so on. Guilt is normal. If you let yourself be driven by guilt, you will run around like a chicken with your head cut off and never handle things in an organized and rational way. If you have a plan for how things will be handled, follow your plan. Do not listen to that little voice inside you that suggests maybe you shouldn't skip a visit to the nursing home so you can go shopping with your daughter. If you are satisfied that your plan is rational and solid, follow it and ignore that little voice.

Remind yourself of all you do for your parent and that you cannot be everything to everyone all the time. You cannot do it all, and trying to will just wear you out. Decide to do the best you can and not worry about the rest.

Battling Resentment

It can be hard to face the fact that in many ways you are resentful. It is common to resent your parent for all the extra responsibilities and burdens he or she has added to your life. You may also resent your spouse, children, or other relatives for not doing enough and not understanding what you are handling. All of these feelings are normal and it is okay to have them. The key is finding a way to manage them without hurting other people. You probably do not want to end up shouting at your father, "I'm sick and tired of you talking about how lonely you are when I come up here four times a week to see you even when I don't have time or want to!"

Take your resentment and wallow in it—get good and upset, cry, yell, and moan at home. Then pick yourself up and dust yourself off and realize you have to move on. Think about ways to make changes so you won't feel so much resentment. Ask others for help and make more time for yourself.

Battling Anger

Anger is another common reaction to the things you are facing. You may feel angry with your parent for being weak, for being sick, or for being stubborn. You may also at times experience anger toward your spouse, children, relatives, and coworkers for demands they make or for a lack of understanding. It is also common to feel anger toward the professionals in your parent's life. You may feel angry with the doctor for not fully explaining what the recovery time would be like for your parent, at nursing home staff for not being responsive enough, or toward hospital staff for a medication mix-up.

In many of these situations, your anger is probably justified. You do need to remember that because you are under a lot of stress and because you have a lot on your mind, it is easy to overreact and allow your feelings about the entire situation to become focused on one person at one moment.

Look at your anger and examine the situation. Are there ways to effect change without blowing up? Can you speak to the director of the nursing home about your concerns? Can you suggest to your adult children that they find another weekend baby-sitter for their kids while all of this is going on? Look for solutions to solve the underlying problem you are facing.

Dealing with Grief and Loss

As your parent ages, you experience loss. Each step along the road of life does bring us closer to the end. But the best way to cope is not to keep squinting to try to see and anticipate the end of the path, but instead to enjoy the moment and the things we see and do along the way. Try not to overreact about a future you can't predict. Focus instead on today and what you can do to make life enjoyable for you and your parent.

At some point you will have to cope with the loss of your parent, and there will be nothing easy about it. If you have enjoyed every moment and helped your parent experience joy in life each day, you will have less to feel badly about. Deal with loss when it happens—not today.

Maintaining Your Relationships

An important part of keeping your equilibrium involves devoting time and energy to relationships in your life that are important. Certainly your parent is important to you and you are probably devoting a lot of time and energy to him or her. Think about the other relationships in your life. If you have a spouse or partner, make time for him or her. Have a quiet dinner alone together once a week or go for walks together. Make sure you have time to connect as a couple and time to talk and share. The emotional support you receive will really give you strength to deal with other things in your life.

If you have children, make time for them. The same goes for grandchildren. Set time aside to see them or do things together. Maintain phone contact. If you have a pet, do not forget to make time for it. Animals can provide a lot of comfort and can help relieve stress.

Talk to and see your close friends and make room for them in your life. They are a great resource for venting about everyone and everything you are dealing with.

Finding Help

Remember that you cannot do it all on your own and you should not have to. Other chapters in this book tell you where to find practical hands-on help for your parent. You may find that you need emotional help as well, though. Use the resources in Appendix B to find support groups, online groups, or organizations that can help you. Talking to or interacting with other people who are in similar situations and share similar concerns is an important way to feel as if you are not alone and to find understanding. It can also be a good way to gather information and get leads on how to find things out or how to do certain things.

Check out Appendix B for a listing of caregiver support organizations.

Helping Your Children Cope

As difficult as it is for you to cope with the changes, situations, and happenings in your parent's life, it is equally hard for your children. Whether they are kids, teens, or adults, your children are probably not as involved in your parent's life as you are. They may not see your parent as often, and thus changes that seem gradual to you can seem sudden and unexpected to them.

It is important to be honest with your children about your parent and his or her situation. If your parent will be moving from a senior residence to an assisted-living facility, talk to your children and explain what is happening and why. If your parent has a hospital stay, explain everything to your children. Be honest about diagnoses and plans.

Encourage your children to spend time with your parent, but do not expect them to be as involved as you are. Encourage them to go on with their lives, but help them see that their presence is needed sometimes.

Holidays

Holidays are fraught with emotion for everyone. They are even more loaded when your parent is elderly. You want to include your parent in holidays. It may be difficult to feel as if you are taking over managing the family's holidays when in the past your parents were in charge of this. Include your parent in decisions and plans so that he or she is still very much a part of the holiday.

Keep your parent's limitations in mind. It may not be practical to think you can bring your parent from the assisted-living facility for an entire day to spend with your family. This may be overwhelming or too tiring. Talk to your parent about the plans and how he or she would like to participate. Sometimes a senior may insist that he or she doesn't want to come, but really may want you to convince him or her how essential he or she is to the celebration. Do everything you can to encourage your parent to come.

Plan things in a way that will make the holiday more manageable for your parent. An all-day open house for family and friends may be too long, so plan a family meal instead. Have Thanksgiving dinner at 2 p.m. instead of 6 p.m. if your parent tires by evening. Be sensitive to his or her needs and feelings, and try not to expect him or her to be the same as in the past.

It may be hard to get through the holidays if you are always looking back on how things used to be. Some reminiscing is good for everyone, but avoid becoming stuck on the "good old days." Focus instead on the joys of this particular holiday as it is in the present. Keep your parent comfortable and be flexible. If Dad nods off during the gift exchange, put his gifts aside until he wakes up. If Mom wants to go home early, take her.

Do not let the entire holiday hinge around your parent. Develop new traditions, do the things that are important to your family, and make sure that everyone who is part of the holiday is included and happy.

Thinking About Your Future

As you focus on keeping your life together while helping your parent, give some thought to how you will keep your life alive as you become older and face some of the challenges your parent faces. Think about what you can do now that will help you be happy then. One important thing is maintaining your relationships with those whom you love. Don't get too busy now to take care of those important relationships. You will want those people around when you are older.

Remember to keep your own interests alive as well so that you have things you like to do that can remain a part of your life when you are older.

Think about your attitude toward life and toward aging. Try to make your attitude a positive and tolerant one. Accept that things will change in your life as they have in your parent's life. Focus on making your life a happy one, and one with little regrets.

Use this book to help you plan for your own senior years and all the decisions and situations that will arise.

SENIOR COUPLES

You may be in the position of being fortunate enough to have both your parents still with you, or perhaps your one remaining parent has remarried at some point. Much of the information in this book will apply to your situation, but you may also find that there are some issues that come up that are solely related to couples.

If you are married, you are probably planning to live out your senior years with your spouse. This chapter will help you consider how you can help each other and how you can plan for a life together.

How to Talk to a Couple

Talking to a couple is different than talking to an individual senior. You might already know that you need to speak one way or explain things in a certain way to one parent and in a different way to the other parent. It is usually best to have discussions about important decisions and about the future with both your parents together. If you have one parent who understands less than the other, you may find it best to explain everything to the more aware parent and a pared-down version to the parent who has trouble grasping things. See *Tips for Dealing with Senior Couples* at the end of this chapter on page 262 for more information on talking to elderly couples.

Helping Them Make Decisions Together

Often, there is one partner who is more involved in certain kinds of decisions. ("If your father thinks it is best, then it's fine with me" or "Ask your mother—she'll know what to do.") While this may be how your parents have always functioned, it is important to make sure they both understand the decisions or concerns you are talking about since they affect both of their lives.

Encourage both parents to consider the options and choices. Encourage each of them to give feedback and discuss their concerns and questions. Give them each a turn to express their opinions.

If your parents can't agree about something, think about whom the decision affects the most. If you are discussing whether your father needs a home health care aide and he agrees to it and your mother is opposed to it and you believe this is something he really needs, you may need to convince her to come around to your way of thinking. But if your dad is the one opposed, an aide isn't going to get far if he isn't cooperating. If you believe he needs the help, you will have to help convince him that it is necessary.

Helping Them Face Each Other's Situations

Sometimes a spouse can turn a blind eye to the other's condition and refuse to acknowledge the truth of the situation. Your dad may insist your mom is just forgetful and not want to accept that she is displaying signs of early Alzheimer's. Your mother may not really see the trouble your dad has feeding himself. In these kinds of situations, you need to help the parent face the truth of the other's condition. It is usually best if you can have someone back you up on this—such as a geriatric care manager, a health care worker, or another family member.

You do not want to upset or frighten your parent, but if a potentially dangerous situation continues to be denied, the parent with the condition could have a bad outcome if he or she does not get the care needed.

How They Can Help Each Other

Often couples are able to complement each other quite well. Your mom may not be able to stand in front of the stove and cook, but she can sit in the kitchen and tell your dad what to do to make dinner. Your father may not be able to get in and out of the tub without assistance, but your mother is able to help guide him in and out. If your parents can help each other without risking injury to each other, then you should encourage them. Keep in mind, though, that if ever the stronger parent is not there, the other parent will need immediate assistance from someone.

Be aware that when a couple is able to compensate for each other's weaknesses, it may conceal serious problems. For example, if your father is having trouble driving, your mother may always be with him in the car and constantly give him instructions and directions to prevent accidents. To detect these kinds of problems, you have to keep your eyes open and ask a lot of questions.

The Effect of Aging on Their Relationship

Some couples continue to have the same kind of relationship they have always had when they reach senior years. For some couples, dynamics change. If one parent is very dependant on the other, the stronger parent may resent the burden.

It is important to keep in mind that even though your parents may have been together for what seems like forever, serious problems can develop in their relationship as in any other marriage. Should this happen, marriage counseling can definitely help.

The Desire to Stay Together

Your parents probably are insistent that they will remain together and reside together the rest of their lives. This is a natural instinct and one that needs to be respected.

If one parent reaches a point where he or she can no longer be cared for at home, there are many options available that will allow your parents to remain together. Senior residences and assisted-living facilities do have space for couples. You will need to inquire about what is available and what kinds of care can be provided in this setting. (See chapters 9 and 10 for more information.)

When one parent must enter a long-term care facility to receive medical care, it is very important that the other parent have frequent (if not daily) visits with the resident parent. Talk to your parent about how frequently he or she wants to go and monitor him or her for signs of stress and tiredness, since constant visiting can be very draining.

Respecting Their Relationship

No matter where your parents are living, it is paramount that everyone respect their relationship and their need to be together. This includes you, family, friends, health care workers, and staff. Your parents are married adults and deserve to have time together alone, in private if at all possible. Insist that staff and caregivers grant them this.

Decision Making

If a decision must be made about one parent's care, you will need to work closely with your other parent to reach that decision. If at all possible, you want the healthy parent to have control of the choices (with a lot of input from you) if he or she wants it. Work with your parent to present all the choices and options and offer your opinion.

Managing Temporary Separations

If one parent is hospitalized or in a nursing home for a short time, you will need to help your other parent cope. Consider whether he or she needs help with daily living activities. Enlist friends and family to help. This can become complicated because family members will be spending a lot of time with the ill parent, but you cannot forget the needs of the well parent. He or she may be at home or in a residence and be quite worried without the other parent. Let him or her visit the ill parent. Being together is very important for both of them and can help hasten healing or help them find closure if the end of life is near.

Offer the well parent a lot of support and watch closely to be sure he or she is continuing to eat, bathe, and stay active. It is very easy to become depressed when your spouse is ill.

Dealing with Grief

Should the time come that you lose one of your parents, the surviving parent will need a tremendous amount of support. In the short-term, he or she will need help making decisions about the funeral and end-of-life issues. Family and friends will probably be very available at this time. As time passes, however, he or she will need continued attention. He or she may become quite lonely, and may require increasing assistance at home or at the residence where he or she resides. Grieving is a long-term process, and being there for your parent in the weeks following a death is not enough. The months ahead are quite difficult.

TIPS FOR DEALING WITH SENIOR COUPLES

- Respect their relationship and their need for each other.

- Encourage them both to become informed about each other's needs and conditions.

- Involve both of them in important decisions that need to be made.

- Understand that separations can be extremely difficult.

- Try to make plans that will meet both of their needs.

- Watch for dangerous compensation where one elder is able to conceal another's weaknesses.

LONG-DISTANCE MANAGEMENT | 18

Many parents and children do not live in the same town or the same state. Through the years, you have probably found ways to maintain your relationship despite the distance, through phone calls, the Internet, and visits. Things become more complicated once your parent needs your assistance. It is very difficult to try to manage or monitor your parent's health, finances, and daily life from far away.

If you and your children live far apart, they will have difficulties staying involved in your life and helping you with any assistance you may need as you age. For this reason, some people choose to move near their children after they retire. Understanding the difficulties of the situation will help you plan for your own future, as well as manage your parent's future.

Understanding Your Limitations

Because you and your parent are not in the same town, you cannot stop over every few days to see how things are going. You don't bump into neighbors on the sidewalk who can tell you their impressions, and you don't have the opportunity to chat with a nurse in the hallway. You rely on your parent, relatives, or friends who live near your parent and on doctors or nursing home personnel to keep you informed. You probably visit as often as you can, but it probably isn't often enough to have a true sense of how things are going.

Because of where you live, you probably cannot be as involved in helping your parent as you would like to be. You are not going to be the one who takes him or her to the grocery store once a week and you cannot just stop in unexpectedly at the senior residence to see what's going on.

You can, however, be involved in helping your parent and directing care. If you are an only child or the only child able to be actively involved, you can find ways to manage care even though you may not be able to do it in person. One way to do so is to hire a *geriatric care manager*. He or she can keep you informed and help you make any decisions. He or she can be your eyes and ears. It is best if you can hire him or her while you are in town, but you can do so by phone if there is no choice.

> You can also rely on a network of family and friends. They can gather information, do the footwork, and let you make decisions, in consultation with your parent.

Making Decisions and Getting Information from a Distance

Being far away does not mean you have to be distant from information. You can speak to your parent every day by phone. You can speak to doctors and other health care workers by phone. If your parent is in a facility, the staff can keep you up to date.

When making decisions from a distance, it is sometimes difficult to know if you are doing the right thing without firsthand, in-person experience and knowledge. You cannot see your parent and observe what is happening with him or her, so it is hard to feel as if you have enough information to make important decisions.

If you are in the position of being the person who has to decide, then you must make the best decisions you can with the information you can gather. Talk to doctors, nurses, people who have visited your parent, and especially to your parent. Do your research. If a health decision is involved, get on the Internet and learn everything you can. Go to the library and ask a librarian for help finding the information you need. Do not be afraid to ask questions of doctors, nurses, and staff.

Finding Local Help

If you have family in the area, contact them and ask them for whatever help your parent needs. Maybe Cousin Mark can drive your dad to the cardiologist. Perhaps Aunt Donna can interview home health aides. Talk to your parent's neighbors and friends. Find out if the next-door neighbor can pop in on your mom at the nursing home once a week.

If you do not have a local network of people to call on or no one is available, contact the local agency on aging and find out what services are available. If your parent is in a facility, speak to the staff social worker and ask for help.

Considering a Move

You may think that the best answer is for you and your parent to live closer to each other. Most people assume it would be easier for their parent to move than for them. After all, you have a job, a family, and responsibilities. It is important to remember that your parent is probably quite attached to where he or she lives. He or she may have lived there most of his or her life. Asking your parent to move may be met with staunch resistance. Your parent would have to live in an area where he or she has no friends and where everything is unfamiliar. If your parent is suffering from dementia or Alzheimer's, this may make everything worse. You need to think carefully about relocating your parent. Can he or she handle the change? Can you handle living so close to him or her? Do you have room at your home or have you researched the local living options? Do you feel comfortable switching your parent's doctors? Is this what your parent really wants?

You may believe that it would be best if you relocated to be near your parent. Obviously this would make things easier for your parent, but you need to consider the ramifications on your own life. Do you have a job lined up? Where would you live? If you have children or a spouse, how would they react to the relocation? Would you be happy there?

Dealing with Your Emotions

When your parent ages and you live far away, you may feel guilt, frustration, isolation, worry, relief, and many other emotions. It is important to remind yourself that the circumstances are that you are far away, and because of this you are limited in what you can do from this distance. You cannot be the one at your parent's bedside on a daily basis or the one to shovel his or her driveway. You need to focus on what you can do from where you are. Stay in touch with your parent, other relatives, and any home care workers or medical personnel. Give yourself permission to go on living. You probably have a job and a family to think about. You can't spend every moment obsessing about what is happening with your parent.

Dealing with Family Members

If you have brothers or sisters or other close family members who do live closer to your parent, you can be sure that at some point they will feel resentment toward you. Because of your location, you are probably not as involved in the day-to-day problems involved with your parent's life. Your relative may feel that an unfair percentage of the burden falls on him or her while you are getting off scot-free. Be sympathetic to his or her frustration, but be sure to point out the difficulties of your situation. You feel out of the loop, you feel guilty, and you worry constantly. You may be using up all your vacation or sick time to travel to see your parent. There is a great impact on your life as well.

> Let your relative know what you are able to handle from a distance. Take on what responsibility is feasible for you to handle from where you are.

Getting Medical Updates

It can be frustrating when your parent is ill or receiving long-term medical care and you are out of town. It is important that you have a signed release from your parent (see Chapter 3). Send a copy of it to each care provider with a letter. Explain that you live out of town and will be calling him or her for updates. Request that he or she call you with any important or urgent changes.

Handling Finances from a Distance

It may seem impossible, but it is possible for you to handle your parent's finances from a distance. If there is another relative in town, it would be easier for him or her to manage this, but if you have no choice, it can be done. Get a power of attorney from your parent (see Chapter 4) and get several copies of it. Give copies to utility companies, banks, credit card companies, insurance companies, doctor's offices, hospitals, nursing homes or care facilities, and anyone else who may be sending your parent a bill. Explain that your address is to be used as the billing address and request that this be changed in the system. Inform the bank that you will now be using the account. You will also need to make sure that any bills or other financial paperwork that is not sent to you can be forwarded by your parent, another relative, or the care facility where your parent resides. (See Chapter 3 for information on organizing bills and records.)

Staying in Touch

You may feel out of the loop if you live out of town. You can't see with your own eyes what is happening. It is important that you find someone you trust who can be your eyes and ears. Maybe another relative, a friend, neighbor, or staff member at your parent's facility will be able to do this for you. Call and check in with this person often and make sure he or she will contact you immediately with any problems or concerns. Call your parent on a regular basis and, if he or she is able, make sure he or she has your number and a calling card to use to contact you. Stay close to your parent by sending photographs, cards, notes, small gifts, and other things through the mail. Encourage your children or spouse to stay in contact in similar ways as well.

When to Visit

It can be hard to know when to plan on visiting your parent. On the one hand, you want to see him or her frequently, but on the other hand, you probably have a limited amount of vacation time or funds for travel. You also probably want to be able to take real vacations sometimes. It is difficult to know what to do because you may feel you should save sick time, vacation time, or money for travel should your parent become critically ill or need you present for some equally pressing reason.

You have to find a balance that works for you. The fact of the matter is that you can't see your parent as often as you might wish because of the distance. Instead of planning to come and visit for a couple weeks in the summer, try to come more frequently for shorter visits if possible. If you are employed and your company is large enough to be covered by the *Family and Medical Leave Act*, you will always be able to take time off in an emergency to care for your parent even if you have no sick or vacation time left.

Reduce travel costs by using frequent flyer plans, taking a train or bus, or driving. See if you can stay at your parent's home or with relatives or friends when you visit.

CONCLUSION

My grandfather always said, "It doesn't pay to get old." Aging may not be something we look forward to, but it is definitely something we can plan for, think about, and manage. There are more and more choices, options, and resources available for seniors today than ever before.

Whether you are making decisions for a parent, a spouse, another family member, or yourself, taking the time to gather information and find resources and support will help you make well-reasoned decisions that can make the senior years comfortable, happy, and enjoyable.

It may not pay to get old, but the senior years can and should be just as well-planned, financially affordable, and carefully managed as all the other phases of life.

GLOSSARY

A

accelerated benefits. Life insurance benefits that can be used while the insured person is still alive; also called *living benefits*.

ADL. Activities of daily living, such as eating, personal hygiene, and using the bathroom.

aging in place. Continuing to live in one's own home as one becomes older.

ALJ. Administrative law judge; a judge who hears a Medicaid appeal.

Alzheimer's disease. A disease of the brain that causes memory loss.

AMA. Against medical advice; when a patient chooses to leave a hospital or refuses treatment that is recommended.

annuity. Financial arrangement where a bank pays a yearly sum in exchange for equity interest in a home.

appeal. Asking another court to decide that a court decision is wrong.

assisted living. A facility that provides assistance with activities of daily living, but not skilled-nursing care.

B

beneficiary. A person who receives a benefit, such as someone who received something based on a will.

bereavement counselor. A counselor who is trained and experienced in helping people cope with grief.

C

capital gains tax. A tax based on the increase in value of an asset.

charge nurse. A nurse in charge of a shift in a medical facility.

community spouse resource amount. The amount of assets the spouse of a person receiving Medicaid may keep.

compassion fatigue. A condition where a person is worn out from caring for another.

continuing care community. A long-term choice that provides all levels of care for residents from senior living to skilled-nursing care.

cremation. The process in which a body is turned to ash.

custodial care facility. Assisted-living facility.

D

dementia. Any of a family of illnesses causing mental confusion.

discharge planner. A hospital employee who helps patients make plans for when they leave the hospital.

do not resuscitate (DNR) order. An order that can be placed on a patient's chart indicating that emergency lifesaving treatment is not to be administered.

durable power of attorney. A type of power of attorney that becomes effective immediately.

E

emergency room (ER). The part of a hospital that provides urgent care.

estate planning. Planning how assets will be divided after a person's death, including finding ways of maximizing them.

exempt assets. Assets not considered when one applies for Medicaid.

F

Family and Medical Leave Act. The federal law permitting twelve weeks of unpaid leave from work to care for a family member.

family council. A group of family members of nursing home residents who meet to discuss issues and problems at the home.

Federal Funeral Rule. Governs what funeral homes may tell clients and how they can charge for services.

G

geriatric assessment. An evaluation of an elderly person's abilities, needs, and physical and mental condition.

geriatric care manager. A trained professional who can help elderly people find resources, locate medical care, arrange for assistance, and do anything else that may be needed.

geriatrician. A medical doctor who specializes in caring for elderly patients.

gerontologist. A social scientist who studies the elderly.

guardianship. A legal determination that a person cannot make decisions for him- or herself and requires a guardian to make them for him or her.

H

health care proxy. A legal document giving someone else the authority to make health care decisions for a person if he or she is unable to do so him- or herself.

home equity conversion mortgage. A reverse mortgage, where the financial institution pays a lump sum to the homeowner and gets ownership in the home.

home health care aide. A worker trained to assist people with bathing, meal preparation, and household tasks.

hospice. A program or organization that cares for terminally ill patients in a way that focuses on pain management and improving quality of life; also called *palliative care*.

I

IADL. Instrumental activity of daily living, such as shopping, preparing food, and housekeeping.

intestate. Dying without a will.

irrevocable. Something that cannot be changed.

L

licensed practical nurse (LPN). A nurse who has had medical training and obtained a license to provide care.

lien. A legal hold placed on real estate to ensure payment of a debt.

life estate. Ownership in property for the term of a person's life; a person who owns a life estate has no ownership to distribute after his or her death.

living benefits. A type of life insurance benefits that can be accessed while the insured person is still alive; also called *accelerated benefits*.

living will. A legal document describing what type of medical care and intervention a person authorizes for him- or herself.

long-term care insurance. Private insurance that pays for nursing home care.

look-back period. The thirty-six months before one applies for Medicaid from which all financial records must be provided to help determine eligibility.

M

Medicaid planner. A person experienced in helping others distribute and manage assets so as to become eligible for Medicaid.

Medicaid. State-run medical insurance programs for people with low incomes.

Medicare. Federally sponsored medical insurance for people age 65 and up.

Medigap. Private insurance that covers things Medicare does not.

memorial service. A nonreligious ceremony where people share memories of one who has died.

N

nonexempt assets. Assets that must be considered when applying for Medicaid.

nursing home. A facility that provides skilled-nursing care to short-term or long-term residents.

O

obituary. A death notice in a newspaper.

ombudsman. A state employee who works to represent the concerns of citizens.

P

palliative care. Medical care that seeks to limit pain; also called *hospice*.

pastoral care. Religious services provided by clergy.

peer review organization. A group of medical professionals who review claims and medical decisions.

Phone Assistance League (PAL). An organization that will call an elderly person daily to check on him or her.

physician assistant (PA). A trained medical provider who can prescribe medication and offer some medical care.

power of attorney. A legal document giving someone else authority to handle another person's financial affairs for him or her.

private duty nurse. A nurse employed by the patient and not the hospital or facility the patient is in.

probate. The court process through which the terms of a will are made legal.

Q

Qualified Medicare Beneficiary Program. A state-sponsored program that pays Medicare premiums and co-pays.

R

registered nurse (RN). A nurse who is able to administer medication and perform some medical procedures.

release. A legal form that allows a doctor to share a patient's medical information with another person.

resident council. A group of nursing home patients who meet to discuss issues and problems associated with the nursing home.

respite care. When someone else cares for an elderly person so the primary caregiver can have time away.

reverse mortgage. An arrangement where a financial institution gets title to a home and in return makes monthly or lump-sum payments to the homeowner.

S

sandwich generation. People who are caring for aging parents while still raising a family.

senior apartment. Another name for a senior-living facility.

senior living. Independent living units for seniors that provide daily staff contact and group activities.

skilled-nursing facility. A nursing home that provides nursing care to long- or short-term residents.

spending down. Using up one's assets in order to qualify for Medicaid.

springing power of attorney. A power of attorney that becomes effective only upon the happening of an event named in it.

state surveys. State inspections of nursing homes.

T

triage. A method of prioritizing medical care based on urgency.

trust. A legal entity that holds assets for another person.

trustee. The person who administers or manages a trust.

V

veteran's benefits. Health insurance benefits provided to honorably discharged military personnel.

Vial of Life. A program run by many sheriff departments, where a person keeps a vial in the refrigerator with health information and emergency contact information.

W

will. A legal document directing how to divide a person's belongings after death.

STATE-SPECIFIC RESOURCES

State Agencies on Aging

ALABAMA

Region IV
Irene Collins, Executive Director
Alabama Department of Senior Services
P.O. Box 301851
770 Washington Ave., Ste. 470
Montgomery, AL 36130
334-242-5743 or 800-243-5463
Fax: 334-242-5594
E-mail:
Irene.collins@adss.alabama.gov

ALASKA

Region X
Denise Daniello, Executive Director
Alaska Commission on Aging
Department of Health and Social Services
150 Third St., No. 103
P.O. Box 110693
Juneau, AK 99811
907-465-4879
Fax: 907-465-4716
E-mail: denise_daniello@health.state.ak.us

AMERICAN SAMOA

Region IX
Taesalialii F. Lutu, Director
Territorial Administration on Aging
American Samoa Government
Pago Pago, American Samoa 96799
011 684-633-1251 or 633-1252
Fax: 011 684-633–2533

ARIZONA

Region IX
Rex Critchfield, Acting Assistant
Director
**Arizona Aging and Adult
Administration**
Department of Economic Security
1789 W. Jefferson, No. 950A
Phoenix, AZ 85007
602-542-4446
Fax: 602-542-6575
E-mail: rcritchfield@azdes.gov

ARKANSAS

Region VI
Herb Sanderson, Director
**Arkansas Division of Aging and
Adult Services**

Department of Health & Human
Services
P.O. Box 1437
700 Main St., 5th Floor, S530
Little Rock, AR 72203
(FedEx zip code 72201)
501-682-2441
Fax: 501-682-8155
E-mail: Herb.sanderson@mail.state.
ar.us

CALIFORNIA

Region IX
Lynn Daucher, Director
California Department of Aging
1300 National Dr., #200
Sacramento, CA 95834
916-419-7500
Fax: 916-928-2268
E-mail: ldaucher@aging.ca.gov

COLORADO

Region VIII
Jeanette Hensley, Director
**Colorado Division of Aging and
Adult Services**
Department of Human Services
1575 Sherman St., 10th Floor

Denver, CO 80203
303-866-2636
Fax: 303-866-2696
E-mail: Jeanette.Hensley@state.co.us

CONNECTICUT
Region I
Pamela Giannini, Director
Connecticut Bureau of Aging
Community & Social Work Services
Department of Social Services
25 Sigourney St.
Hartford, CT 06106
860-424-5277
Fax: 860-424-4957
E-mail: Pamela.giannini@po.state.ct.us

DELAWARE
Region III
Guy Perrotti, Director
Delaware Division of Services for
Aging and Adults with Physical
Disabilities
Department of Health and Social
Services
1901 N. Du Pont Hwy.
New Castle, DE 19720
302-255-9390

Fax: 302-255-4445
e-mail: Guy.perrotti@state.de.us

DISTRICT OF COLUMBIA
Region III
Clarence Brown, Director
District of Columbia Office on Aging
One Judiciary Square
441 4th St., NW, 9th Floor
Washington, DC 20001
202-724-5622
Fax: 202-724-4979
E-mail: Clarence.brown@dc.gov

FLORIDA
Region IV
Doug Beach, Secretary
Florida Department of Elder Affairs
4040 Esplanade Way, Ste. 315
Tallahassee, FL 32399
850-414-2000
Fax: 850-414-2004
E-mail: beachd@elderaffairs.org

GEORGIA
Region IV
Maria Greene, Director
Georgia Division for Aging Services

2 Peachtree St. NW, 9th Floor
Atlanta, GA 30303
404-657-5258
Fax: 404-657-5285
E-mail: magreene@dhr.state.ga.us

GUAM
Region IX
Arthur U. San Agustin, Senior
Citizens Administrator
Guam Division of Senior Citizens
Department of Public Health and
Social Services
Government of Guam
P.O. Box 2816
Hagaina, Guam 96932
011-671-735-7382
Fax: 671-735-7416
E-mail: chiefdsc@dphss.govguam.net

HAWAII
Region IX
Noemi Pendleton, Director
Hawaii Executive Office on Aging
No. 1 Capitol District
250 S. Hotel Street, Ste. 406
Honolulu, HI 96813
808-586-0100

Fax: 808-586-0185
E-mail: Noemi.pendleton@doh.hawaii.
gov

IDAHO
Region X
Kim Toryanski, Administrator
Idaho Commission on Aging
3380 Americana Terrace, No. 120
P.O. Box 83720
Boise, ID 83720
208-334-3833
Fax: 208-334-3033
E-mail: ktoryanski@aging.idaho.gov

ILLINOIS
Region V
Charles D. Johnson, Director
Illinois Department on Aging
421 E. Capitol Ave.
Springfield, IL 62701
217-785-2870
Fax: 217-785-4477
E-mail: Charles.Johnson@aging.state.
il.us

INDIANA
Region V
Stephen Smith, Director
Indiana Division of Aging
Family and Services Administration
402 W. Washington St.
P.O. Box 7083
Indianapolis, IN 46207
317-232-7123
Fax: 317-232-7867
E-mail: Stephen.smith@fssa.in.gov

IOWA
Region VII
John McCalley, Director
Iowa Department of Elder Affairs
Jessie Parker Building
510 E. 12th St., Ste. 2
Des Moines, IA 50319
515-725-3301
Fax: 515-725-3300
E-mail: John.mccalley@iowa.gov

KANSAS
Region VII
Kathy Greenlee, Secretary
Kansas Department on Aging
New England Building
503 S. Kansas Ave.
Topeka, KS 66603
785-296-5222
Fax: 785-296-0256
E-mail:
kathygreenlee@aging.state.ks.us

KENTUCKY
Region IV
Deborah Anderson, Commissioner
Department For Aging & Independent Living
Cabinet for Health & Family Services
275 E. Main St., 3W-F
Frankfort, KY 40621
502-564-6930
Fax: 502-564-4595
E-mail: Deborah.anderson2@ky.gov

LOUISIANA
Region VI
Godfrey White, Executive Director
Louisiana Governor's Office of Elderly Affairs
P.O. Box 61 (zip 70821)
412 N. 4th St.
Baton Rouge, LA 70802
225-342-7100
Fax: 225-342-7133
E-mail: gpwhite@goea.state.la.us

MAINE

Region I
Diana Scully, Director
Maine Office of Elder Services
Department of Health & Human
Services
442 Civic Center Dr.
11 State House Station
Augusta, ME 04333
207-287-9200
Fax: 207-287-9230
E-mail: Diana.scully@maine.gov

MARIANA ISLANDS

Region IX
Tony Agulto, Acting Director
CNMI Office on Aging
Commonwealth of the Northern
Mariana Islands
P.O. Box 502178
Saipan, MP 96950
670-233-1320 or 670-233-1321
Fax: 670-233-1327
E-mail: aging@vzpacifica.net

MARYLAND

Region III
Gloria Lawlah, Secretary
Maryland Department of Aging

301 W. Preston St., Ste. 1007
Baltimore, MD 21201
410-767-1100
Fax: 410-333-7943
E-mail: ggl@ooa.state.md.us

MASSACHUSETTS

Region I
Michael Festa, Secretary
**Massachusetts Executive Office of
Elder Affairs**
One Ashburton Place
Boston, MA 02108
617-222-7451
Fax: 617-727-6944
E-mail: Michael.Festa@state.ma.us

MICHIGAN

Region V
Sharon Gire, Executive Director
**Michigan Office of Services to the
Aging**
P.O. Box 30676
7109 W. Saginaw, First Floor
Lansing, MI 48909
(FedEx zip 48917)
517-373-8230
Fax: 517-373-4092
E-mail: OSADirector@michigan.gov

MINNESOTA

Region V

Jean Wood, Director

Minnesota Board on Aging

Department of Human Services

P.O. Box 64976

St. Paul, MN 55164

651-431-2500 or 800-882-6262

Fax: 651-431-7453

E-mail: jean.wood@state.mn.us

MISSISSIPPI

Region IV

Marion Dunn Tutor, Director

Mississippi Council on Aging

Division of Aging and Adult Services

750 N. State St.

Jackson, MS 39202

601-359-4925

Fax: 601-359-4370

E-mail: Mdunntutor@mdhs.state.ms.us

MISSOURI

Region VII

Brenda Campbell, Division Director

**Missouri Division of Senior &
Dis-ability Services**

Department of Health & Senior
Services

P.O. Box 570

Jefferson City, MO 65102

573-526-3626

Fax: 573-751-8687

Email: Brenda.campbell@dhss.mo.gov

MONTANA

Region VIII

Charles Rehbein, Aging Services
Bureau Chief

Montana Office on Aging

Senior and Long Term Care Division

Department of Public Health and
Human Services

111 Sanders St.

P.O. Box 4210

Helena, MT 59604

406-444-7788 or 800-551-3191

Fax: 406-444-7743

E-mail: crehbein@mt.gov

NEBRASKA

Region VII

Joann Weis, Director

**Nebraska Health and Human
Services—State Unit on Aging**

P.O. Box 95044

301 Centennial Mall—South

Lincoln, NE 68509

402-471-2307
Fax: 402-471-4619
E-mail: Joann.weis@hhss.ne.gov

NEVADA

Region IX
Carol Sala, Administrator
Nevada Division for Aging Services
Department of Health & Human
Services
3416 Goni Rd., Building D-132
Carson City, NV 89706
775-687-4210 Ext 226
Fax: 775-687-4264
E-mail: csala@aging.nv.gov

NEW HAMPSHIRE

Region I
Kathleen F. Otte, Administrator
**New Hampshire Bureau of Elderly
and Adult Services**
Brown Building—129 Pleasant St.
Concord, NH 03301
603-271-4394
Fax: 603-271-4643
E-mail: Kathleen.F.Otte@dhhs.state.
nh.us

NEW JERSEY

Region II
Patricia Polansky, Assistant
Commissioner
**New Jersey Division of Aging &
Community Services**
Department of Health & Senior
Services
240 W. State St.
P.O. Box 807
Trenton, NJ 08625
(FedEx zip 08608)
609-292-4027
Fax: 609-943-3343
E-mail: patricia.polansky@doh.state.
nj.us

NEW MEXICO

Region VI
Deborah Armstrong, Cabinet
Secretary
**New Mexico Aging and Long-Term
Services Department**
2550 Cerrillos Rd.
Santa Fe, NM 87505
505-476-4799 (main)
505-476-4755 (direct)
Department Fax: 505-476-4836

Office of the Secretary Fax:
505-476–4750
E-mail: Debbie.Armstrong@state.nm.us

NEW YORK

Region II
Michael Burgess, Director
New York State Office for the Aging
Two Empire State Plaza
Albany, NY 12223
518-474-7012
Fax: 518-474-1398
E-mail: mike.burgess@ofa.state.ny.us

NORTH CAROLINA

Region IV
Dennis W. Streets, Director
**North Carolina Division of Aging &
Adult Services**
Department of Health and Human
Services
2101 Mail Service Center
693 Palmer Dr.
Raleigh, NC 27699
(FedEx zip 27603)
919-733-3983
Fax: 919-733-0443
E-mail: Dennis.Streets@ncmail.net

NORTH DAKOTA

Region VIII
Linda Wright, Director
North Dakota Aging Services Division
Department of Human Services
600 E. Boulevard Ave.
Department 325
Bismarck, ND 58505
701-328-4601
Fax: 701-328-4061
E-mail: sowril@nd.gov

OHIO

Region V
Barbara E. Riley, Director
Ohio Department of Aging
50 W. Broad St., 9th Floor
Columbus, OH 43215
614-466-7246
Fax: 614-995-1049
E-mail: briley@age.state.oh.us

OKLAHOMA

Region VI
Lance Robertson, Director
Oklahoma Aging Services Division
OK Department of Human Services
2401 NW 23rd St., Ste. 40

Oklahoma City, OK 73107
405-521-2281
Fax: 405-521-2086
E-mail: lance.robertson@okdhs.org

OREGON
Region X
James Toews, Assistant Director
**Oregon Seniors and People With
Dis-abilities**
Department of Human Services
500 Summer St., NE, E02
Salem, OR 97301
503-945-6478
Fax: 503-373-7823
E-mail: James.d.toews@state.or.us

PENNSYLVANIA
Region III
Nora Dowd, Secretary
Pennsylvania Department of Aging
555 Walnut St., 5th Floor
Harrisburg, PA 17101
717-783-1550
Fax: 717-772-3382
E-mail: ndowd@state.pa.us

PUERTO RICO
Region II

Rossana López León, Executive Director
**Puerto Rico Governor's Office for
El-derly Affairs**
P.O. Box 191179
San Juan, PR 00919–1179
787-721-5710
Fax: 787-721-6510
E-mail: rlopez@ogave.gobierno.pr

RHODE ISLAND
Region I
Corinne Calise Russo, Director
**Rhode Island Department of Elderly
Affairs**
John O. Pastore Center
Benjamin Rush Building, No. 55
35 Howard Ave.
Cranston, RI 02920
401-462-0501 or 401-462-0565
Fax: 401-462-0503
E-mail: crusso@dea.state.ri.us

SOUTH CAROLINA
Region IV
Curtis M. Loftis Jr., Director
**South Carolina Lieutenant Gover-
nor's Office on Aging**
Bureau of Senior Services
1301 Gervais St.

Suite 200
Columbia, SC 29201
803-734-9900
Fax: 803-734-9886
E-mail: cloftis@aging.sc.gov

SOUTH DAKOTA

Region VIII
Marilyn Kinsman, Administrator
South Dakota Office of Adult
Services & Aging
Department of Social Services
700 Governors Dr.
Pierre, SD 57501
605-773-3656
Fax: 605-773-6834
E-mail: Marilyn.kinsman@state.sd.us

TENNESSEE

Region IV
Kathy Zamata, Acting Director
Tennessee Commission on Aging and
Disability
Andrew Jackson Building
500 Deaderick St., No. 825
Nashville, TN 37243
615-741-2056
Fax: 615-741-3309
E-mail: kathy.zamata@state.tn.us

TEXAS

Region VI
Adelaide Horn, Commissioner
Texas Department of Aging &
Dis-ability Services
P.O. Box 149030 (W-619)
Austin, TX 78714
512-438-3030
Fax: 512-438-4220
e-mail: Adelaide.horn@dads.state.tx.us

U.S. VIRGIN ISLANDS

Region II
Eva Williams, Administrator
Virgin Islands Senior Citizen Affairs
Administration
Department of Human Services
3011 Golden Rock
Christiansted, St. Croix, VI 00820
340-772-9811
Fax: 340-772-9849
E-mail: dhssca@yahoo.com

UTAH

Region VIII
Alan Ormsby, Director
Utah Division of Aging & Adult
Services
Department of Human Services

120 North 200 West, Room 325
Salt Lake City, UT 84103
801-538-3910
877-424-4640
Fax: 801-538-4395
E-mail: akormsby@utah.gov

VERMONT
Region I
Joan Senecal, Commissioner
**Vermont Department of Disabilities,
Aging and Independent Living**
Weeks Building
103 S. Main St.
Waterbury, VT 05676
802-241-2401
Fax: 802-241-2325
E-mail: joan.senecal@dail.state.vt.us

VIRGINIA
Region III
Linda Nablo, Commissioner
Virginia Department for the Aging
1610 Forest Ave., Ste. 100
Richmond, VA 23229
804-662-9333
Fax: 804-662-7035
E-mail: linda.nablo@vda.virginia.gov

WASHINGTON
Region X
Kathy Leitch, Assistant Secretary
**Washington Aging and Disability
Services**
Department of Social & Health
Services
640 Woodland Square Loop SE
Lacey, WA 98503
P.O. Box 45600
Olympia, WA 98504
360-725-2260
Fax: 360-407-0304
E-mail: leitckj@dshs.wa.gov

WEST VIRGINIA
Region III
Sandra Vanin, Commissioner
**West Virginia Bureau of Senior
Services**
1900 Kanawha Blvd., East
3003 Town Center Mall
Charleston, WV 25305
(FedEx zip 25389)
304-558-3317
Fax: 304-558-609
E-mail: svanin@boss.state.wv.us

WISCONSIN

Region V

Donna McDowell, Director

Wisconsin Bureau of Aging and Disability Resources

Department of Health and Family Services

One West Wilson St., Room 450

(FedEx zip 53702)

P.O. Box 7851

Madison, WI 53707

608-266-3840

Fax: 608-267-3203

E-mail: mcdowdb@dhfs.state.wi.us

WYOMING

Region VIII

Beverly Morrow, Administrator

Wyoming Aging Division

Department of Health

6101 Yellowstone Rd., Ste. 259B

Cheyenne, WY 82002

307-777-7986 or 800-442-2766

Fax: 307-777-5340

E-mail: Beverly.morrow@health.wyo.gov

State Hospice Associations

Alabama Hospice Organization
1040 14th St., Ste. B
Calera, AL 35040
205-668-0460
800-355-1973
Fax: 205-668-0470
www.alhospice.org

**Arizona Hospice and Palliative Care
Organization**
815 N. First Ave., Ste. One
Phoenix, AZ 85003
602-712-9822
Fax: 602-712-1252
www.arizonahospice.org

**Arkansas State Hospice and
Palliative Care Organization**
P.O. Box 251507
Little Rock, AK 72225
866-742-1541
Fax: 877-779-6472
www.arkansasstatehospice.org

**California Hospice and Palliative
Care Association**
3841 North Freeway Blvd., Ste. 225
Sacramento, CA 95834

916-925-3770
888-252-1010
Fax: 916-925-3780
www.calhospice.org

Colorado Hospice Organization
P.O. Box 50888
Colorado Springs, CO 80949
719-594-9233
Fax: 719-594-9203
www.coloradohospice.org

**Connecticut Council for Hospice &
Palliative Care**
110 Barnes Rd., Box 90
Wallingford, CT 06492
203-265-5923
www.cthospice.org

**Florida Hospices and Palliative Care,
Inc.**
2000 Apalachee Pkwy., Ste. 200
Tallahassee, FL 32301
850-878-2632
800-282-6560
Fax: 850-878-5688
www.floridahospices.org

Georgia Hospice Organization
Five Concourse Pkwy., Ste. 3000
Atlanta, GA 30328
877-924-6073
Fax: 703-837-1233
www.ghpco.org

Hawaii Islands Hospice Organization
P.O. Box 62155
Honolulu, HI 96839
808-585-9977
800-474-2113
Fax: 808-988-3877
www.hospicehawaii.org

Idaho State Hospice Organization
190 E. Bannock
Boise, ID 83712
208-772-7994
Fax: 208-726-7688
www.hospiceidaho.org

Illinois Hospice and Palliative Care
Organization
1525 East 53rd St., Ste. 400
Chicago, IL 60615
888-844-7706
Fax: 888-844-7697
www.il-hpco.org

Indiana Hospice and Palliative Care
Organization, Inc.
Ten West Market St., Ste. 1720
Indianapolis, IN 46204
317-464-5145
866-254-1910
Fax: 317-464-5146
www.ihpco.org

Iowa Hospice Organization
100 E. Grand Ave., Ste. 120
Des Moines, IA 50309
515-243-1046
Fax: 515-283-9366
www.iowahospice.org

Kansas Hospice and Palliative Care
Organization
1901 W. University St.
Wichita, KS 67213
316-263-6380
888-202-5433
Fax: 316-263-6542
www.lifeproject.org/akh.htm

The Kentucky Association of
Hospice and Palliative Care
305 Ann St., Ste. 308
Frankfort, KY 40601

888-322-7317
Fax: 888-755-6531
www.kah.org

Lousiana—Mississippi Hospice and Palliative Care Organization
717 Kerlerec St.
New Orleans, LA 70116
504-945-2414
888-546-1500
Fax: 504-948-3908
www.lmhpco.org

Maine Hospice Council
P.O. Box 2239
Augusta, ME 04338
207-626-0651
800-438-5963
Fax: 207-622-1274
www.mainehospicecouncil.org

Hospice Network of Maryland
408 Headquarters Dr., Ste. 3-H
Millersville, MD 21108
410-729-4571
Fax: 410-729-4574
www.hnmd.org

Hospice and Palliative Care Federation of Massachusetts
1420 Providence Hwy., Ste. 277
Norwood, MA 02602
781-255-7077
800-962-2973
Fax: 781-255-7078
www.hospicefed.org

Michigan Hospice and Palliative Care Organization
5123 W. Saint Joseph Hwy., Ste. 204
Lansing, MI 48917
517-886-6667
800-536-6300
Fax: 517-886-6737
www.mihospice.org

Hospice Minnesota
2365 McKnight Rd. North, Ste. 2
North Saint Paul, MN 55109
651-659-0423
800-214-9597
Fax: 651-659-9126
www.hospicemn.org

Missouri Hospice and Palliative Care Association
3905 Stonewall Ave.

Independence, MO 64055
816-350-7702
Fax: 816-350-7708
www.mohospice.org

**MHA—An Association of Montana
Health Care Providers**
P.O. Box 5119
Helena, MT 59604
406-442-1911
Fax: 406-443-3894
www.mtha.org

**Nebraska Hospice and Palliative
Care Association**
4720 Randolph St., Bethel Bldg.
Lincoln, NE 68510
402-477-0204
Fax: 402-477-0204
www.nehospice.org

Hospice Association of Nevada
P.O. Box 160087
Sacramento, CA 95816
916-441-3770
888-252-1010
Fax: 916-441-4720

**New Hampshire Hospice and
Palliative Care Organization**
125 Airport Rd.
Concord, NH 03301
877-646-7742
Fax: 603-863-6780
www.nhhpco.org

**New Jersey Hospice and Palliative
Care Organization**
175 Glenside Ave.
Scotch Plains, NJ 07076
908-233-0060
Fax: 908-233-1630
www.njhospice.org

**The Carolinas Center for Hospice
and End of Life Care (North
Carolina)**
P.O. Box 4449
Cary, NC 27519
919-677-4100
800-662-8859
Fax: 919-677-4199
www.carolinasendoflifecare.org

**Hospice and Palliative Care
Asso-ciation of New York State**
21 Aviation Rd., Ste. 9

Albany, NY 12205
518-446-1483
800-431-8988
Fax: 518-446-1484
www.hpcanys.org

North Dakota Hospice Organization
c/o Sakakawea Hospice
510 8th Ave. NE
Hazen, ND 58545
701-748-7381
Fax: 701-748-6004
www.ndhospice.com

Ohio Hospice & Palliative Care Organization
555 Metro Pl. North, Ste. 650
Dublin, OH 43017
614-763-0036
800-776-9513
Fax: 614-763-0050
www.ohpco.org

Oklahoma Hospice & Palliative Care Association
P.O. Box 54586
Oklahoma City, OK 73154
405-606-4442
800-456-8201
Fax: 405-604-2830
www.okhospice.org

Pennsylvania Hospice Network
475 W. Governor Rd., Ste. 7
Hershey, PA 17033
717-533-4002
866-554-6774
Fax: 717-533-4007
www.pahospice.org

Oregon Hospice Association
P.O. Box 10796
Portland, OR 97926
503-228-2104
888-229-2104
Fax: 503-222-4907
www.oregonhospice.org

Puerto Rico Home Health and Hos-pice State Association
P.O. Box 192152
San Juan, PR 00919
787-281-0064
Fax: 787-765-9876

The Carolinas Center for Hospice and End of Life Care (South Carolina)
1000 Center Point Rd.
Columbia, SC 29210
803-791-4220
800-662-8859
Fax: 803-791-5664
www.carolinasendoflifecare.org

South Dakota Hospice Organization
200 E. Dakota, Ste. 1
Pierre, SD 57501
605-224-3214
Fax: 605-224-3208
www.southdakotahospice.org

Tennessee Hospice Organization
500 Interstate Blvd. South
Nashville, TN 37210
615-401-7402
800-258-9541
Fax: 615-242-4803
www.tha.com/tho

Texas and New Mexico Hospice
Organization
P.O. Box 15465
Austin, TX 78761
512-454-1247
800-580-9270
Fax: 512-454-1248
www.txnmhospice.org

Utah Hospice and Palliative Care
Organization
1327 South 900 East
Salt Lake City, UT 84105
801-582-2245
888-325-4150
www.utahhospice.org

Hospice and Palliative Care Council
of Vermont
10 Main St.
Montpelier, VT 05602
802-229-0579
Fax: 802-223-6218
www.hpccv.org

The Virginia Association for Hospices
P.O. Box 70025
Richmond, VA 23255
804-740-1344
Fax: 804-559-2677
www.virginiahospices.org

Washington State Hospice and Palliative Care Organization
1911 Southwest Campus Dr., # 316
Federal Way, WA 98023
253-661-3739
866-661-3739
Fax: 253-551-3584 (West) or
509-928-6812 (East)
www.wshpco.org

Hospice Council of West Virginia
c/o Hospice of the Panhandle
122 Waverly Ct.
Martinsburg, WV 25401
304-264-0406
800-345-6538

Fax: 304-264-0409
www.hospicecouncilofwv.org

The Hospice Organization and Palliative Experts of Wisconsin (HOPE)
3240 University Ave., Ste. 2
Madison, WI 53705
608-233-7166
800-210-0220
Fax: 608-233-7169
www.wisconsinhospice.org

Wyoming Hospice Organization
319 S. Wilson, Ste. D
Casper, WY 82601
307-577-4832
Fax: 307-352-6769

State Home Care Associations

Alabama

EXECUTIVE DIRECTOR	PRESIDENT/CHAIRPERSON
Melanie Golson	Debra Veal
Home Care Association of Alabama	Lanier Home Health Services
P.O. Box 3238	1806 44th St.
Montgomery, AL 36109	Valley, AL 36854
334-395-9949	334-756-1950
800-934-4312	334-756-1970 fax
Fax: 334-395-9959	E-mail: dveal@lanierhospital.com
E-mail:	
executivedirector@homecarealabama.org	
www.homecarealabama.org	

Alaska

EXECUTIVE DIRECTOR	PRESIDENT/CHAIRPERSON
N/A	Diane Anderson
Alaska Home Care Association	Pacific Home Health
4155 Tudor Centre Dr., Ste. 103	4155 Tudor Centre Dr., Ste. 103
Anchorage, AK 99508	Anchorage, AK 99508
	907-729-2492
	Fax: 907-729-2489
	E-mail: djanderson@anmc.org

Arizona

EXECUTIVE DIRECTOR	PRESIDENT/CHAIRPERSON
Marie Fredetta	Karen Jeselun
Arizona Association for Home Care	Arizona Home Care
2302 N. Third St.	4615 S. 33rd Pl.
Phoenix, AZ 85004	Phoenix, AZ 85040
602-712-9812	602-252-5000, ext. 202
Fax: 602-252-5265	Fax: 602-323-5070
E-mail: marie@capitolconsultingaz.com	E-mail: karen@azhomecare.com

Arkansas

EXECUTIVE DIRECTOR	PRESIDENT/CHAIRPERSON
Nancy Elphingstone	Susan Carter
Home Care Association of Arkansas	Home Health Professionals
411 S. Victory	P.O. Box 704
Suite 205	Blytheville, AR 72316
Little Rock, AR 72201	870-762-1825
501-376-2273	Fax: 870-762-2299
Fax: 501-376-7107	E-mail:hhp@sbcglobal.net
E-mail: hcaaark@sbcglobal.net	
EXECUTIVE DIRECTOR	PRESIDENT/CHAIRPERSON
Don Adams	Arkansas Hospital Association
Arkansas Hospital Association	419 Natural Resources Dr.
419 Natural Resources Dr.	Little Rock, AR 72205
Little Rock, AR 72205	501-224-7878
501-224-7878	Fax: 501-224-0519
Fax: 501-224-0519	
E-mail: donadams@arkhospitals.org	
www.arkhospitals.org	

California

EXECUTIVE DIRECTOR	PRESIDENT CHAIRPERSON
Joseph Hafkenschiel	Carolyn Bonner
California Association for Health Services at Home	Area Administrator, San Diego Home Health & Hospice
3780 Rosin Ct.	Kaiser Foundation Hospital Home Health
Suite 190	10992 San Diego Mission Rd. 3rd Floor
Sacramento, CA 95834	San Diego, CA 92108
916-641-5795	619-641-4663
Fax: 916-641-5881	619-641-4110
E-mail: jhafkenschiel@cahsah.org	E-mail: Carolyn.m.bonner@kp.org
www.cahsah.org	

Colorado

EXECUTIVE DIRECTOR	PRESIDENT CHAIRPERSON
Ellen Caruso	Susan E. Birch
Home Care Association of Colorado	Northwest Colorado VNA/HQ
7853 E. Arapahoe Rd.	940 Central Park Dr., Ste. 101
Suite 2100	Steamboat Springs, CO 80487
Englewood, CO 80112	970-879-1632
303-694-4728	Fax: 970-870-1326
Fax: 303-694-4869	
E-mail: ecaruso@assnoffice.com	
www.hcaconline.org	

Connecticut

EXECUTIVE DIRECTOR	PRESIDENT/CHAIRPERSON
Brian Ellsworth	Kathryn Roby, BSN, MA, MS, CHCE
Connecticut Association for Home Care, Inc.	New England Home Care
110 Barnes Rd.	136 Berlin Rd.
P.O. Box 90	Cromwell, CT 06416
Wallingford, CT06492–0090	860-632-3928
203-265-9931	Fax: 860-632-3536
Fax: 203-949-0031	E-mail: kroby@newenglandhomecare.
E-mail: ellsworth@chime.org	com
www.cthomecare.org	

Delaware

EXECUTIVE DIRECTOR	PRESIDENT/CHAIRPERSON
N/A	Ruth Hansen
Delaware Association of Home and Community Care	St. Francis Hospital Home Health Care Program
Home Health Corp of America	Seventh and Clayton Streets
260 Chapman Rd., #200	Wilmington, DE 19805
Commonwealth Bldg.	302-575-8231
Newark, DE 19702	Fax: 302-575-8239
	E-mail: rhansen@chi-east.org
EXECUTIVE DIRECTOR	PRESIDENT/CHAIRPERSON
Susan Lloyd	Delaware Hospice Association
Delaware Hospice Association	3515 Silverside Rd., Ste. 100
3515 Silverside Rd., Ste. 100	Wilmington, DE 19810

Wilmington, DE 19810 302-478-5707 800-838-9800 Fax: 302-479-2586	302-478-5707 800-838-9800 Fax: 302-479-2586

Florida

EXECUTIVE DIRECTOR	PRESIDENT/CHAIRPERSON
Gene Tischer Associated Home Health Industries of Florida, Inc. 1331 E. Lafayette St., Ste. C Tallahassee, FL 32301 850-222-8967 Fax: 850-222-9251 E-mail: gtischer@ahhif.org www.ahhif.org	Jimmie Culpepper MedSouth Home Health 112 W. Virginia Ave. Bonifay, FL 32425 850-547-5549 Fax: 850-657-5458 E-mail: balddaddy@comcast.net

Georgia

EXECUTIVE DIRECTOR	PRESIDENT/CHAIRPERSON
Judy Adams Georgia Association for Home Health Agencies, Inc. 2100 Roswell Rd. Suite 200C—PMB 1107 Marietta, GA 30062 770-565-4531 Fax: 770-565-1739	Rod Windley Healthfield, Inc. 6666 Powers Ferry Rd. Atlanta, GA 30339 770-951-6106 Fax: 770-541-3776 E-mail: rod.windley@healthfield.com

Fax: 770-565-1739
E-mail: gahomehealth@earthlink.net
www.gahha.org

EXECUTIVE DIRECTOR
Melissa Pelfrey
Georgia Association of Community
Care Providers
168 N. Johnston St.
Suite 304
Dallas, GA 30132
770-445-6640
Fax: 770-445-3893
E-mail: email@gaccp.org
www.gaccp.org

EXECUTIVE DIRECTOR
Christie Carpenter
Georgia Home Care Association
168 N. Johnston St., Ste. 304
Dallas, GA 30132
770-445-3180
Fax: 770-445-3893
E-mail: gahcassn@aol.com
www.gahca.org

PRESIDENT/CHAIRPERSON
Joyce Barlow
Englewood Home Health Care
P.O. Box 1743
Albany, GA 31702
229-435-2109
229-435-0729
E-mail: jdgb@bellsouth.net

PRESIDENT/CHAIRPERSON
Ruth Bruner
Nursing Care, Inc.
205 Boulevard NE
Gainesville, GA 30501
770-536-0484
Fax: 770-536-3003
E-mail: ruthbruner@aol.com

Hawaii

EXECUTIVE DIRECTOR	PRESIDENT/CHAIRPERSON
Coral Andrews	Emilie Smith
Healthcare Association of Hawaii	Administrator
932 Ward Ave., Ste. 430	CareResource Hawaii
Honolulu, HI 96814	680 Iwilei Rd., Ste. 660
808-521-8961	Honolulu, HI 96817
Fax: 808-599-2879	808-599-4999
E-mail: candrews@hah.org	808-531-2832
www.hahc.org	E-mail: esmith@queens.org
	www.careresourcehawaii.org

Idaho

EXECUTIVE DIRECTOR	PRESIDENT/CHAIRPERSON
Liz Barnett	Shane Loar
Idaho Association of Home Health Agencies	Guardian Home Care
10400 Overland Rd., Ste. 144	119 S. Valley Dr., Ste. C
Boise, ID 83709	Nampa, ID 83686
208-362-8190	208-461-1600
Fax: 208-562-1366	E-mail: guardian@micron.net
E-mail: homecare@iahha.org	

Illinois

EXECUTIVE DIRECTOR	PRESIDENT/CHAIRPERSON
Nancy Nelson Illinois Home Care Council 1926 Waukegan Rd., Ste. 1 Glenview, IL 60025 847-657-6960 Fax: 847-657-6963 E-mail: nancyn@tcag.com www.ilhomecare.org	Tom Galluppi Resurrection Home Health Services 4930 W. Oakton St. Skokie, IL 60077 847-568-8524 Fax: 847-568-8537 E-mail: tgalluppi@reshealthcare.org

Indiana

EXECUTIVE DIRECTOR	PRESIDENT/CHAIRPERSON
Todd Stallings Indiana Association for Home and Hospice Care, Inc. 8604 Allisonville Rd., Ste. 260 Indianapolis, IN 46250 317-844-6630 Fax: 317-575-8751 E-mail: todd@ind-homecare.org www.ind-homecare.org	Karen Wade St. Margaret Mercy Home Care 5454 Hohman Ave. Hammond, IN 46320 219-933-6663 Fax: 219-933-2641 E-mail: karen.wade@ssfhs.org

Iowa

EXECUTIVE DIRECTOR	PRESIDENT/CHAIRPERSON
Larry Breeding	Denise Schrader
Iowa Association for Home Care	Visiting Nurse Association
1520 High St., Ste. 203-B	611 N. 2nd St.
Des Moines, IA 50309	Clinton, IA 52732
515-282-3965	563-242-7165
Fax: 515-282-8034	Fax: 563-242-7197
E-mail: iahc@iowahomecare.org	
www.iowahomecare.org	

Kansas

EXECUTIVE DIRECTOR	PRESIDENT/CHAIRPERSON
Linda Lubensky	Karen Elliott
Kansas Home Care Association	Community Home Health
1512 B Legend Trail Dr.	100 W. 8th
Lawrence, KS 66047	Onaga, KS 66521
785-841-8611	785-889-7200
Fax: 785-749-5414	Fax: 785-889-4808
E-mail: khca@kshomecare.org	E-mail: elliotk@chcs-ks.org
www.kshomecare.org	

Kentucky

EXECUTIVE DIRECTOR	PRESIDENT/CHAIRPERSON
Karen Hinkle	Mary Lynn Spalding
Kentucky Home Health Association	Visiting Nurse Association/JHHS
154 Patchen Dr., Ste. 90	101 W. Chestnut St., Ste. 90
Lexington, KY 40517	Louisville, KY 40202

859-268-2574	502-581-8702
Fax: 859-269-1124	Fax: 502-585-7600
E-mail: homecare@khha.org	E-mail: mary.spalding@jhhs.org
www.khha.org	

Louisiana

EXECUTIVE DIRECTOR	PRESIDENT/CHAIRPERSON
Warren Hebert, CHCE	Richard Chandler, CHCE
HomeCare Association of Louisiana	Southland HH of Shreveport
233-A E. Main St.	8870 Youree Dr., Ste. 110
New Iberia, LA 70562	Shreveport, LA 71115
337-560-9610	318-798-1755
Fax: 337-560-9606 fax	Fax: 318-798-1754
E-mail: warren@hclanet.org	E-Mail: southhhs@bellsouth.net
www.hclanet.org	

Maine

EXECUTIVE DIRECTOR	PRESIDENT/CHAIRPERSON
Vicki Purgavie	Elaine Brady
Home Care Alliance of Maine	SMMC Visiting Nurses
20 Middle St.	P.O. Box 739
Augusta, ME 04330	72 Main St.
207-623-0345	Kennebunk, ME 04043
Fax: 207-623-7141	207-985-1000
Email: vicki@homecarealliance.org	800-794-3546
www.homecarealliance.org	Fax: 207-985-6715
	E-mail: smh.emb@smmc.org

Maryland/District of Columbia

EXECUTIVE DIRECTOR	PRESIDENT/CHAIRPERSON
Maryland National Capital Homecare Association 6919 Baltimore National Pike, Ste. F Frederick, MD 21702 301-473-9801 Fax: 301-473-9803	Mara Benner Gentiva Health Services 1227 25th Street, NW Washington, DC 20037 703-340-1633 E-mail: Mara.Benner@gentiva.com

Massachusetts

EXECUTIVE DIRECTOR	PRESIDENT/CHAIRPERSON
Patricia McDonald Kelleher Home & Health Care Association of Massachusetts 31 James Ave., Ste. 780 Boston, MA 02116 617-482-8830 Fax: 617-426-0509 E-mail: pkelleher@mass-homehealth.org www.mass-homehealth.org	Nancy L. Pettinelli VNA of Greater Lowell P.O. Box 1965 Lowell, MA 01853 978-459-9343 Fax: 978-441-0007
EXECUTIVE DIRECTOR Lisa Gurgone Massachusetts Council for Home Care Aide Services 31 New Chardon St. Boston, MA 02114 617-227-6641 Fax: 617-227-1190 E-mail: lgurgone@jfcsboston.org	PRESIDENT/CHAIRPERSON Wendy Drastel HomeCare, Inc. 360 Merrimack St., Bldg. #9 Lawrence, MA 01843 978-552-4701 978-552-4730

Michigan

EXECUTIVE DIRECTOR	PRESIDENT/CHAIRPERSON
Harvey Zuckerberg	Steve Slater
Michigan Home Health Association	Airway Oxygen
2140 University Park Dr., Ste. 220	2935 Madison SE
Okemos, MI 48864	Grand Rapids, MI 49548
517-349-8089	877-632-0730, ext. 208
Fax: 517-349-8090	Fax: 616-452-7404
E-mail: zuckerberg.harvey@mhha.org	Email: sslater@airwayoxygeninc.com
www.mhha.org	

Minnesota

EXECUTIVE DIRECTOR	PRESIDENT/CHAIRPERSON
Neil Johnson	Kathy Lucas
Minnesota HomeCare Association	Fairview Home Care and Hospice
1711 W. County Road B, Ste. 211S	2450—26th Avenue S.
St. Paul, Minnesota 55113	Minneapolis, Minnesota 55406
651-635-0607	612-721-2491
Fax: 651-635-0043	Fax: 612-728-2400
E-mail: njohnson@mnhomecare.org	Email: klucas1@fairview.org
www.mnhomecare.org	

Mississippi

EXECUTIVE DIRECTOR	PRESIDENT/CHAIRPERSON
N/A	Curtis Bray
Mississippi Association for Home Care	Gilbert Home Health
P.O. Box 1468	605 2nd Ave., North #203

Ridgeland, MS 39158
601-853-7533
Fax: 601-853-7582
E-mail: mahc1975@aol.com
www.mahc.org

Columbus, MS 39701
662-327-9669
Fax: 662-239-2015
E-mail: cbray@hhca.com

Missouri

EXECUTIVE DIRECTOR
Mary Schantz
Missouri Alliance for Home Care
2420 Hyde Park Rd., Ste. A
Jefferson City, MO 65109
573-634-7772
Fax: 573-634-4374
E-mail: mary@homecaremissouri.org
www.homecaremissouri.org

PRESIDENT/CHAIRPERSON
Sandy Morgan
John Knox Village Home Health
400 Northwest Murray Rd.
Lee's Summit, MO 64081
816-524-1133
Fax: 816-524-9177

EXECUTIVE DIRECTOR
Sharon Burnett
Missouri Hospital Home Health
Council
P.O. Box 60
Jefferson City, MO 65102
573-893-3700
Fax: 573-893-2809

PRESIDENT/CHAIRPERSON
N/A
Missouri Hospital Home Health
Council
P.O. Box 60
Jefferson City, MO 65102
573-893-3700
Fax: 573-893-2809

Montana

EXECUTIVE DIRECTOR	PRESIDENT/CHAIRPERSON
Casey Blumenthal	Jane Hron
Montana Hospital Association: An Association of Montana Health Care Providers	Marcus Daley Home Care and Hospice
P.O. Box 5119	1200 Westwood Dr.
Helena, MT 59604	Hamilton, MT 59840
406-442-1911	406-363-6503
Fax: 406-443-3894	Fax: 406-363-2866
E-mail: casey@mtha.org	E-mail: jhron@mdmh.org
www.mtha.org	

Nebraska

EXECUTIVE DIRECTOR	PRESIDENT/CHAIRPERSON
Kimberle Hall	Marjorie Jones
Nebraska Association of Home and Community Health Agencies	Saint Francis Medical Center Home Care Services
7421 Forbes Dr.	2116 W. Faidley Ave.
Lincoln, NE 68516	Grand Island, NE 68802
402-489-1117	308-398-5470
Fax: 402-489-1117	Fax: 308-398-5363
E-mail: khall@nebraskahomecare.org	E-mail: mjones@sfmc-gi.org
www.nebraskahomecare.org	

Nevada

EXECUTIVE DIRECTOR	PRESIDENT/CHAIRPERSON
N/A	Pamela Rossen
Home Health Care Assn of Nevada	Colonial Home Care
Washoe Home Care	5516 Boulder Hwy.
780 Kuenzli, Ste. 200	#2-F PMB185
Reno, NV 89502	Las Vegas, NV 89122
	702-733-8498
	Fax: 702-733-8498
	E-mail: prossen@chscares.com

New Hampshire

EXECUTIVE DIRECTOR	PRESIDENT/CHAIRPERSON
Susan Young	Mary Palmer
Home Care Association of New	Rockingham VNA & Hospice
Hampshire	137 Epping Rd.
8 Green St.	Exeter, New Hampshire 03079
Concord, New Hampshire 03301	603-893-2900
603-225-5597	Fax: 603-382-6246
Fax: 603-225-5817	
E-mail: syoung@homecarenh.org	
www.homecarenh.org	

New Jersey

EXECUTIVE DIRECTOR	PRESIDENT/CHAIRPERSON
Carol Kientz	Mary Ann Christopher
The Home Care Association of New	VNA of Central Jersey, Inc.
Jersey	141 Bodman Place
14 Washington Rd., Ste. 211	Redbank, NJ 07701

Princeton Junction, NJ 08550
609-275-6100
Fax: 609-936-9349
E-mail: carol@homecarenj.org
www.homecarenj.org

732-747-1204
Fax: 732-224-0843

EXECUTIVE DIRECTOR
Valerie Sellers
New Jersey Hospital Association
760 Alexander Rd.
P.O. Box 1
Princeton, NJ 08543
609-275-4000
Fax: 609-275-4265
E-mail: vseller@njha.com
www.njha.com

PRESIDENT/CHAIRPERSON
Theresa Edelstein
New Jersey Hospital Association
760 Alexander Rd.
P.O. Box 1
Princeton, NJ 08543
609-275-4000
Fax: 609-275-4265

New Mexico

EXECUTIVE DIRECTOR
Joie Glenn, RN, MBA, CAE
New Mexico Association for Home
and Hospice Care
3200 Carlisle Blvd., NE, Ste. 117
Albuquerque, NM 87110
505-889-4556
Fax: 505-889-4928
E-mail: joieg@nmahc.org
www.nmahc.org

PRESIDENT/CHAIRPERSON
Helen Karns
Lovelace Sandia Home Care
5403 Gibson SE
Albuquerque, NM 87108
505-872-6500
Fax: 505-872-6547
E-mail: helen.karns@lovelacesandia.
com

New York

EXECUTIVE DIRECTOR	PRESIDENT/CHAIRPERSON
Carol Rodat	Michele Quirolo
Home Care Association of New York State, Inc.	President/Chief Executive Officer
	VNA of Hudson Valley, Inc.
194 Washington Ave., Ste. 400	100 S. Bedford Rd.
Albany, NY 12210	Mount Kisco, NY 10549
518-426-8764	914-666-7616, ext. 187
Fax: 518-426-8788	Fax: 914-666-9514
E-mail: crodat@earthlink.net	E-mail: mquirolo@vnahv.org
www.hcanys.org	
EXECUTIVE DIRECTOR	PRESIDENT/CHAIRPERSON
Phyllis Wang	Robert Callaghan
New York State Association of Health Care Providers, Inc.	New York Nursing Care
	527 Townline Rd., Ste. 302
99 Troy Rd., Ste. 200	Hauppauge, NY 11788
East Greenbush, NY 12061	631-979-2200
518-463-1118	Fax: 631-979-2265
Fax: 518-463-1606	
E-mail: hcp@nyshcp.org	
www.nyshcp.org	
EXECUTIVE DIRECTOR	PRESIDENT/CHAIRPERSON
Laura Leeds	J. Ronald Gaudreault
Health Care Association of New York State	President and CEO
	Huntington Hospital
One Empire Dr.	270 Park Ave.

Rensselaer, NY12144
518-431-7600
Fax: 518-431-7915
E-mail: lleeds@hanys.org
www.hanys.org

EXECUTIVE DIRECTOR
Joe Campanella
Home Care Council of New York City
25 W. 43rd St., 3rd Fl.
New York, NY 10036
646-366-0860
Fax: 646-366-0864
E-mail: hccnyc@earthlink.net

Huntington, NY 11743
631-351-2200
Fax: 631-351-2586

PRESIDENT/CHAIRPERSON
George Cortes
Union Settlement Home Care
219 E. 115 St.
New York, NY 10029
212-828-6182, ext. 204
Fax: 212-828-6190

North Carolina

EXECUTIVE DIRECTOR
Timothy Rogers
Association for Home Care and
Hospice of North Carolina, Inc.
3101 Industrial Dr.
Raleigh, NC 27609
919-848-3450
Fax: 919-848-2355
E-mail: timrogers@homeandhospice-
care.org
www.homeandhospicecare.org

PRESIDENT/CHAIRPERSON
Sherry Hedrick
President
Piedmont Home Care
P.O. Box 1624
Lexington, NC 27293
336-248-8212
Fax: 336-248-4937
E-mail: piedhomecare@lexcominc.net

EXECUTIVE DIRECTOR	
Larry Smith	
The Carolinas Center for Hospice and End of Life Care	
2400 Weston Pkwy.	
Cary, NC 27513	
919-677-4115	
Fax: 919-677-4199	
www.carolinasendoflifecare.org	

North Dakota

EXECUTIVE DIRECTOR	PRESIDENT CHAIRPERSON
Ken Tupa	Marcia Sjulstad
North Dakota Association for Home Care	MeritCare Home Care
c/o APT, Inc.	1711 S. University Dr.
P.O. Box 2175	Fargo, ND 58103
Bismarck, ND 58502	701-280-4027
701-224-1815	Fax: 701-280-4030
Fax: 701-224-9824	E-mail: marcia.sjulstad@meritcare.com
E-mail: ktupa@aptnd.com	
www.aptnd.com/ndahc	

Ohio

EXECUTIVE DIRECTOR	PRESIDENT/CHAIRPERSON
Kathleen Anderson	Karen Thompson
Ohio Council for Home Care	Administrator
1395 E. Dublin Granville Rd., Ste. 350	SOMC Home Health Services
Columbus, OH 43229	727 8th St.
	Portsmouth, OH 45662

614-885-0434
Fax: 614-885-0413
E-mail: kka@homecareohio.org
www.homecareohio.org

EXECUTIVE DIRECTOR
Jeffrey Lycan
Ohio Hospice & Palliative Care
Organization
555 Metro Place North, Ste. 650
Dublin, OH 43017
614-763-0036
Fax: 614-763-0050
E-mail: hospiceoh@aol.com
www.ohpco.org

740-356-4663
Fax: 740-353-5956
E-mail: marshalk@somc.org

PRESIDENT/CHAIRPERSON
Bridget Montana
Hospice of the Western Reserve
300 E. 185th St.
Cleveland, OH 44119
216-383-2222
Fax: 216-383-3730
E-mail: bmontana@hospicewr.org

Oklahoma

EXECUTIVE DIRECTOR
Stan Sweeney
Oklahoma Association for Home Care
8108 NW Tenth, Ste. C3
Oklahoma City, OK 73127
405-495-5995
Fax: 405-495-5993
E-mail: sweeneyok@aol.com
www.oahc.com

PRESIDENT/CHAIRPERSON
Eric Drennan, RN
Director of Operations
May House Call
P.O. Box 940
Antlers, OK 74523
580-298-3947
Fax: 580-298-2443
E-mail: May95@yahoo.com

Oregon

EXECUTIVE DIRECTOR	PRESIDENT/CHAIRPERSON
Sarah Myers	Debra Robinson
Oregon Association for Home Care	Cascade Home Care
1249 Commercial St. SE	2500 NE Neff Rd.
Salem, OR 97302	Bend, OR 97701
503-364-2733	541-388-7796
Fax: 503-399-1029	Fax: 541-318-4955
E-mail: sarah@oahc.org	E-mail: drobinson@scmc.org
www.oahc.org	

Pennsylvania

EXECUTIVE DIRECTOR	PRESIDENT/CHAIRPERSON
Vicki Hoak	Elissa Della Monica, Director
Pennsylvania Homecare Association	Abington Memorial Hospital Home
20 Erford Rd., Ste. 115	Care
Lemoyne, PA 17043	2510 Maryland Rd., Ste. 250
717-975-9448	Willow Grove, PA 19090
Fax: 717-975-9456	215-481-5800
E-mail: vhoak@pahomecare.org	Fax: 215-481-5850
www.pahomecare.org	

Rhode Island

EXECUTIVE DIRECTOR	PRESIDENT/CHAIRPERSON
Alan Tavares Rhode Island	Mary Linn Hamilton
Partnership for Home Care, Inc.	VNA Rhode Island
334 East Ave.	622 George Washginton Hwy.

Pawtucket, RI 02860	Lincoln Mall
401-722-9090	Lincoln, RI 02865
Fax: 401-728-6509	401-335-2493
E-mail: riphc@AOL.com	Fax: 401-335-9030

South Carolina

EXECUTIVE DIRECTOR	PRESIDENT/CHAIRPERSON
N/A	Nancy Boyle
	Carolinas Community Hospice, Inc.
	3096 Sunset Blvd.
	West Columbia, SC 29169
	803-454-0365
	Fax: 803-454-0366
	E-mail: nancy@agapesenior.com

South Dakota

EXECUTIVE DIRECTOR	PRESIDENT/CHAIRPERSON
Ken Senger	Jean Hunhoff
South Dakota Association of	Avera Scared Heart Health Care
Healthcare Organizations	Services
3708 Brooks Place	501 Summit
Sioux Falls, SD 57106	Yankton, SD 57078
605-361-2281	605-668-8312
Fax: 605-361-5175	Fax: 605-665-0170
E-mail: ksenger@sdaho.org	E-mail: jhunhoff@shhservices.com
www.sdaho.org	

Tennessee

EXECUTIVE DIRECTOR	PRESIDENT/CHAIRPERSON
Gayla Sasser	Carolyn Foster
Tennessee Association for Home Care, Inc.	UT Medical Center Home Health
	2220 Southerland Ave.
131 Donelson Pike	Suite 102
Nashville, TN 37214	Knoxville, TN 37919
615-885-3399	865-544-6200
Fax: 615-885-4191	Fax: 865-544-6240
E-mail: gayla.sasser@tahc-net.org	
www.tahc-net.org	
EXECUTIVE DIRECTOR	PRESIDENT/CHAIRPERSON
Mike Dietrich	Laura Beth "LB" Brown
Tennessee Hospital Association Home Care Alliance	Vanderbilt Home Care
	Vanderbilt University Medical Center
500 Interstate Blvd., South	Nashville, TN
Nashville, TN 37210	615-936-0336
615-256-8240	
Fax: 615-242-4803	
E-mail: mdietrich@tha.com	

Texas

EXECUTIVE DIRECTOR	PRESIDENT/CHAIRPERSON
Anita Bradberry	Diana Farmer, CHCE
Texas Association for Home Care	North Central Texas Home Care, Inc.
3737 Executive Center Dr., Ste. 268	5608 Malvey, Ste. 300
Austin, TX 78731	Fort Worth, TX 76107

512-338-9293
512-338-9496
E-mail: anita@tahc.org
www.tahc.org

800-648-0854
Fax: 817-377-0948

Utah

EXECUTIVE DIRECTOR	PRESIDENT/CHAIRPERSON
Dan Hull	Rick Hall
Utah Association for Home Care	Applegate HomeCare & Hospice
1327 South 900 East	1740 Combe Rd., Ste. 1
Salt Lake City, UT 84105	Ogden, UT 84403
801-466-7210	801-621-4027
E-mail: homecareconnection@msn.com	Fax: 801-627-6226
www.ua4hc.org	E-mail : rickh@applegatehomecare. com

Vermont

EXECUTIVE DIRECTOR	PRESIDENT/CHAIRPERSON
Peter Cobb	Ron Cioffi, CEO
Vermont Assembly of Home Health Agencies	Rutland Area VNA and Hospice
10 Main St.	P.O. Box 787
Montpelier, VT 05602	Rutland, VT
802-229-0579	802-775-0568
Fax: 802-223-6218	E-mail: rcioffi@sover.net
E-mail: vahha@adelphia.net	
www.vnavt.com	

Virginia

EXECUTIVE DIRECTOR	PRESIDENT/CHAIRPERSON
Marcie Tetterton	Lisa Sprinkel
Virginia Association for Home Care	Carilion Home Care Services
8001 Franklin Farms Dr.	1917 Franklin Rd., Ste. C
Suite 110	Roanoke, VA 24014
Richmond, VA 23229	540-224-4800
804-285-8636	Fax: 540-982-5785
800-755-8636	E-mail: lsprinkel@carilion.com
Fax: 804-288-3303	
E-mail: mtetterton@vahc.org	
www.vahc.org	
EXECUTIVE DIRECTOR	PRESIDENT/CHAIRPERSON
Susan Ward	Larry Sartoris
Virginia Hospital and Health Care	Virginia Hospital and Health Care
Association	Association
P.O. Box 31394	P.O. Box 31394
Richmond, Virginia 23294	Richmond, Virginia 23294
804-965-1249	804-965-1216
804-965-0475	Fax: 804-965-0475
E-mail: sward@vhha.com	E-mail: lsartoris@vhha.com
www.vhha.com	

Washington

EXECUTIVE DIRECTOR	PRESIDENT/CHAIRPERSON
Donna Cameron	Linda Dahl
Home Care Association of	Group Health Cooperative Home &
Washington	Community Services
P.O. Box 2016	1600 E. John St., M/S CMB-140
Edmonds, WA 98020	

425-775-8120 Fax: 425-771-9588 E-mail: HomeCareWA@aol.com www.hcaw.org	Seattle, WA 98122 206-326-4828 Fax: 206-326-4555 E-mail: dahl.l@ghc.org

West Virginia

EXECUTIVE DIRECTOR	PRESIDENT/CHAIRPERSON
Laura Friend West Virginia Council of Home Care Agencies, Inc. Route 1 Box 190 Elk Fork Rd. Middlebourne, WV 26149 304-758-4312 Fax: 304-758-4354 E-mail: wvchha@mountain.net www.wvhomecare.com	Debora V. Henry Panhandle Home Health 1161–2 Winchester Ave. Martinsburg, WV 25401 304-263-5680 Fax: 304-267-1532 E-mail: phhi@intrepid.net

Wisconsin

EXECUTIVE DIRECTOR	PRESIDENT/CHAIRMAN
Russell King, MBA, CAE Wisconsin Homecare Organization 5610 Medical Circle, Ste. 33 Madison, WI 53719 608-278-1115 Fax: 608-278-4009 E-mail: WIShomecare@earthlink.net www.wishomecare.org	Caralynn Hodgson 412 W. Kinne St. Ellsworth, WI 54011 715-273-6756 Fax: 715-273-6854 E-mail: chodgson@co.pierce.wi.us

Wyoming

EXECUTIVE DIRECTOR	PRESIDENT/CHAIRPERSON
Janace Chapman, RN	Deborah Kaufman
Home Health Care Alliance of Wyoming	Central Wyoming Home Care
1515 S. Spruce St.	401 E. Main
Casper, WY 82601	Riverton, WY 82501
307-237-7042 (phone and fax)	307-857-0599
E-mail: jac@rmisp.com	Fax: 307-857-2778
	E-mail: cwhc@rmisp.com

General Resources

Organizations

Abledata Assistive Technology
8630 Fenton St., Ste. 930
Silver Spring, MD 20910
800-227-0216
www.abledata.com

**National Institute on Aging
Alzheimer's Disease Education and
Referral Service**
National Institute on Aging
Building 31, Room 5C27
31 Center Dr., MSC 2292
Bethesda, MD 20892
800-438-4380
www.nia.nih.gov/alzheimers

Alzheimer's Association
919 N. Michigan Ave.
Chicago, IL 60611
www.alz.org
800-272-3900

**Alzheimer's Association MedicAlert
and Safe Return Program**
888-572-8566
www.alz.org/we_can_help_medicalert_
safereturn.asp

**American Association for Geriatric
Psychiatry (AAGP)**
7910 Woodmont Ave.
Bethesda, MD 20814
301-654-7850
www.aagpgpa.org

American Association of Homes and Services for the Aging (AAHSA)
2519 Connecticut Ave., NW
Washington, DC 20008
202-783-2242
www.aahsa.org

American Association of Retired People (AARP)
601 E Street, NW
Washington, DC 20049
888-687-2277
www.aarp.org

American Geriatrics Society (AGS)
350 Fifth Ave.
New York, NY 10118
212-308-1414
www.americangeriatrics.org

Arthritis Foundation
P.O. Box 7669
Atlanta, GA 30357
800-283-7800
www.arthritis.org

Assisted Living Federation of America
1650 King St., Ste. 602,

Alexandria, VA 22314
703.894.1805
www.alfa.org

The Centers for Medicare and Medicaid Services
7500 Security Blvd.
Baltimore, MD 21244
800-MEDICARE
410-786-3000 (Medicare hotline)
www.medicare.gov

Children of Aging Parents
1609 Woodburne Rd.
Levittown, PA 19507
800-227-7294
www.caps4caregivers.org

Clearinghouse on Abuse and Neglect of the Elderly (CANE)
c/o Center for Community Research and Services
University of Delaware
297 Graham Hall
Newark, DE 19716
800-677-1116
www.ncea.aoa.gov

U.S. Department of Health and Human Services
200 Independence Ave., SW
Washington, DC 20201
877-696-6775
www.dhhs.gov

Department of Veterans Affairs (VA)
Office of Public Affairs
810 Vermont Ave., NW
Washington, DC 20420
800-827-1000
www.va.gov

Family Caregiver Alliance
690 Market St., Ste. 600
San Francisco, CA 94104
415-434-3388
www.caregiver.org

Hearing Loss Association of America
7910 Woodmont Ave, Suite 1200,
Bethesda, MD 20814
301-657-2248
www.shhh.org

HUD for Seniors
451 7th St. SW
Washington, DC 20410

202-708-1112
www.hud.gov/groups/seniors.cfm

Legal Services for the Elderly (LSE)
130 W. 42nd St., 17th Fl.
New York, NY 10036
212-391-0120

Meals on Wheels Association of America
1414 Prince St.
Alexandria, VA 22314
703-548-5558
www.mowaa.org

Medic Alert
2323 Colorado Ave.
Turlock, CA 95382
888-633-4298
www.medicalert.org

National Academy of Elder Law Attorneys, Inc. (NAELA)
1604 N. Country Club Rd.
Tucson, AZ 85716
520-881-4005
www.naela.org

National Adult Day Services
Association
85 S. Washington, Ste. 316
Seattle, WA 98104
800-558-5301.
www.nadsa.org

National Asian Pacific Center on
Aging (NAPCA)
1511 3rd Ave., Ste. 914
Seattle, WA 98101
206-624-1221
www.napcaonline.org

National Association of Area
Agencies on Aging
927 15th St. NW, 6th Fl.
Washington, DC 20005
202-296-8130
www.n4a.org

National Association for Hispanic
Elderly (Asociación Nacional Por
Personas Mayores)
234 E. Colorado Blvd.
Pasadena, CA 91101
626-564-1988

National Association for Home Care
228 7th St. SE
Washington, DC 20003
202-547-7424
www.nahc.org

National Association of Professional
Geriatric Care Managers
(NAPGCM)
1604 N. Country Club Rd.
Tucson, AZ 85716
520-881-8008
www.caremanager.org

National Association of Social
Security Claimants Representatives
560 Sylvan Ave.
Englewood Cliffs, NJ 07632
800-431-2804
www.nosscr.org

National Association of State Units
on Aging (NASUA)
1225 I St., NW, Ste. 725
Washington, DC 20005
202-898-2578
www.nasua.org

National Caucus and Center on
Black Aged, Inc. (NCBA)
1424 K St., NW, Ste. 500
Washington, DC 20005
202-637-8400
www.ncba-aged.org

National Center for Assisted Living
1201 "L" St., NW
Washington, DC 20005
202-842-4444
www.ncal.org

National Center on Elder Abuse
(NCEA)
1225 I St., NW, Ste. 725
Washington, DC 20005
202-898-2586
www.ncea.aoa.gov/ncearoot/Main_
Site/index.aspx

National Center for Home Equity
Conversion
360 N. Robert, Ste. 403
Saint Paul, MN 55101
www.reverse.org

National Citizen's Coalition for
Nursing Home Reform
1424 16th St., NW, Ste. 202
Washington, DC 20036
202-332-2275
www.nccnhr.org

National Council on Aging, Inc.
409 3rd St., SW, Ste. 200
Washington, DC 20024
202-479-1200
www.ncoa.org

National Family Caregivers
Association (NFCA)
10400 Connecticut Ave.
Kensington, MD 20895
800-896-3650
www.nfcacares.org

National Funeral Director's
Association
13625 Bishop's Dr.
Brookfield, WI 53005
800-228-6332
www.nfda.org

National Hispanic Council on Aging (NHCOA)
2713 Ontario Rd., NW
Washington, DC 20009
202-265-1288
www.nhcoa.org

National Hospice and Palliative Care Organization (NHPCO)
1700 Diagonal Rd., Ste. 300
Alexandria, VA 22314
800-658-8898
www.nhpco.org

National Hospice Foundation
1700 Diagonal Road, Ste. 300
Alexandria, VA 22314
800-338-8619
www.hospiceinfo.org

National Indian Council on Aging
10501 Montgomery Blvd. NE
Albuquerque, NM 87111
508-292-2001
www.nicoa.org

National Institute on Aging
Building 31, Room 5C27
31 Center Dr., MSC 2292
Bethesda, MD 20892
301-496-1752
www.nih.gov/nia

National Long-Term Care Resource Center (NLTCRC)
Division of Health Services,
University of Minnesota School
of Public Health
420 Delaware St., SE
Minneapolis, MN 55455
612-624-5171
www.hpm.umn.edu/ltcresourcecenter

National Network of Estate Planning Attorneys
410 17th St., Ste. 1260
Denver, CO 80202
800-638-8681
www.netplanning.com

National Resource Center on Native American Aging (NRCNAA)
P.O. Box 9037
Grand Forks, ND 58202
800-896-7628
http://ruralhealth.und.edu/projects/
nrcnaa

National Resource Center on
Suppor-tive Housing & Home
Modifications
3715 McClintock Ave.
Los Angeles, CA 90089
213-740-1364
www.homemods.org

National Senior Citizens Law Center
1101 14th St., NW, Ste. 400
Washington, DC 20005
202-289-6976
www.nsclc.org

National Sleep Foundation
1522 K St., NW, Ste. 500
Washington, DC 20005
202-347-3471
www.sleepfoundation.org

Partnership for Caring, Inc. (PFC)
America's Voices for the Dying
1620 Eye St., NW, Ste. 202
Washington, DC 20006
800-989-9455
www.partnershipforcaring.org

Social Security Administration
Office of Public Inquiries

6401 Security Blvd.
Baltimore, MD 21235
800-772-1213
www.ssa.gov

State Elder Abuse Hotlines
www.ncea.aoa.gov/NCEAroot/Main_
Site/Find_Help/Help_Hotline.aspx

State Long-Term Care Insurance
Partnerships
www.aarp.org/research/
longtermcare/insurance/fs124_ltc_06.
html

Visiting Nurse Association of
America (VNAA)
11 Beacon St., Ste. 910
Boston, MA 02108
888-866-8773
www.vnaa.org

Well Spouse Foundation
P.O. Box 30093
Elkins Park, PA 19027
800-838-0879
www.wellspouse.org

Websites

55 Alive Driving Program from the AARP
www.aarp.org/55alive

Ageline Database
research.aarp.org/ageline/home.html

Aging Parents and Adult Children Living Together Guide
www.feddesk.com/freehand-books/1014–4.pdf

Alzheimer's Disease Fact Sheet
www.alzheimers.org/pubs/adfact.html

Alzheimer's Disease Program Directory
www.nia.nih.gov/Alzheimers/Research Information/ResearchCenters

Benefits Check Up
www.benefitscheckup.org

Buying Drugs Online
www.pueblo.gsa.gov/cic_text/health/buydrugs-online/100_online.html

Care Guide
www.careguide.com

Caregiver Guide for Families of Alzheimer Patients
www.nia.nih.gov/Alzheimers/Caregiving/HomeAndFamily

Care Scout
www.carescout.com

Caring for an Aging Loved One
www.pueblo.gsa.gov/cic_text/family/aging/lovedones.htm

Carrier Alert Program
www.nalc.org/commun/alert/howcalt.html

Eldercare Locator
www.eldercare.gov
800-677-1116

Elderweb
www.elderweb.com

First Gov for Seniors
www.seniors.gov

FTC's Guide to Viatical Settlements
http://library.findlaw.com/1998/
May/1/126790.html

Guide to Choosing a Nursing Home
www.medicare.gov/Publications/Pubs/
pdf/02174.pdf

Guide to Long Term Care Insurance
http://www.pueblo.gsa.gov/cic_text/
health/ltc/guide.htm

Insurance company ratings
www.ambest.com

Medicaid
www.cms.hhs.gov

Medicare
www.ssa.gov/mediinfo.htm

Medicare Participating Physician
Finder
www.medicare.gov/Physician/Home.asp

Medicare Participating Supplier
Finder
www.medicare.gov/Supplier/Home.asp

Medicare Personal Plan Finder
www.medicare.gov/MPPF/Home.asp

Medicare Prescription Drug Assistance Programs
www.medicare.gov/Prescription/
Home.asp

Medicare Prescription Drug Plan
Finder
www.medicare.gov/MPDPF/Public/
Include/DataSection/Questions/MPDPF
Intro.asp?version=default&browser=IE
%7C7%7CWinXP&language=English
&default-status=0&pagelist=Home&
ViewType=Public&PDPYear=2008&
MAPDYear=2008&MPDPF%5FMPPF
%5FIntegrate=N

Medicare State Contacts
www.medicare.gov/contacts/home.asp

National Council on Aging
www.benefitscheckup.org

Nursing Home Checklist
www.medicare.gov/nursing/checklist.asp

Nursing Home Inspection Reports and Comparisons
www.medicare.gov/NHCompare/Include/
DataSection/Questions/SearchCriteria
.asp?version=default&browser=IE%7C7
%7CWinXP&language=English&default
status=0&pagelist=Home&Cookies
EnabledStatus=True

Patient's Bill of Rights (American Hospital Association)
www.injuredworker.org/Library/
Patient_Bill_of_Rights.htm

Senior Housing Finder
www.seniorhousingnet.com/seniors

Senior Living
www.seniorliving.about.com

Senior Resource Directory
www.seniorresource.com

Ten Things to Know for an Emergency with Aging Parents
www.mayoclinic.com/health/senior-
health/HA00029

Vial of Life Form and Instructions
www.vialoflife.com

Online Medical Research

Centers for Disease Control
www.cdc.gov/az/a.html

Clinical Trials
www.clinicaltrials.gov

Healthfinder
www.healthfinder.gov

Johns Hopkins
www.hopkinshospital.org/health_info

Mayo Clinic
www.mayoclinic.com

Medline Plus
www.nlm.nih.gov/medlineplus

Medscape
www.medscape.com

Merck
www.merck.com

National Institutes of Health
www.nih.gov

National Women's Health Information
Center
www.4women.gov

PubMed
www.ncbi.nlm.nih.gov/entrez/query.
fcgi

Wed MD
www.webmd.com

Magazines

Modern Maturity Magazine
(free to AARP members)
www.aarp.org

Today's Caregiver Magazine
800-829-2734
www.caregiver.com

For Additional Reading

Aging

Aging and Mental Health (Understanding Aging)
by Sara H. Qualls

Aging Well: The Complete Guide to Physical and Emotional Health
by Jeanne Wei and Sue Levkoff

Beating the Senior Blues: How to Feel Better and Enjoy Life Again
by Leslie Eckford and Amanda Lambert

Chicken Soup for the Golden Soul: Heartwarming Stories for People 60 and Over
edited by Jack Canfield, Mark Victor Hansen, Paul J. Meyer, and Barbara Chesser

Growing Older, Growing Better: Daily Meditations for Celebrating Aging
by Amy E. Dean

Healthy Aging: Challenges and Solutions
by Ken Dychtwald

Seniors' Rights: Your Legal Guide to Living Life to the Fullest
by Brette McWhorter Sember

Still Here: Embracing Aging, Changing, and Dying
by Ram Dass

When I Am an Old Woman I Shall Wear Purple
by Sandra Haldeman Martz

Aging in Place

Aging in Place: Designing, Adapting, and Enhancing the Home Environment
edited by Ellen D. Taira and Jodi L. Carlson

Making Aging in Place Work
edited by Leon A. Pastalan

Alzheimer's

The 36-Hour Day: A Family Guide to Caring for People with Alzheimer Disease, Other Dementias, and Memory Loss in Later Life
by Nancy L. Mace and Peter V. Rabins, MD

Living With Alzheimer's Disease: Overcoming Common Problems
by Dr. Tom Smith

The Loss of Self: A Family Resource for the Care of Alzheimer's Disease and Related Disorders
by Donna Cohen and Carl Eisdorfer

Talking to Alzheimer's: Simple Ways to Connect When You Visit with a Family Member or Friend
by Claudia J. Strauss

Caregiving

Elder Care: A Six Step Guide to Balancing Elder Care and Work
by John Paul Marosy

Elder Rage or Take My Father...Please!: How to Survive Caring for Aging Parents
by Jacqueline Marcell

A Caregiver's Companion: Ministering to Older Adults
by J. Daniel Dymski

Coping With Your Difficult Older Parent: A Guide for Stressed-Out Children
by Grace Lebow, Barbara Kane, and Irwin Lebow

Daily Comforts for Caregivers
by Pat Samples

A Field Guide For Families: How to Assist Your Older Loved Ones When You Don't Live Next Door
by Jane Yousey

Loving Voice II: A Caregiver's Book of More Read-Aloud Stories for the Elderly
edited by Carolyn Banks and Janis Rizzo

Pitching In: When Your Elderly Parents Need Help
by S.B. Ross

The Sandwich Generation: Caught Between Growing Children and Aging Parents
by H. Michael Zal

Should Mom Live with Us? And is Happiness Possible if She Does?
by Vivian F. Carlin and Vivian E. Greenberg

Couples

Couples Who Take Care: Elders Weathering the Years with Strength and Love
by Lou Dunn Diekemper

Death and Dying

Dying Unafraid
by Fran Moreland Johns

Final Gifts: Understanding the Special Awareness, Needs, and Communications of the Dying
by Maggie Callanan and Patricia Kelley

Do I Know You? Living Through the End of a Parent's Life
by Bette Ann Moskowitz

Handbook for Mortals: Guidance for People Facing Serious Illness
by Joanne Lynn

The Needs of the Dying: A Guide for Bringing Hope, Comfort, and Love to Life's Final Chapter
by David Kessler

On Death and Dying: What the Dying Have to Teach Doctors, Nurses, Clergy, and Their Own Families
by Elisabeth Kubler-Ross

Saying Goodbye: You & Your Aging Parents
by David H. Klein, PhD

What Dying People Want: Practical Wisdom for the End of Life
by David Kuhl

Dementia
Care That Works: A Relationship Approach to Persons with Dementia
by Jitka M. Zgola

Keeping Busy: A Handbook of Activities for Persons with Dementia
by James R. Dowling

The Validation Breakthrough: Simple Techniques for Communicating with People With "Alzheimer's-Type Dementia"
by Naomi Feil

Drugs
Complete Guide to Prescription & Nonprescription Drugs (2008)
by A. Winter Griffith, MD

Finances

Funding Your Dreams Generation to Generation: Intergenerational Financial Planning to Ensure Your Family's Health, Wealth, and Personal Values
by Carol Akright, CFP

Set for Life: Financial Peace for People Over 50
by Bambi Holzer

Food

Mealtime Manual for People with Disabilities and the Aging
by Judith Lannefeld Klinger

I-Can't-Chew Cookbook: Delicious Soft-Diet Recipes for People with Chewing, Swallowing and Dry-Mouth Disorders
by J. Randy Wilson

Funerals

Creating Your Own Funeral or Memorial Service: A Workbook
by Stephanie West Allen

Grief

Awakening from Grief: Finding the Road Back to Joy
by John E. Welshons

Finding Your Way after Your Spouse Dies
by Marta Felber

The Grief Recovery Handbook: The Action Program for Moving Beyond Death, Divorce, and Other Losses
by John James and Russell Friedman

I Remember You: A Grief Journal
by Laynee Gilbert

I Wasn't Ready to Say Goodbye: Surviving, Coping & Healing After the Sudden Death of a Loved One
by Brook Noel and Pamela D. Blair, PhD

Health Care

A Senior's Health Journal: A Personal Record of Vital Health and Medical Information
by Joann Lamb, MSN, and Ina Yalof

Home Care

Circles of Care: How to Set Up Quality Home Care for Our Elders
by Ann Cason

In-Home Care for Senior Citizens (A Bedside Companion)
by Shirley M. Baker-Davis

Hospice

The Family Handbook of Hospice Care
Fairview Health Services

A Practical Guide to Palliative Care
by Jerry L. Old and Daniel L. Swagerty

Insurance

The Medicaid Handbook 2007: Protecting Your Assets from Nursing Home Costs
by Sean W. Scott

Long-Term Care: How to Plan & Pay for It
by Attorney Joseph L. Matthews

Understanding Managed Healthcare: A Guide for Seniors on Medicare
by William J. Pokluda

Medical Care

Healthwise for Life: Medical Self-Care for People Age 50 and Better
by Molly Mettler and Donald W. Kemper

Nursing Homes

Living Well in a Nursing Home: Everything You and Your Folks Need to Know
by Lynn Dickinson, MA, and Xenia Vosen, PhD

Nursing Homes: The Family's Journey
by Peter S. Silin

Selling the Home

Dress Your House for Success: 5 Fast, Easy Steps to Selling Your House, Apartment, or Condo for the Highest Possible Price!
by Martha Webb and Sarah Parsons Zackheim

Sell Your Home Without a Broker: Insider's Advice to Selling Smart, Fast and for Top Dollar!
by Joseph P. DiBlasi, Attorney at Law

Senior Living

Simplifying Life as a Senior Citizen: Hundreds of Tips to Make Everyday Living Easier
by Joan Cleveland

Social Security

The Social Security Answer Book
by Stanley Tomkiel III

The Social Security Benefits Handbook, 5E
by Stanley Tomkiel III

Widowhood

The Widow's Resource: How to Solve the Financial and Legal Problems That Occur Within the First Six to Nine Months of Your Husband's Death
by Julie A. Calligaro

Widow to Widow: Thoughtful, Practical Ideas for Rebuilding Your Life
by Genevieve Davis Ginsburg, MS

Widower: When Men Are Left Alone (Death, Value and Meaning)
by Scott Campbell and Phyllis R. Silverman

A Handbook for Widowers
by Ed Ames

Nursing Home Residents' Rights in the United States

Background

The following nursing home residents' rights must be adhered to by all nursing homes in the United States that wish to participate in the government's Medicare or Medicaid program. This requirement was enacted by the U.S. Congress on December 22, 1987, as part of Public Law 100–203, the *Consolidated Omnibus Budget Reconciliation Act*. For further information, contact:

Mr. Vic Santoro
Division of Outcomes and Improvements
Nursing Home Branch
Health Care Financing Administration
7500 Security Blvd, S2–11–07
Baltimore, MD 21244
Phone: 410-786-6778
E-mail: vsantoro@HCFA.gov

Nursing Home Residents' Rights in the United States

As a resident of this facility, you have the right to a dignified existence and to communicate with individuals and representatives of choice. The facility will protect and promote your rights as designated below.

Exercise of Rights

You have the right and freedom to exercise your rights as a resident of this facility and as a citizen or resident of the United States without fear of discrimination, restraint, interference, coercion, or reprisal.

If you are unable to act in your own behalf, your rights are exercised by the person appointed under state law to act in your behalf.

Notice of Rights and Services

You will be informed of your rights and of all rules and regulations governing resident conduct and responsibilities both orally and in writing.

You have the right to inspect and purchase photocopies of your records.

You have the right to be fully informed of your total health status.

You have the right to refuse treatment and the right to refuse to participate in experimental research.

You have the right to formulate an advance directive in accordance with facility policy.

You will be informed of Medicare and Medicaid benefits. This information will be posted.

You will be informed of facility services and charges.

The facility will inform you of procedures for protecting personal funds. If you deem necessary, you may file a complaint with the state survey and certification agency.

You will be informed of your physician, his or her specialty, and ways of contacting him or her.

The facility must consult with you and notify your physician and interested family member of any significant change in your condition or treatment, or of any decision to transfer or discharge.

The facility will notify you and interested family members of a room or roommate change.

You have the right to refuse room changes requested by the facility.

The facility will periodically update the address and telephone number of your legal representative or interested family member.

The facility will notify you and interested family members of any change in your rights as a resident.

Protection of Funds

You may manage your own financial affairs. You are not required to deposit personal funds with the facility.

The facility must manage your deposited funds with your best interests in mind. Your money will not be commingled with facility funds.

The facility will provide you with an individualized financial report quarterly and upon your request.

Any remaining estate will be conveyed to your named successor.

All funds held by the facility will be protected by a security bond.

Free Choice

You may choose your own personal physician.

You will be informed of and may participate in your care and treatment and any resulting changes.

Privacy

You have the right of privacy over your personal and clinical records.

Your privacy will include: personal care, medical treatments, telephone use, visits, letters, and meetings of family and resident groups.

You may approve or refuse the release of your records except in the event of a transfer or legal situation.

Grievances

You may voice grievances concerning your care without fear of discrimination or reprisal.

You may expect prompt efforts for the resolution of grievances.

Examination of Survey Results

You may examine survey results and the plan of correction. These, or a notice of their location, will be posted in a readily accessible place.

You may contact client advocate agencies and receive information from them.

Work

You may perform or refuse to perform services for the facility.

All services performed must be well-documented in the care plan to include the nature of the work and compensation.

Mail

You may promptly send and receive your mail unopened and have access to writing supplies.

Access and Visitation Rights

You have the right to receive or deny visitors.

You have the right and the facility must provide access to visit with any relevant agency of the state or any entity providing health, social, legal, or other services.

Telephone

You have the right to use the telephone in private.

Personal Property

You can retain and use personal possessions as space permits.

Married Couples

A married couple may share a room.

Self-Administration of Drugs

You may self-administer drugs unless determined unsafe by the interdisciplinary team.

Admission, Transfer, and Discharge Rights

Transfer and Discharge

You may not be transferred or discharged unless your needs cannot be met, safety is endangered, services are no longer required, or payment has not been made.

Notice of and reason(s) for transfer or discharge must be provided to you in an understandable manner.

Notice of transfer or discharge must be given thirty days prior, except in case of health and safety needs.

The transfer or discharge notice must include the name, address, and telephone number of the appropriate, responsible protective agency.

A facility must provide sufficient preparation to ensure a safe transfer or discharge.

Notice of Bed-Hold Policy and Readmission

You and a family member must receive written notice of state and facility bed-hold policies before and at the time of a transfer.

The facility must follow a written policy for readmittance if the bed-hold period is exceeded.

Equal Access to Quality Care

The facility must use identical policies regarding transfer, discharge, and services for all residents.

The facility may determine charges for a non-Medicaid resident as long as written notice was provided at the time of admission.

Admission Policy

The facility must not require a third-party guarantee of payment or accept any gifts as a condition of admission or continued stay.

This facility cannot require you to waive your right to receive or apply for Medicare or Medicaid benefits.

The facility may obtain legal financial access for payment without incurring your personal liability.

The facility may charge a Medicaid-eligible resident for items and services requested.

The facility may only accept contributions if they are not a condition of admission or continued stay.

Resident Behavior and Facility Practices

Restraints

The facility may not use physical restraints or psychoactive drugs for discipline or convenience or when they are not required to treat medical symptoms.

Abuse

You have the right to be free from verbal, sexual, physical or mental abuse, corporal punishment, and involuntary seclusion.

Staff Treatment

The facility must implement procedures that protect you from abuse, neglect, or mistreatment, and misappropriation of your property.

In the event of an alleged violation involving your treatment, the facility is required to report it to the appropriate officials.

All alleged violations must be thoroughly investigated and the results reported.

Quality of Life

The facility must care for you in a manner that enhances your quality of life.

Dignity

The facility will treat you with dignity and respect in full recognition of your individuality.

Self-Determination

You may choose your own activities, schedules, and health care, and any other aspect affecting your life within the facility.

You may interact with visitors of your choice.

Participation in Resident and Family Groups

You may organize or participate in groups of choice.

Families have the right to visit with other families.

The facility must provide a private space for group meetings.

Staff or visitors may attend meetings at the group's invitation.

The facility will provide a staff person to assist and follow up with the group's requests.

The facility must listen to and act upon requests or concerns of the group.

Participation in Other Activities

You have the right to participate in activities of choice that do not interfere with the rights of other residents.

Accommodation of Needs

You have the right as a resident to receive services with reasonable accommodations to individual needs and preferences.

You will be notified of room or roommate changes.

You have the right to make choices about aspects of your life in the facility that are important to you.

Activities

The facility will provide a program of activities designed to meet your needs and interests.

Social Services

The facility will provide social services to attain or maintain your highest level of well-being.

Environment

The facility must provide a safe, clean, comfortable, home-like environment, allowing you the opportunity to use your personal belongings to the extent possible.

The facility will provide housekeeping and maintenance services.

The facility will assure you have clean bath and bed linens and that they are in good repair.

The facility will provide you with private closet space as space permits.

The facility will provide you with adequate and comfortable lighting and sound levels.

The facility will provide you with comfortable and safe temperature levels.

Nursing Home Checklist

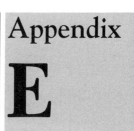
*Nursing Home Checklist from **www.Medicare.gov***

Checklists can help you evaluate the nursing homes that you call or visit. Use a new checklist for each home you call or visit. Then, compare the scores. This will help you select a nursing home that is a good choice for you or your relative.

Nursing Home Name: _____

Date Visited: _____

Address: _____

I. Basic Information

Is the facility Medicare-certified?

_____(yes) _____(no)

Is the facility Medicaid-certified?

_____(yes) _____(no)

Is this a skilled-nursing facility?

____(yes) _____(no)

Is the facility accepting new patients?

____(yes) _____(no)

Is there a waiting period for admission?

____(yes) _____(no)

Is a skilled bed available to you?

____(yes) _____(no)

Useful Tips

- Generally, skilled-nursing care is available only for a short period of time after a hospitalization. Custodial care is for a much longer period of time. If a facility offers both types of care, learn if residents may transfer between levels of care within the nursing home without having to move from their old room or from the nursing home.

- Nursing homes that only take Medicaid residents might offer longer-term, but less intensive, levels of care. Nursing homes that do not accept Medicaid payment may make a resident move when Medicare or the resident's own money runs out.

- An *occupancy rate* is the total number of residents currently living in a nursing home divided by the home's total number of beds. Occupancy rates vary by area, depending on the overall number of available nursing home beds.

II. Nursing Home Information

Is the home and the current administrator licensed?

____(yes) _____(no)

Does the home conduct background checks on all staff?

____(yes) _____(no)

Does the home have special services units?

____(yes) _____(no)

Does the home have abuse prevention training?

____(yes) _____(no)

Useful Tips

- **Licensure.** The nursing home and its administrator should be licensed by the state to operate.

- **Background Checks.** Do the nursing home's procedures to screen potential employees for a history of abuse meet your state's requirements? Your state's ombudsman program might be able to help you with this information.

- **Special Services.** Some nursing homes have special service units like rehabilitation, Alzheimer's, and hospice. Learn if there are separate waiting periods or facility guidelines for when residents would be moved on or off the special unit.

- **Staff Training.** Do the nursing home's training programs educate em-ployees about how to recognize resident abuse and neglect, how to deal with aggressive or difficult residents, and how to deal with the stress of caring for so many needs? Are there clear procedures to identify events or trends that might lead to abuse and neglect, and on how to investigate, report, and resolve your complaints?

- **Loss Prevention.** Are there policies or procedures to safeguard residents' possessions?

For Sections III through VI, give the nursing home a grade from one to five. One is worst, five is best.

III. Quality of Life

1 2 3 4 5   1. Residents can make choices about their daily routine. Examples are when to go to bed or get up, when to bathe, or when to eat.

1 2 3 4 5   2. The interaction between staff and patient is warm and respectful.

1 2 3 4 5   3. The home is easy to visit for friends and family.

1 2 3 4 5   4. The nursing home meets your cultural, religious, or language needs.

1 2 3 4 5   5. The nursing home smells and looks clean and has good lighting.

1 2 3 4 5   6. The home maintains comfortable temperatures.

1 2 3 4 5   7. The resident rooms have personal articles and furniture.

1 2 3 4 5   8. The public and resident rooms have comfortable furniture.

1 2 3 4 5   9. The nursing home and its dining room are generally quiet.

1 2 3 4 5   10. Residents may choose from a variety of activities that they like.

1 2 3 4 5   11. The nursing home has outside volunteer groups.

1 2 3 4 5   12. The nursing home has outdoor areas for resident use and helps residents to get outside.

Total: _____ (best possible score: 60)

IV. Quality of Care

1 2 3 4 5   1. The facility corrected any quality of care deficiencies that were in the state inspection report.

1 2 3 4 5   2. Residents may continue to see their personal physician.

1 2 3 4 5   3. Residents are clean, appropriately dressed, and well-groomed.

1 2 3 4 5   4. Nursing home staff respond quickly to requests for help.

1 2 3 4 5   5. The administrator and staff seem comfortable with each other and with the residents.

1 2 3 4 5   6. Residents have the same caregivers on a daily basis.

1 2 3 4 5   7. There are enough staff at night and on weekends or holidays to care for each resident.

1 2 3 4 5   8. The home has an arrangement for emergency situations with a nearby hospital.

1 2 3 4 5   9. The family and resident councils are independent from the nursing home's management.

1 2 3 4 5   10. Care plan meetings are held at times that are easy for residents and their family members to attend.

Total: _____ (best possible score: 50)

Useful Tips

Good care plans are essential to good care. They should be put together by a team of providers and family and updated as often as necessary.

V. Nutrition and Hydration (Diet and Fluids)

1 2 3 4 5   1. The home corrected any deficiencies in these areas that were on the recent state inspection report.

1 2 3 4 5   2. There are enough staff to assist each resident who requires help with eating.

1 2 3 4 5   3. The food smells and looks good and is served at proper temperatures.

1 2 3 4 5   4. Residents are offered choices of food at mealtimes.

1 2 3 4 5   5. Residents' weight is routinely monitored.

1 2 3 4 5   6. There are water pitchers and glasses on tables in the rooms.

1 2 3 4 5   7. Staff help residents drink if they are not able to do so on their own.

1 2 3 4 5   8. Nutritious snacks are available during the day and evening.

1 2 3 4 5   9. The environment in the dining room encourages residents to relax, socialize, and enjoy their food.

Total: _____ (best possible score: 45)

Useful Tips

- Ask the professional staff how the medicine a resident takes can affect what they eat and how often they may want something to drink.

- Visit at mealtime. Are residents rushed through meals or do they have time to finish eating and to use the meal as an opportunity to socialize with one another?

- Sometimes the food a home serves is fine, but a resident still will not eat. Nursing home residents may like some control over their diet. Can they select their meals from a menu or select their mealtime? If residents need help eating, do care plans specify what type of assistance they will receive?

VI. Safety

1 2 3 4 5   1. There are handrails in the hallways and grab bars in the bathrooms.

1 2 3 4 5   2. Exits are clearly marked.

1 2 3 4 5   3. Spills and other accidents are cleaned up quickly.

1 2 3 4 5   4. Hallways are free of clutter and have good lighting.

1 2 3 4 5   5. There are enough staff to help move residents quickly in an emergency.

1 2 3 4 5   6. The nursing home has smoke detectors and sprinklers.

Total: _____ (best possible score: 30)

Useful Tips Relating to Information in Nursing Home Compare

Nursing Home Compare contains summary information about nursing homes from their last state inspection. It also contains information that was reported by the nursing homes prior to the last state inspection including nursing home and resident characteristics.

If you have questions or concerns about the information on a nursing home, you should discuss them during your visit. This section contains useful tips and questions that you may want to ask the nursing home staff, family members, and residents of the nursing home during your visit.

Nursing Home Compare Information on Results of Nursing Home Inspections

Bring a copy of the Nursing Home Compare inspection results for the nursing home. Ask whether the deficiencies have been corrected. Ask to see a copy of the most recent nursing home inspection report.

Nursing Home Compare Information on Resident and Nursing Home Characteristics

For the Measure: Residents with Physical Restraints

- Does it appear that there is sufficient staff to assist residents who need help in moving or getting in and out of chairs and bed?

- Ask the director of nursing who is involved in the decisions about physical restraints.

- When physical restraints are used, do the staff remove the physical restraints on a regular basis to help residents with moving and activities of daily living?

- Do the staff help residents with physical restraints to get in and out of bed and chairs when they want to get up?

- Do staff help residents with physical restraints to move as much as they would like to?

For the Measure: Residents with Pressure (Bed) Sores

- Ask the staff how they identify if a resident is at risk for skin breakdown.

- Ask the staff what they do to prevent pressure sores for the residents at risk.

- Ask the staff about the percentage of their residents that have pressure sores and why.

- Do you see staff helping residents change their positions in wheelchairs, chairs, and beds?

For the Measure: Residents with Bowel and Bladder Incontinence

- Does the nursing home smell clean?

- Ask the staff what steps they take to prevent bowel and bladder incontinence for residents who are at risk.

For the Measure: Residents Who Are Very Dependent in Eating

- Look at your response to Question 2 in Section V.

- Observe residents who need help in eating. Are they able to finish their meals or is the food returned to the kitchen uneaten?

For the Measure: Residents Who Are Bedfast

- Ask the director of nursing how staff are assigned to care for these residents.

For the Measure: Residents With Restricted Joint Motion

- Ask the director of nursing how the nursing home cares for residents with restricted joint motion.

- Do the residents get help with getting out of chairs and beds when they want to get up?

For the Measure: Residents with Unplanned Weight Gain or Loss

Look at your responses to Questions 2, 3, 4, 5, 8, and 9 in Section V.

For the Measure: Residents with Behavioral Symptoms

- What management and/or medical approaches for behavioral symptoms are being used by the nursing home?

- How does staff handle residents who have behavioral symptoms such as calling out or yelling?

- Ask whether residents with behavioral symptoms are checked by a doctor or behavioral specialist.

- Ask whether staff get special training to help them to provide care to residents with behavioral symptoms.

Nursing Home Compare Information on Nursing Staff

Caring, competent nursing staff who respect each resident and family member are very important in assuring that residents get needed care and enjoy the best possible quality of life. Adequate nursing staff is needed to assess resident needs, plan and give them care, and help them with eating, bathing, and other activities. Some residents (e.g., those who are more dependent in eating or who are bedfast) need more help than other residents, depending on their conditions.

The combinations of registered nurses (RNs), licensed practical and vocational nurses (LPNs/LVNs), and certified nursing assistants (CNAs) that nursing homes may have vary depending on the type of care that residents need and the number of residents in the nursing home.

Look at your responses to Questions 2 and 5 in Section III and Questions 4, 5, and 10 in Section IV. Also look at your responses to Questions 2 and 7 in Section V.

- Are nursing staff members courteous and friendly to residents and to other staff?

- Do nursing staff respond timely to residents' calls for assistance such as help getting in and out of bed, dressing, and going to the bathroom?

- Observe meal times. Do all residents who need assistance with eating get help? Do staff give each resident enough time to chew food thoroughly and complete the meal?

- Which nursing staff members are involved in planning the residents' individual care? (Are they the same ones who give the care to residents?)

- Ask questions about staff turnover. Is there frequent turnover among certified nursing assistants (CNAs)? What about nurses and supervisors, including the director of nursing and the administrator? If staff changes frequently, ask why.

- While the number of nursing staff members is important to good care, also consider other factors, such as education and training. How many registered nurses (RNs) are on the staff, and how many available on each shift? What kind of training do certified nursing assistants (CNAs) receive? How does the nursing home ensure that all staff receive continuing education and keep their knowledge and skills up to date?

Sample Forms

PERMISSION TO RELEASE MEDICAL INFORMATION

To: Dr. _____

I, _____ (parent's name), request that
_____ (caretaker's name), my son/
daughter/_____(other relationship), be given full access to all of
my medical records maintained by your office, now and in the future. I request
that all medical and office personnel speak freely with _____
(caretaker's name) about my health and medical information.

Check if applicable:

_____ I request that this office contact _____ (caretaker)
directly by phone (at the following number: _____) instead
of me with test results, appointment information, and all other telephone communication. I also request that all written correspondence be directed to him or her
at the following address: _____

_____ I request that this office contact _____ (caretaker) as well
as me by phone (at the following number: _____) with
test results, appointment information, and all other telephone communication.
I also request that all written correspondence be copied to him or her at this
address: _____.

_____   _____
Signature   Date

List of Medical Contacts

Name: _____

Address: _____

Phone Number: _____ Type of Provider/Specialty: _____

Name: _____

Address: _____

Phone Number: _____ Type of Provider/Specialty: _____

Name: _____

Address: _____

Phone Number: _____ Type of Provider/Specialty: _____

Name: _____

Address: _____

Phone Number: _____ Type of Provider/Specialty: _____

Name: _____

Address: _____

Phone Number: _____ Type of Provider/Specialty: _____

Name: _____

Address: _____

Phone Number: _____ Type of Provider/Specialty: _____

Name: _____

Address: _____

Phone Number: _____ Type of Provider/Specialty: _____

Transportation Telephone List

Name   Phone Number

_____   _____

_____   _____

_____   _____

_____   _____

_____   _____

_____   _____

_____   _____

_____   _____

_____   _____

_____   _____

_____   _____

_____   _____

_____   _____

_____   _____

Prescription Drug Dosage List

Drug Allergies: _____

Drug	Doctor	Dosage	Condition	Instructions

BASIC INFORMATION ORGANIZATION SHEET

I. General Information

Name: _____

Name at birth if different: _____

Address: _____

_____

Phone number: _____

Previous addresses: _____

_____

Social Security number: _____

Date of birth: _____

II. Health Insurance

Medicare number: _____

Medicaid number: _____

Other health insurance (list number, group number, company, and type of insurance):

_____

_____

_____

III. Income Information

Monthly Social Security income: _____

Pension income: _____

Veterans income: _____

Other income: _____

Source: _____

IV. Real Estate

(a)Primary residence: _____

_____

Value: _____

Equity: _____ Mortgage amount: _____

Bank: _____

Names on account: _____

(b) Other residences or property: _____

Value: _____

Equity: _____ Mortgage amount: _____

Bank: _____

Names on account: _____

(c) Other residences or property: _____

Value: _____

Equity: _____ Mortgage amount: _____

Bank: _____

Names on account: _____

V. Banks

(a) Savings account number: _____ Bank: _____

Current balance: _____

Names on account: _____

(b) Checking account number: _____ Bank: _____

Current balance: _____

Names on account: _____

_____

_____

(c) Other bank account number: _____ Bank: _____
Current balance: _____
Names on account: _____

(d) Other bank account number: _____ Bank: _____
Current balance: _____
Names on account: _____

(e) CD account number: _____ Bank: _____
Current balance: _____
Names on account: _____

(f) CD account number: _____ Bank: _____
Current balance: _____
Names on account: _____

VI. Investments

(a) Account number: _____

_____

Name of institution, fund, or stock: _____
Current balance: _____
Names on account: _____

_____

(b) Account number: _____

_____

Name of institution, fund, or stock: _____
Current balance: _____
Names on account: _____

_____

VII. Insurance

(a) Life insurance policy number: _____

Company: _____

Face value: _____ Beneficiary: _____

(b) Life insurance policy number: _____

Company: _____

Face value: _____ Beneficiary: _____

(c) Homeowner's or renter's insurance policy number: _____

Company: _____

Property insured: _____

VIII. Vehicles

(a) Type of vehicle: _____ Year: _____

Approximate value: _____ Name on title: _____

Insurance policy number: _____ Company: _____

(b) Type of vehicle: _____ Year: _____

Approximate value: _____ Name on title: _____

Insurance policy number: _____ Company: _____

IX. Personal Property

(a) Safety-deposit box number: _____

Location: _____ Contents: _____

Location of key or password: _____

(b) Safety-deposit box number: _____

Location: _____ Contents: _____

Location of key or password: _____

(c) Important or valuable item of property: _____

Value: _____ Location: _____

(d) Important or valuable item of property: _____

Value: _____ Location: _____

(e) Important or valuable item of property: _____

Value: _____ Location: _____

(f) Important or valuable item of property: _____

Value: _____ Location: _____

X. Other Assets

Please list all other assets of value or importance, including interest in a business, loans owned, investment property, and any other asset or property not previously listed. Specify the location of the item and value.

_____

_____

_____

_____

_____

_____

_____

_____

_____

_____

Meals

HOME LIVING PLAN

Fill in name of person or organization providing each, if needed.

Day	Breakfast	Lunch	Dinner	Snacks
Sunday				
Monday				
Tuesday				
Wednesday				
Thursday				
Friday				
Saturday				

Housekeeping

(Such as cleaning, laundry, dishes, and household organization)

(a) Name: _____ Services: _____

Availability: _____

Phone number: _____

(b) Name: _____ Services: _____

Availability: _____

Phone number: _____

(c) Name: _____ Services: _____

Availability: _____

Phone number: _____

Agency/Professional Assistance

Name: _____ Rate: _____

Services: _____ Phone number: _____

Availability: _____

Home Repairs

(a) Name: _____ Type: _____

Availability: _____

Phone number: _____

(b) Name: _____ Type: _____

Availability: _____

Phone number: _____

(c) Name: _____ Type: _____

Availability: _____

Phone number: _____

(d) Name: _____ Type: _____

Availability: _____

Phone number: _____

Professional Assistance

Electrician: _____ Phone number: _____

Plumber: _____ Phone number: _____

Contractor: _____ Phone number: _____

Lawn care: _____ Phone number: _____

Snow removal: _____ Phone number: _____

Personal Care

(Such as bathing, dressing, exercising, hair care, shaving, manicures, medication assistance, in-home health care)

(a) Name: _____ Type: _____

Availability: _____

Phone number: _____

(b) Name: _____ Type: _____

Availability: _____

Phone number: _____

(c) Name: _____ Type: _____

Availability: _____

Phone number: _____

(d) Agency/professional: _____

Type: _____

Availability: _____

Rate: _____ Phone number: _____

Miscellaneous Help

(Such as assistance with shopping, writing, reaching things, scheduling appointments, paying bills, etc.)

(a) Name: _____ Type: _____

Availability: _____

Phone number: _____

(b) Name: _____ Type: _____

Availability: _____

Phone number: _____

(c) Name: _____ Type: _____

Availability: _____

Phone number: _____

(d) Name: _____ Type: _____

Availability: _____

Phone number: _____

(e) Name: _____ Type: _____

Availability: _____

Phone number: _____

(f) Agency/professional help: _____

Type: _____

Rate: _____ Phone number: _____

Emergency Contacts

Name: _____

Phone number: _____

Name: _____

Phone number: _____

Name: _____

Phone number: _____

Name: _____

Phone number: _____

Name: _____

Phone number: _____

INDEX

ABOUT THE AUTHOR

Brette McWhorter Sember received her law degree from the State University of New York at Buffalo. She is a former New York state attorney and skilled mediator. She was on the Law Guardian panel in four counties and acted as a volunteer mediator for the Better Business Bureau.

Sember is experienced in helping seniors sort through options and evaluate choices that involve lifestyle, care facilities, finances, and estate and health planning. Her one-to-one experience with seniors gave her understanding about the deeply personal nature of senior planning and also developed her belief that senior planning is an issue for the entire family. Additionally, her own family experience with aging grandparents makes senior care a day-to-day issue.

Sember is an expert at explaining and simplifying business concepts. She has written more than thirty books, including *File for Divorce in New York*, *The Complete Credit Repair Kit*, and *Seniors' Rights*.

Her website is **www.BretteSember.com**.